David Tarrant's

PACIFIC

Ga·r·d·e·n·i·n·g

GUIDE

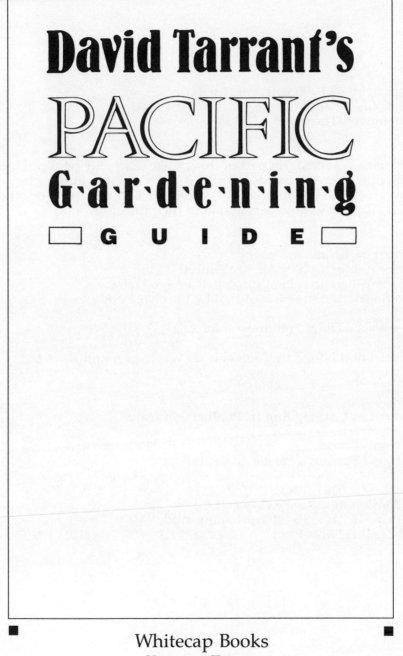

David Tarrant's PACIFIC Gardening GUIDE

Whitecap Books

Vancouver/Toronto

Edited by Brian Scrivener
Cover photograph by Michael Burch
Cover design and illustration by Carolyn Deby
Interior design and illustration by Carolyn Deby

Typeset by Opus Productions Inc.

Printed and bound in Canada by D.W. Friesen and Sons Ltd.

Canadian Cataloguing in Publication Data

Tarrant, David
    David Tarrant's Pacific gardening guide

ISBN 0-921061-77-3
1. Gardening - Pacific Coast (B.C.).
I. Title. II. Title: Pacific gardening guide.
SB453.3.C2T37 1990   635'.09711'31   C90-091171-9

For Cathie Perkins

CONTENTS

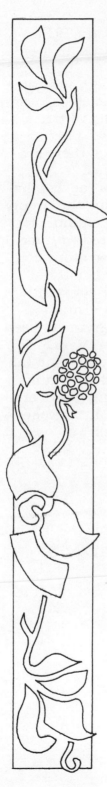

When I was asked to write this book I really had to think it over for awhile, as it seems to me that there are more and more gardening books being written all the time. And really, was another one going to help? But while the basics of gardening are the same the world over, there are little local tips that can really help when you start to garden in our part of the world. So many people retire here from other areas and are quite mystified by our climate, especially the long growing season. Once you have got used to the rain, it really makes sense to think of the Pacific Coast as the land of eternal spring, with a few hot days in the summer for a change.

I have always loved gardening and came from a country where there are a lot of gardens. But I'll let you in on a secret—not all Britons are great gardeners. However, the tried and tested techniques of classic English gardening really do work. It is these that I have tried to adapt for our coastal gardens.

On this coast, we really do have a unique climate for gardening. Just think about it. Temperate plants from such exotic places as the Himalayas love it here. Bulbs from Europe and Asia start blooming here in February and do so in succession until May. Shrubs and trees from China and Japan bloom during the grey months of November through February. No wonder this is known as Lotus Land!

I really do believe that gardening should be a fun and enjoyable experience, not all locked up in computers and text books, but something that you just get outside and do. Gardening is challenging, and it is a continuous experiment. If things do not work we can blame it on the weather. Best of all if someone tells you that you cannot grow something here, you can damn well go out and do it, so there! That's why there are palm trees at VanDusen Botanical Garden, kiwi

fruit vines growing up cedar trees at UBC Botanical Garden and figs in backyards all over the city of Vancouver.

I hope that this book will help both first-time gardeners and newcomers to the Pacific Coast to get out and plant and weed and dig with a vengeance. People who garden have a better understanding of nature. Perhaps if there are enough of us we can save the planet.

I would like to thank so many of the wonderful gardeners that I have met during the twenty years that I have lived in British Columbia for the knowledge that they have shared with me. In particular I would like to thank two of my colleagues at the UBC Botanical Garden: Judy Newton for allowing me to bug her constantly, bouncing ideas for this book off her, and to Gerald Straley for his patience in trying to keep me straight on plant nomenclature. VanDusen Botanical Garden very kindly allowed us to take the cover photograph in their garden. Thanks also to Launi Lucas for transcribing hours of tape, and last but not least to Brian Scrivener for his diligence in editing my work.

Soils and Fertilizers

Soil is the very essence of gardening. Without good soil we would not be able to grow many of the plants we know and love. In large commercial nurseries it is common to use soil-less mixes, but what I am going to write about in this book is that black or brown stuff right outside in our backyards.

Soil can be scarce, particularly in mountainous regions on the coast which were densely forested just over a hundred years ago. If you live in an older established neighbourhood where there have been gardens for the past fifty to a hundred years, the probability of having decent gardening soil is good. However, if you live in a new development where there is very little top soil, then you are going to have to do a lot of work to improve the soil or do something about bringing soil into your garden.

■ SOIL

If you do not have good quality soil in your garden then you will have to resort to buying a load of top soil. The best advice I can give to anyone is to make

1

sure that you see the soil before you purchase it. Once you have a load of top soil dumped into your driveway, you have very few avenues left open for getting it back to the supplier.

Although it is important that you look at the soil, keep in mind that you cannot judge it by looks alone. There is a fallacy that dark soil is the best possible soil in the world. I am sure we have all visited gardens from time to time that have had wonderful vegetables in them, and perhaps your mother or grandmother has said to you, "no wonder the vegetables are so good, look at the colour of the soil." Colour, however, has nothing to do with it. In Hawaii the soil is very red. If you travel through the Maritime provinces, the soil is red in some areas and pale yellow in others. It is what is in the soil that counts, not the colour of it.

When you look at soil make sure it is not more than 30 percent sawdust. Sawdust is a very dangerous thing to put in a garden. It can be useful because it does break down eventually, but putting a lot of sawdust in your garden will cause many problems. Any wood particles added to the soil use up a tremendous amount of nitrogen in their rotting process.

I remember when we first put in the food garden at the University of British Columbia Botanical Garden, we had a terrible problem. We added manure that came from some very nice stables which were cleaned out daily. This gave us little manure and masses of sawdust. When we put our vegetables in they germinated but hardly grew at all. They were tiny pale-green plants that took forever to develop, and for two years we had no decent vegetables from that area. So, I

would strongly recommend that you do not get top soil that has a lot of sawdust in it. Also, be leery of very fine soil. To test it, pick some up in your hands and rub it through your fingers. If it has been overly sifted it will be silt-like. This means that it contains very little humus. When you put it on your garden or raised bed, it will compact down and nothing will grow in it.

If you know the nursery or source where you buy your soil, talk to them about what they put into it. If they are honest they will tell you. If it has a lot of mushroom manure added to it, then that is what I would buy. I do not think you can go wrong with a mixture of 50 percent mushroom manure and 50 percent soil. Always be sure to look at the soil before you have it delivered.

A good soil mixture to use for raised beds (and one that I use in my outdoor patio boxes) is three parts rich top soil, two parts bulk peat and one part sand. Bulk peat can be purchased from large garden centres where it is sold in the pile rather than in bales. There is nothing wrong with baled peat except that many of the fibres have been removed, and you will need some good fibre in your soil. Sand is not always easy to get. In recent years a lot of people have been using perlite as a substitute for sand. However, if you live near a builder's yard and have access to sand then do buy some. Do not buy sand that is too fine as it will push out the air from your soil. It should be gritty to the feel and may even have small pebbles in it. If I am going to be growing vegetables, I often substitute one part of the soil with mushroom manure. The mixture would then be two parts of soil, one part of mushroom manure, two parts of peat and one part of sand or perlite. This mixed well together will yield a very good basis for growing vegetables or flowers for the first year in a raised bed, tub or patio pot.

Soil Acidity

A problem that seems to worry people about the soil on our coast is that it is very acidic. This is true of many high-rainfall areas of the world. Acidity may seem a little alarming, but many plants are happy with a high acidic content. Because I believe that gardening should be fun, I do not think a lot of time should be spent worrying about the acidic content of the soil.

Acidity is measured on a pH scale of 0-14, seven being neutral. A pH above seven is called alkaline and a pH below 6.5 is called acid. Soil ratings above 8.5 and below 4.5 are rare, and most plants prefer a soil in the range of 6.5 to 7, which is probably what you will find in an average established garden on our coast. So go ahead and cultivate some plants and see how well they do. If you run into problems I would recommend that you have your soil tested. There are home soil test kits, but I would advise having it done by a soil test laboratory, particularly if you think that there may be major problems.

Soil Moisture

Although most of the soil in our part of the West Coast is very well drained, there can be problems in low lying areas where, during our long, wet winters, there is standing water. If it is possible, you may want to add an underground drainage system. In the old days we used to get clay tile drains and bury them under the soil. They were buried about 18 in. (45 cm) deep in among trenches of gravel and laid out in a feather or branch pattern. These trenches would drain the water into a ditch on the lower side of the property. Nowadays, prefabricated pipes with drainage holes are available. They can be substituted for clay tiles and are easier to lay. If you have moved into a new area and are not sure about the water drainage in your garden, keep notes during the winter rains to see exactly where the water sits. If it is a major problem, as when all the property around you is at a higher level and there is no low point to take your drainage ditch to, then you will have to resort to raised bed gardening.

Soil Compaction

Soil compaction occurs in high rainfall areas where the soil gets tamped down by people walking on it or rolling heavy machinery over it. If the soil is moist, it is pushed closer and closer together so that it becomes cement-like and nothing will grow on it. In a public garden where I used to work years ago we had a terrible time with soil compaction. It was a garden with lawns, trees and shrubs to represent contemporary plants used in everyday landscaping. The landscape contractors began to develop the area using heavy machinery. They would use certain tracks over and over again to come in and out of the garden, and we had a very difficult time getting some things to grow. To combat the problem we applied a good top dressing of well-rotted manure in the fall.

To lessen the occurrence of soil compaction in your home garden I suggest that you do your digging early in the fall when the weather is drier. If it is very wet, then leave it because you will do more harm than good by walking around on the soggy soil. If you feel that you simply have to dig and you cannot wait for the weather to dry up, then get some boards or a sheet of plywood and work from a platform. This will help the soil to stay light and well drained.

■ HUMUS

In an established garden, on an annual basis, we need to add to our garden soil that wonderful thing called humus. Humus is an old English gardening term for well-rotted compost, which is made from all the biodegradable things such as weeds, old plants, potato and apple peelings that we tend to throw away in the garbage. We should in fact be putting these back into the garden year after year.

Humus is essential to the soil. It is a dark-brown crumbly organic matter, consisting of plant and animal remains. Throughout their various stages of decay they ensure the continued survival of bacteria in the soil. This is necessary to keep the soil fertile. Humus helps to retain moisture, keeps the soil well aerated and is an excellent source of plant nutrients.

On cultivated ground humus breaks down more quickly than it would if left alone. That is why it is very important to replenish soil with well-rotted manure, compost, leaf mould or other forms of humus whenever possible. In all the great gardens of the world, including gardens that have been established for thousands of years, compost is added to the soil on a yearly basis.

In more temperate regions the best time of the year to dig your soil and add humus is in the fall, any time from October through to November. In the interior, which gets a lot of frost, it would be advisable to leave it until February. This, however, does not apply to preparing the

1. Digging a trench.

Turning the soil over.

Working in old crops, weeds and manure.

soil around shrubs and trees, but to annual flower beds and vegetable gardens only. I will talk about soil preparation for shrubs and trees later in this chapter.

After your flowers and vegetables are finished for the season, cut them off and chop them up. With a good spade or shovel remove some of the old plants and dig out a trench about 18 in. (45 cm) deep and 12 in. (30 cm) wide. The soil from that trench should be put into a wheelbarrow and taken to the other end of your garden and dumped. Go back to where you have dug your trench and scrape off the weeds and old cabbage or flowers or whatever vegetation is there. Take about a spade's width of adjacent soil and push this into the trench. If possible, stand in the trench and turn the old debris under one more time. This is not always possible in shallow soil, but try to turn it under. Then dig out a new trench by turning the soil upside down on top of the other, burying the first trench with all the weeds and compost in it. Now you are ready to start again.

This business of digging may sound terribly labour intensive, but if you begin digging in October and do not get the patch finished until November, that is no cause to worry. I am not against using rototillers or any of the modern tilling equipment, but there is a problem you should be aware of if you use them. If a rototiller is used time after time, it allows hard pan to form on the base as the blades only till the soil to a constant depth. As the blades reach the bottom they will form a basin. When digging by hand, you hit different levels of soil at different times, allowing you to chip away and break up the hard pan underneath.

Another problem with using a rototiller is that as you mix weeds and their seeds back into the soil, some seeds end up near the surface. Once the weather warms up in the spring they will germinate very quickly. If you dig by hand, as you turn each spade of soil completely upside down, bury the surface weed seeds at least 12 in. (30 cm) underground. They should then be too deep to germinate the following year.

You may, on reading through old English gardening books, come across the term loam. Loam is made by piling sod upside down and leaving it to rot for a season. This forms a fibrous top soil once the grass has rotted down. If you move into a home where there has been a large lawn and not much of a garden, then you could use this method by turning over the lawn to make your flower beds and borders. But there is one thing to watch out for. If the previous owners used a lot of lawn fertilizer and herbicides on the lawn I would not recommend that you grow vegetables during the first year. Some of the herbicides that are used in lawn care products can build up in the soil and cause problems for vegetables. So, for the first season or two grow flowers in those beds instead of vegetables. After one or two seasons, as long as you see no major problems with irregular flower growth, you could use these beds for a safe vegetable garden.

Another very good reason for adding humus and compost to soil on an annual basis is for moisture retention. It never ceases to amaze me that in the Vancouver area, when we get about ten days in a row of sunny weather in the summer, everything dries up and browns very quickly.

This is because there is very little moisture retention in the soil. To have a successful garden you must add, on an annual basis, organic material. Compost, peat, leaf mould, chopped-up sod or rotted manure are all suitable additions. If you can get good fresh manure that will be useful too.

In addition to adding compost in the fall, some people like to put in what is called a green manure crop. This can be oats, mustard or alfalfa. Alfalfa is used because it has good nitrogen fixation nodules on the root. If you choose to do this, spread seed on your garden after you have dug it in the fall. It will germinate and start to grow as soon as the weather warms up in the spring. Then dig under the green crop, providing a further addition of natural organic material to your soil. For more ideas on what to dig into your garden soil read the section on fertilizers and manures.

In an established flower bed or shrub border...one which includes perennials such as delphiniums and poppies...obviously you cannot dig it in every year and add humus. In this case, use well-rotted manure, mushroom manure or compost as a mulch. Apply it in the spring when the perennials begin to put up their annual growth. The average depth for a top dressing or a mulch would be about 3-4 in. (8-10 cm)...not so deep that you suffocate the surface roots of your perennials. This is also very important for shrub borders. Shrubs such as the rhododendron prefer a top dressing or mulch, but their surface roots are very important and should not be disturbed.

One thing I often see in shrub beds, where there has been a lot of weeding, is mounding up of soil. There is a terrible tendency, while hand or hoe weeding, not to shake all the soil from the plants. The result is that the shrubs end up growing on small mounds of soil because the top soil keeps being taken away. If this has happened in your garden, then apply a mulch in the spring just before the flower buds open on the rhododendrons and before the magnolia comes into bloom.

■ RAISED BEDS

Raised bed gardening is useful in poorly drained gardens and also in areas where there is little top soil, or where there are a lot of trees. If you find it difficult to get up and down and work in your garden, it is also advantageous to have a raised bed. Raised garden beds can be built to whatever height you wish. It can be at table height, suitable for standing or sitting at while working.

All kinds of materials can be used for building raised beds. The most popular in recent years have been railroad ties. These are fine as long as they are old. It is very important that they do not have creosote seeping out of them. Creosote can be detrimental to flowering plants and is not

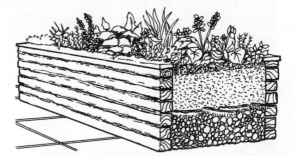

2. Wooden raised bed built from railroad ties.

good to have among food plants. If your railroad ties seep creosote, line the raised beds with plastic or use some other kind of lumber to build with. You can use any kind of treated lumber. Most lumber is treated with a material called copper naphthenate, which is very harmful to plants. However, if it has been absorbed into the wood and is dry then there is absolutely no problem. Creosote is only toxic to plants if it directly contacts the roots or foliage. Make sure that the wood has been treated one to two months before using it to allow for absorption.

It is perfectly alright to build raised beds out of cement blocks or insulation blocks used in the building industry. I have also seen metal sides used, although they are not the easiest thing to obtain. Most importantly, when planning raised garden beds, think about how you are actually going to use them. They can be as long as you like but should be no wider than twice your arm's length. You should be able to reach into the centre of your raised bed from either side so that you do not have to get up and walk around on the soil. This can cause problems with soil compaction.

Having said that raised beds can be as deep or as high as you need them, you may be thinking "how on earth can I afford to buy top soil to fill them?" However, you do not need to have good soil from the base to the top. As long as the top 18 in. (45 cm) is of good quality the rest can be absolute rubbish. It can be old rocks picked up from around the garden or soil from construction sites. It should be fairly well drained material, but you could use just about anything.

■ COMPOST

In North America, we are very tidy gardeners and tend to throw away much of our garden waste. With this waste we could be making a wonderful humus and soil conditioner for our garden right in our own backyard. I even have friends who make compost on their balconies. One makes compost in plastic bags from her twelfth-storey apartment. The plastic bags keep the smell down and she hides them behind planters so they are not too visible. Organic material breaks down very quickly and can be usable compost within a month and a half. By making our own compost not only do we have a free source of soil conditioner but also the amount of waste that we send to our landfills is reduced. Almost any organic material is suitable for putting in a compost pile. Plant trimmings such as dead leaves from houseplants or yellowed leaves from cabbages and cauliflowers can be added. Weeds are also good if they are annual weeds. You do not want to add couch grass or mare's tail to your compost pile. Some people worry about weed seeds in their compost pile, but if you add only immature weeds there should be no problem. As long as the weeds have flower buds and no seed yet they will not germinate in your compost pile. Kitchen waste such as vegetable and fruit peelings and egg shells are wonderful things for adding to compost. Coffee grounds, tea bags and tea leaves will also add moisture. Ashes from wood burning fires, potato peelings, grapefruit, orange and apple peels, all these things make up a good soil conditioner for the garden. Grass clippings are also excellent to add to a compost pile. If you have a lawn you will have large amounts of grass clippings at regular intervals. These should be mixed thoroughly into your compost pile to allow them to rot down quickly. Do not just dump grass clippings onto the compost heap—it will take much longer for them to rot down. Be careful not to use grass from a lawn which has been treated with herbicide.

The best location for a compost pile is

the day. It should not be sited in deep shade beneath trees where it will get no sunlight. Sunlight is important to activate the bacteria to heat up the compost pile, which will make it break down much faster.

If you have a permanent space to develop your compost then I would definitely recommend putting in a concrete base on which to build your compost bin. It may be costly but it will be something

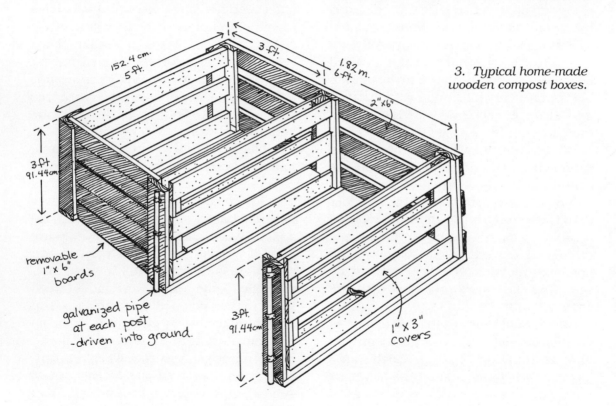

152.4 cm. 5 ft.

3 ft.

1.82 m. 6 ft.

2" x 6"

3 ft. 91.44 cm

3. *Typical home-made wooden compost boxes.*

removable 1" x 6" boards

galvanized pipe at each post -driven into ground.

3 ft. 91.44 cm

1" x 3" covers

in a convenient but inconspicuous place. It should be down towards the bottom of the garden near the garage or shed, or in behind some high-growing plants, perhaps behind a shrub border or pole beans. Wherever you put it, it is important that a compost pile gets sunshine at least half

you will use year after year and which will become an integral part of your gardening. A minimum size for the base is approximately 6.5 ft. (2 m) long by 3 ft. (1 m) wide. Build two wooden bins or boxes side by side, each 3 ft. (1 m) square. Again, the lumber should be treated, preferably treated cedar. Keep in mind that it should be nice and dry before using. The boards on the side of the boxes need not meet. This will allow extra air into the compost pile. For the front of the box it is important that the boards be slotted in such a way that they can be lifted out. When it comes time to use your compost you will then be able to shovel it cleanly and freely out of the bin without getting hung up on the sides.

To begin your compost pile mix together grass clippings, cabbage leaves, potato peelings—organic material. If they are dry add some moisture, then sprinkle on a handful of ammonium sulphate. Ammonium sulphate is nitrogen fertilizer and breaks things down very quickly. Compost additives introduce bacteria into your compost pile, and you can buy numerous types of compost-making agents at any garden centre. I suggest that you discuss options with one of their gardeners. For those of you who live in the country you may have access to manure. Chicken manure is very high in nitrogen when it is fresh. Sprinkle some of that in, just enough to get the bacteria started. After the first 6 in. (15 cm) layer of green debris, add an inch or two (2.5-5 cm) of soil. This is not absolutely necessary, but I find it a good idea to put a light layer of soil over the top. It will help keep rodents out and the smell in. This soil does not have to be good quality and can even be subsoil from your garden. After spending some time in the compost pile it will be wonderful.

Continue to build your compost in 6 in. (15 cm) layers with a bit of soil in between. When the box is half full, it is a good idea to poke bamboo canes down into the centre. Four canes poked into the box will give good air circulation, which will help the bacteria to activate and encourage rot. Some people cover their compost pile with plastic, but I prefer leaving it exposed with the canes sticking up. It may, however, be a good idea to cover your compost pile with plastic in a particularly dry or wet season. You do not want your compost to dry out, yet too much rain can leach out a lot of the goodness. In a small compost pile such as this you do not need to turn it. I am sure you have read about turning compost to make it rot more quickly, but provided you have broken up the material into small enough pieces and have added a rotting agent it will break down fairly quickly without turning.

When breaking up material to add to your compost heap, you may want to use a shredder. Many garden catalogues advertise hand-driven shredders built like old-fashioned meat grinders. For a small compost a shredder is not necessary. However, if you have large-leafed trees and have difficulty breaking up these large leaves in the fall, a shredder could be useful. Large leaves can be a real problem when they are put into a compost pile if they are not broken up properly. They will sit on top of each other, allowing no air between them. Then when you uncover your compost three or four months later, they are preserved exactly as you put them in.

If you have no room to put in a large compost pile you can make them up seasonally. Fall is a good time, when you will have access to lots of organic debris left over from the season—spent annuals, dried-up vegetable plants, fall leaves and things like that from around the garden. All these make a good seasonal compost pile. Get wide-mesh chicken wire and form a circle. Locate an area in the garden that you will not be using during the winter and peg the wire circle down with a few bamboo canes. Put the waste material in exactly as before (6 in./15 cm layers plus soil) and by the spring you will have some very nice compost to dig into your special plants, perhaps beans or tomatoes or any plants that require a little higher nutrition for good growth.

Another good way to get successful crops from deep-rooted plants, such as pole beans, romano beans or sweet peas, is to build a compost pile on site. In the fall, if you have planned your garden and know where your crops are going the following season, you can dig out a trench on site. Make it about 2 ft. (.6 m) wide by at least 2 ft. (.6 m) deep, the deeper the better. Pile the soil around the rim of the trench, and as garden and household waste becomes available, bury it in 6 in. (15 cm) layers. You can do this over the entire winter. A trench opened in October and filled with organic waste throughout the winter would be full by the spring, and you need only level it out a bit. Believe me, when you put those beans in the following year they are going to do a tremendous job for you. It is also a good way of preparing soil without the laborious job of double-digging the trench all in one go.

■ LIME

For growing vegetables, due to our acidic soil content, it is important to add lime, perhaps on an annual basis. However, there are one or two things that you should know. First of all, it is possible to over-lime your garden, so only apply lime when necessary. The best time is during the fall or after you have finished digging your gardens—any time in November. As a general rule, apply lime at one handful to the square yard (1 m^2). One note of caution, and this is very important, is not to spread lime if you have recently put in fresh manure. Lime spread on fresh manure will lock up the phosphates, which results in an undesirable chemical reaction in the soil. By locking up the phosphates you will not get good root action in your garden. There are two widely available lime products. Hydrated lime acts quickly and is safe to use close to plants. If you want something longer lasting then choose dolomite lime, but for general garden use hydrated lime is fine and I recommend it for local use. Interior gardens are often quite alkaline and will not need liming at all.

■ ORGANIC FERTILIZERS

Plant food or fertilizers are divided into two categories: organic manures (which are all the natural forms) and inorganic fertilizers. People have become more and more interested in organic gardening, and there are many natural fertilizers to use. On the coast we have seaweed, which is a wonderful natural fertilizer. Fish fertilizer is also widely used. If you are a true organic gardener you will prefer to use one of the organic fertilizers.

You can never have too much organic material dug into your garden. Humus in its half-decomposed state acts as a sponge in light soils to retain food and moisture.

In heavy soils by river deltas it can be used to provide drainage and allow filtration between soil particles. It is difficult to say exactly how much food is available from homemade composted humus. In the soil, in the latter stages of decomposition the dissolved salts are taken up by the plants. These can include trace elements and all the regular requirements for the plant. There is also a little nitrogen and certainly some phosphates and potash in humus.

However, if possible, it is a good idea to use some animal manures in the garden as well. Well-rotted farmyard manure is very difficult to find, and all animal manures should be well rotted before being used. The Boy Scouts often have manure sales. If the manure is still very smelly then it is fairly fresh. This means that you should put it into your garden in the fall as it will require time for the winter rains to wash out the excess salt. Then, by the time for spring planting, it should be wonderful stuff for the roots to get down into. Leaving fresh manure piled up for the heavy winter rains to wash out the salt is fine if you live in the country, but if you leave it out in your backyard in the city, you will get a lot of complaints from your neighbours. It is also possible to dig in well-rotted manure during the spring before putting in your vegetables. Start in March so that by April everything is ready to go.

Some of you who live near chicken or turkey farms may from time to time have poultry manure available to you. Poultry manure is very rich and must never be used fresh: it should only be dug into a garden during October or November. Mix some up with peat and dig it into your soil. The peat will add texture to a light soil and will improve moisture retention. You should have some lovely vegetables the following year. If you do add poultry manure in the fall you will generally not need to add any other fertilizer in the spring.

Seaweed is probably the next best thing to farmyard manure. It was used by the early settlers to our area, along with starfish and other kinds of marine life. Seaweed contains a reasonable amount of plant nutrients, particularly potash, and decomposes quickly. It may be dug into the ground while wet, or can be composted with garden waste and applied when partially broken down. Some people worry about the salt content in seaweed, but in the sheltered coastal inland waters between Vancouver Island and the Lower Mainland, you are not going to get a tremendous amount of salt. If you put fresh seaweed around your young vegetable plants, the salt will keep the slugs away. Mind you, after the salt is washed off the slugs will flock to the seaweed. It is a good option for short-term protection, and after it breaks down it can be worked into the soil.

Those of you who have lived around the Vancouver area for some time will remember that you once could go to sewage farms and get treated sewage sludge. It was thought to be a wonderful fertilizer for the garden. Today, I would not go anywhere near it. There are far too many chemicals used in the breakdown of sewage which were not used years ago and I do not advise using it. You will end up putting a lot of toxic substances into your garden.

In discussing manures it might seem a

little odd to mention peat. The nutrient value in peat is very low, but the important thing is that it can hold as much as 90 percent water. This can be a very important additive to the soil. Dry summer periods occur regularly in the Lower Mainland area and throughout the Gulf Islands. So if you have access to a source of peat by all means dig it into your garden. If you buy peat from a garden centre and it is dry, moisten it before adding it to the soil. If peat is applied dry and we go through a drought period, even in the winter, it will take a long time for it to absorb that useful moisture.

Leaf mould is another wonderful thing to add to gardens and is readily available. In the fall, street leaves pile up and cars drive over them. Our typical wet weather turns them into a wonderful mushy substance which is almost instant compost. I would strongly recommend that you dig this into your garden. I know that those of you who are organic gardeners will worry about the lead content. However, studies that have been done at the Center for Urban Horticulture at the University of Washington have shown that the lead content is minuscule in high rainfall areas such as Seattle and Vancouver. Most of the lead will be washed out, particularly if you dig the leaves in during the fall. By the time spring comes around any lead content in the soil is going to be minimal.

One of the great successes that we have had at the University of British Columbia's Botanical Garden is making use of leaf refuse. We made an area of the garden available to the city and they brought in truckloads of leaves when they were cleaning the streets. You get a lot of junk in with it such as bottles and

cans, but these can be sorted out. The leaf mould, after it has been piled up for two to three years, is fabulous. We add it to the rhododendrons in the Asian garden and when we put in our fruit trees. Oak and beech leaves make a particularly good leaf mould, but any type is fine to use. Remember when using leaves to break them up before adding them to your compost. If you have a rotary mower, run that over them two or three times and that will chop them up nicely.

Planting a green manure crop is a very useful thing to do if you have major growing problems in your garden or if you have moved into a new home and do not know the nutrient content of your soil. Turn the garden over, and during July and August sow a crop of clover, turnip, alfalfa or peas. This could then be turned under in the fall and should greatly improve the soil quality. A potato crop is another good crop to use this way. Potatoes are very strong-growing plants and will break up the soil as they are forming. This is not the most sophisticated form of green manure crop, but potato plant tops when turned under will be a good conditioner for your soil.

In garden centres you can find a packaged fertilizer called dried blood, or blood meal. Horrible, I know—I do not even want to think about where it comes from. It is, however, very high in nitrogen. If you are gardening organically and do not want to put ammonium sulphate on your compost pile you could substitute dried blood. Also, if you want to give plants an extra boost of nitrogen in the spring, dried blood would be useful to add to your garden. Follow the instructions on the package very carefully and do not overdo it, as you can run into problems by using too much nitrogen.

Another common organic fertilizer is bone meal, which comes in several grades. Coarse bone meal is fairly high in phosphate with about 4 percent nitrogen and takes a long time to break down, so only add coarse bone meal during the fall when planting bulbs as nutrients will become available to them in the spring when they need an extra boost. Coarse bone meal is also good to use when planting shrubs in the fall as it will not burn the roots and will again be available to them in the spring. There is also a slightly faster-acting form of bone meal which has been ground into a finer powder. Without a doubt, bone meal is a good organic fertilizer.

There are several new seaweed products on the market. As with bone meal, these tend to be a little higher in nitrogen. However, they have a good balanced ratio and can be used on a regular basis. Use them in the spring while planting your garden and once a month during the summer. I would strongly recommend any of the seaweed fertilizers as well as fish fertilizers, which have been around for years. One of the things people did not like about fish fertilizers was that they had a rather strong odour. Deodorized fish fertilizer is now available, and I would recommend it over many of the inorganic fertilizers.

Soot and wood ash are also good materials to use for organic gardening. Soot is not readily available, but if you have a wood-burning fireplace, save the soot when you have your chimney swept. It can be used quite effectively in your garden provided you wet it down well. It is fairly high in nitrogen and helps to lighten heavy soil. You may use it as a top dressing in early spring, but be aware that since it is high in nitrogen you will not want to add it if you have put in a lot of manure. This would result in a lot of top growth and no root development. Wood ash is good to put in your garden, and it will also help to keep away the slugs. If you use ash from your stove or fireplace, make sure that you burn only wood in them. It will not be good if you have a habit of burning chemical logs, plastics or trash.

■ INORGANIC FERTILIZERS

If time is too limited to contend with organic forms of fertilizers, there are other options. A trip to the local garden centre, particularly in the spring, will reveal a massive array of packaged fertilizers. Examples are rose food, rhododendron food, lawn food and specialized food for just about every crop you can grow in the garden. However, despite lengthy research and development of these specialized crop fertilizers, I think in a home garden situation it is best to find one balanced fertilizer that works well for you. Everyone will have his or her favourite balanced fertilizer. Mine happens to be 6-8-6.

Let me explain what those numbers mean in a balanced fertilizer. The basic ingredients of commercial fertilizer are nitrogen, phosphate and potash. The amount of each is shown on the package or label as a guaranteed analysis—it has to be there by law. You will see three numbers in a row, always in the same sequence. A very common lawn food is 10-6-4. This means that it has 10 percent nitrogen, 6 percent phosphorus and 4 percent potash. The remainder of it is some sort of inert carrier material. A fertilizer carrying all three elements is commonly known as a complete fertilizer.

The first number is nitrogen. There is a tendency in our area to overfertilize with nitrogen in the spring. Nitrogen overused in high rainfall areas adds acid to our already acidic soil and can create real problems. Some of the older lawns, that have been treated with nitrogen over a number of years, have become so acidic that the grass dies out. Nitrogen is used for good green leaves and stems and is important at certain stages in a plant's growth.

The middle number is phosphate, which is used by plants primarily to build a good root system. Obviously, for any garden plant, lawn, house plant or patio plant, without a healthy root system you will not have a healthy plant. The presence of the middle number is important in all fertilizers that you buy.

The third number is potash. Potash is primarily used for the general health of a plant and is very important when a plant is developing its flowers or fruit. If you have a fruit tree that has not produced flowers for a number of years, it is a good idea to give it some straight potash once in spring and again in August. This will help to promote and produce flower buds for the following year.

So, nitrogen, phosphate and potash are the three major elements in a balanced fertilizer. It is good to know a little about them when sorting out your garden problems. For example, if you find your carrots and radishes have a lot of top growth but underdeveloped roots, you would then know that there is perhaps too much nitrogen in your soil, and you should add a bit more phosphate. This detective work all goes into making gardening fun, and you should feel free to experiment on your own.

The most common source of phosphate is superphosphate, which you will find as a prepackaged fertilizer. There were also some household cleaners with a high phosphate content that people would add to their garden, giving amazing results. However, this all seems to be a thing of the past since most laundry detergents are now phosphate free. When I was a child in Britain I remember my father saving dishwater and laundry water and adding it to the garden during dry spells. It never hurt the garden and in retrospect it probably helped the root systems develop.

Potash can be found in garden centres under the name of sulphate of potash. Recent developments in the potash industry indicate that it will no longer be available, but there should always be some form of potash you can buy. You might think that if you buy nitrogen, phosphate and potash individually, then you could mix up your own fertilizers. However, I think it is much better if you want a general fertilizer to buy one that has been premixed. Again, I find 6-8-6 a good all-purpose blend. I use it at home for my flower and vegetable gardens, and we have used it quite effectively in the Canadian Broadcasting Corporation's (CBC) roof garden in Vancouver. It is not too high in nitrogen, has a stronger middle number for root development and an adequate amount of potash for healthy flowers and fruit.

■ FEEDING YOUR GARDEN

I recommend that you feed your garden on a monthly basis throughout the summer, say at the end of June, July and August. This is especially true if you have raised garden beds. In the roof garden at CBC we had raised beds with no more than an 18 in. (45 cm) soil depth. In the first year of the garden, using fresh soil and mushroom manure, we had tremendous growth in our vegetables and flowers from April to June. In July, when the beds started to fill with roots, the plants began to turn yellow. This is because when growing plants in a restricted area, like a raised bed or patio pot, every watering leaches out a certain amount of fertilizer. So, it is a good idea to adopt a regular feeding program, even if you have an unrestricted soil depth.

In addition to the major elements used by plants for their growth there are trace elements. I would not get too concerned about adding trace elements unless you have a major problem. Gardening should be fun and thinking too much about trace elements could be worrisome. However, as an example, I will mention one symptom I see fairly often that results from a magnesium deficiency. It usually shows up where the veins of a leaf remain very green but the parts in between are yellow. It does not occur a lot in outdoor gardens, but I have seen it on house plants such as the gardenia. A very good source of magnesium is Epsom salts. Add about one teaspoon (5 ml) into 2½ qts. (3 l) of water and water the plants that look to you as if they have magnesium deficiency. It will not hurt them, and if it greens them up then you have solved the problem.

If you are using compost, mushroom manure or leaf mould there is no reason why you would run into deficiencies of trace elements. You can get micronized iron or other trace elements at your garden centre, but do not get too worried about them. If you use a well-balanced fertilizer you should not have any problems. If you do, get advice from an expert. Both of the major botanical gardens in Vancouver will answer home gardening questions. In recent years there has also been a build-up of the master gardener program and very often these master gardeners will be on duty in garden centres in the spring to answer your questions. By adding trace elements to your garden you could upset the balance of your soil. So, first use an organic fertilizer, then as a supplement perhaps dig in some leaves or mushroom manure. Then, during the summer, when you are growing your vegetable crop, use 6-8-6 once a month, applying at a handful per square yard (1 m²). For the average garden, no matter where you live in this region, that should be fine for growing successful flowers and vegetables.

One thing to remember which is extremely important when using inorganic fertilizers on the garden is to water them in well right after applying them. If powdered inorganic fertilizers get on leaves they can burn the plants. So, it is extremely important to do your watering right away to wash all the excess material off the leaves and down into the root area.

■ WATERING YOUR GARDEN

Watering your garden is something that we all have to do in the summertime.

Some of us have limited supplies of water during the summer, but there are things that we can do to help. For example, adding humus to your soil will help retain moisture as will adding a mulch. A mulch can be either well-rotted compost, peat or even grass clippings.

If you have a large lawn which you mow on a regular basis, and as long as you have not put any herbicide products on it, you will have far more grass clippings than you need to put in your compost. In a vegetable garden these clippings can work extremely well as a mulch. Apply mulch on the soil surface particularly around plants such as tomatoes, cabbage and peppers to help stop evaporation. If you spread it on the surface of the soil about 2-3 in. (5-7.5 cm) deep it will keep the sun away from the soil surface and keep moisture down around the root area. I would strongly recommend a mulch in all kinds of gardening, even among flowers. In a perennial bed, for example, if you top dress with well-rotted leaf mould in the spring, your perennials will remain well watered and looking healthy and fine for the summer.

Plastic sheets covered with bark mulch are something else you can use, although I do not care for it. I dislike the use of black plastic and bark mulch in landscaping and think it has been terribly over-used. I prefer to see something more soil-like when I look at a garden. Also, when bark mulch starts to decompose it takes the nitrogen out of the soil in the same way as does sawdust.

When it comes to watering your garden, make sure that you only water the soil areas and not your sidewalk or driveway. I get very cross when I see people wasting tremendous amounts of water, particularly during water shortages. There are many devices that allow you to water at a low height, near your gardens. Drip irrigation watering methods are also quite popular now. The best time of day to water, during the summer months, is first thing in the morning. If you water early in the morning, then as the sun comes up it will dry the excess moisture off the plants and they will be nice and dry by evening. If you water the garden at night, moisture hangs on the leaves, causing problems with powdery mildew, especially in a coastal climate. So, try to give your plants a good soak in the morning and leave them be.

You may have heard people say that you should not water in full sunlight. That is probably true. If the water droplets sit on leaves on a hot sunny day, they will scorch. However, I would say that if your plants are wilted and in need of water during the heat of the day, make sure you water only the root area and not the leaves. You then have no problems with leaf scorching.

■ THINGS TO REMEMBER

The bottom line to good soil is that it should be well drained and deep enough to allow you to dig in annual applications of well-rotted compost, or well-rotted manure to a couple of spades' depth. When choosing a site for a new garden make sure that you take the preparation time to eliminate all the perennial weeds.

Should you run into trouble with drastically poor growth in your first season, then I would strongly recommend having your soil tested professionally.

Lawns

To some people a lawn is one of the most important features of the garden. And I say some, simply because having a perfect lawn on the Pacific Coast takes a lot of work. I well remember from my first visit to the coast in 1968 how the soft green lawns in the parks stuck in my mind. For a family house, on an average-sized city lot, I think a lawn is a must because it is a great place for the children to play and is fun for barbecues.

However, a lawn has to stand a great amount of wear and tear. For example, constant mowing takes an average of 12-18 in. (30-45 cm) of grass away from the lawn every year. And then there is the problem of moss in our coastal lawns, which I will deal with in detail a little later in the chapter.

First of all, let us discuss the establishment of a new lawn. If you have moved into a brand new home where the builders have just left, the possibility of finding any decent top soil in your yard is fairly remote. More likely lumps of cement, bits of wood, pipe and wire will be mixed in with some compacted subsoil and plenty of rocks. Even if a new house has had its yard landscaped or finished off with a load of top soil or bark mulch which has been dumped and raked over for aesthetics, you will still have quite a bit of work to do.

Ideally, if you have a chance to go to the home site before it is built and save the top soil by pushing it to one side, the establishment of your new lawn will be easier. If the lawn area is to be small you could attempt to hand dig the new area, preferably in the fall. However, it may be impossible if the soil has been badly compacted by the builders, so you may well have to have someone come in and plow or till the area before attempting to add any top soil.

The grading of your lawn is also important. If possible, it should slope away from the house just slightly. Since on our hilly coast most lots are naturally sloping this should not be a major problem. However, if the sloping is drastic, then some retainer walls will be necessary to level your lawn. If you have clay subsoil which is poorly drained, then you will need to add drain tile. This is quite a difficult task to undertake in a home garden. The tiles need to be at least 18 in. (45 cm) deep, 16 ft. (5 m) apart and, of course, gently sloping away from the building or garden by a 2 in. (5 cm) drop every 6 in. (15 cm). I think you will agree that it is quite a big job and well worth contracting out. But, on the other hand, if your soil is glacial till and well drained you will not have to deal with drainage. If you are planning to have an irrigation system put in for the future, this is the stage at which it should be incorporated.

Assuming all this has been done throughout the winter, try to remove any debris on the surface, such as pieces of wood and cement. In the spring, perhaps in March when the earth begins to dry out, it will be time to add top soil, either some from your garden or more likely some that has to be purchased. As I mentioned in the soil section, I cannot overemphasize the importance of going to see the top soil before you purchase it. By looking at it first you will have a good idea of what you are getting. How much you purchase will depend on how big an area you need to cover. You should have at least 4 in. (10 cm) of top soil depth over the whole area. Preferably, some organic material such as well-rotted compost or manure should be added in a 2 in. (5 cm) layer on the top before rototilling the whole new lawn site.

If you live in an area that is poorly drained, you may need to add some sand. Avoid putting sawdust into the soil as it robs nitrogen from the top soil when it is rotting down. Nitrogen is very important for green lawns.

Lawns grow best in a soil which has a pH of 6.5, which is slightly on the acid side. If your pH is lower, then you may need to introduce some lime, about a handful per square yard (1 m²), before the rototilling takes place. Early rototilling should be done in March when the soil dries out. This gives the weed seeds a chance to grow. They can then be rototilled or hoed off once germinated before they have a chance to form new seed. Any perennial weeds such as mare's tail should be dug out at this stage also.

During April the site should be raked regularly to remove any large rocks. If it has not rained much, roll and rake or walk and rake as you go to settle the soil since it is very important when it comes to sowing time that the soil be firm and level. Otherwise, dips and hollows will be formed and you will not end up with a nice level lawn. On the other hand, if it has been a wet spring then you will need to lay down boards or planks to walk on to prevent soil compaction. Soil needs to be firm but it does not need to be rock hard like cement so that all the air has been pushed out of it.

■ SEEDING YOUR LAWN

About the third week of April you should be ready to sow your lawn seed, and at this time you should rake the area gently one more time, making sure you get rid of any large rocks. Just before raking add granular 6-8-6 at a handful per square yard (1 m^2).

Now to the seed and what to use. The following four mixtures are recommended by Agriculture Canada for use in southern British Columbia.

Mixture number one consists of 80 percent fine fescue grass and 20 percent Colonial Bent grass, and it should be seeded at 3 lbs. per 100 square yards (1.5 kgs per 100 m^2). This mixture will give a high maintenance, beautiful lawn of fine-textured grasses which is not suitable for heavy traffic.

Mixture number two consists of 30 percent Kentucky Bluegrass, 60 percent fine fescue grass and 10 percent Colonial Bent grass and should be seeded at 3.5 lbs. per 100 square yards (1.8 kgs per 100 m^2). It will give a lawn which is predominantly fine textured but can be managed well with average maintenance. It will give a nice looking lawn but is not recom-

mended for heavy family use.

Mixture number three consists of 40 percent Kentucky Bluegrass and 60 percent fine fescue grass which should be applied at 4 lbs. per 100 square yards (2 kgs per 100 m^2). It is a basic lawn mixture which can tolerate *moderate* shade. Lawns do not generally perform well in deep shade, such as that found under cedars, but this mix is good for the north side of the house, since fescues can tolerate shade better than Bluegrass.

Mixture number four is probably the one that you are looking for if you have a family. It consists of 30 percent Kentucky Bluegrass, 40 percent fine fescue and 30 percent perennial rye grass which should be applied at 5 lbs. per 100 square yards (2.5 kgs per 100 m^2). Because it contains perennial rye grass it has a greater tolerance for wear and tear from ballgames and picnics.

One other mix for heavy use that was recommended to me by a friend is 50 percent Kentucky Bluegrass and 50 percent perennial rye grass. This is sold in garden centres as stadium mix. Apply it at 4 lbs. per 100 square yards (2 kgs per 100 m^2).

Bent grasses tend to dominate lawns in coastal B.C. and they will take over if not controlled. With good management, which means mowing to 1 in. (2.5 cm) or less and a careful regular feeding and watering program, they should not get out of hand. However, never use Creeping Bent grass in coastal lawns. This climate is so good for it, it will just take over completely. If you are tempted to use it, it will only work if you cut your lawn every two days and keep it cut really short, which makes for an ugly and uncomfortable lawn to walk on. So try not to be tempted to use it at all.

The best times for seeding lawns are mid-April to mid-May or late August to mid-September. Sometimes, if the ground needs a lot of work, the late summer sowing leaves adequate preparation time for difficult sites with poorly drained soil or if you have a lot of soil moving to do. Small areas may be seeded by hand using the following method. Divide the seed into halves. Sow one half walking backwards and broadcasting the seed back and forth over the area as you go. Then with the second half walk back and forth at right angles to the previous direction. This should give fairly even coverage, but if you are not sure of yourself, then use a cyclone seeder which you can usually rent from a local garden centre. Again, when using a rotary seeder make sure that you split the seed in half and work in one direction one time and the other direction the next.

After sowing the seed it should be raked lightly but just in one direction, towards you only, working backwards. This will avoid bunching of the seed. You do not want to rake it into little bunches, which results in uneven germination. Then, if possible, roll the area, as this tends to firm the soil around the seed and makes for better germination. Water lightly and frequently but very, very carefully. Do not just leave a sprinkler on and go away because if the water puddles on the ground the seed will get washed about into clumps. In dry seasons I would recommend watering lightly daily until the seeds are well germinated. It is best to water by hand or with a very fine sprinkler.

Once the grass is 3 in. (7.5 cm) tall you may begin to mow. Do not set the mower blade any lower than 2 in. (5 cm) and make sure that you use a sharp mower blade. Otherwise you will be pulling the grass out of the ground because it does not yet have a very large root system. This mowing regime should then be followed for the next seven weeks or so to allow the grass to make a decent root system. Also, it is very important that newly sown grass should be dry when mowing as wet grass can be pulled out of the ground more easily. No matter how careful you have been in preparation of the soil some weeds are bound to germinate with the grass. The mowing should take care of them quite nicely, so do not be tempted to use selective herbicides until the lawn is at least two months old. If it is a fall sowing you should not use any herbicides until the following year. Even then I am not a believer in using any herbicide on lawns because the grass is such a useful thing for compost. In the weed section of this book I will give some alternative ways of keeping your lawn nice and clean without the use of herbicides.

■ SOD

The other way to establish a new lawn is by using sod or turf. This is much more expensive, but it does yield an instant lawn. If you move into a house in the middle of the season and you just cannot wait for all that time to put in your lawn, it is still very important to prepare the site well. Sure, you can buy really nice sod from somewhere, but if the soil has not been well prepared and you do not have that depth for the roots to go down into then you will be wasting your time. Unfortunately, in many areas sod lawns are not put down with the proper preparation and end up being quite a disaster.

It is very important that you purchase your sod from a reputable sod grower who guarantees the variety of grass. Make sure that the sod you buy does not contain any Creeping Bent grass, and that it is a mixture similar to one of those recommended by Agriculture Canada.

I suppose it is fair to say that the preparation of soil to receive sod need not be quite as careful in the amount of rocks that you take out, but try to work it well, and make certain that the ground is level. The sod should be laid as soon as possible after delivery. It must never be allowed to dry out—this is something that you need to watch for because in the spring we tend to get drying winds. If you do have to store it any longer than eight hours, then it should be stored in the shade and covered with wet burlap, or some other material that will allow the air to flow through. Never cover it with plastic because it will start to heat up and rot on the inside like a compost pile. But any covering should only be done in an emergency. It is much better to have your site ready and put the sod down the very first day that it arrives.

Lay your first row of sod in a very straight line along a driveway or a path. If there is no existing border already established around it, then you will need to put in some stakes or canes with strings running between them to determine exactly where your lawn is to go. Try to put in the first row with the ends butted close together. Then indent the second row as if you were building brick work, so that you do not have all the joints lined up

together, and continue on for the other rows.

You must never stretch the sod because it has been cut in exactly the form in which it was growing. If you stretch it, it shrinks on drying and leaves spaces that are easily invaded by weeds. I know the odd time you are going to make a mistake, and you can fill in those little patches with some decent soil and sow some seed in there, but try to do it properly the first time, with the ends really close together so that when they dry out they are still touching.

When all your sod has been laid, roll it with a lawn roller to ensure that you get really good contact between the strips. Make sure that the sod is touching the soil beneath, and then water it thoroughly with a sprinkler, not allowing it to dry out. If it is laid any time from June to August, I would recommend that you water it daily for the first six weeks or so. It is better to lay sod down in the spring or the fall, just as you would seed a lawn, but even then, if it is a hot, dry season make sure that the sod is watered daily.

You will know when the sod is nicely established because the grass will start to grow noticeably. Even though it is sod, it is still best not to cut it any lower than 3 in. (7.5 cm) for the first two to three cuttings because the mower might catch and pull up the newly planted strips.

We have a peculiar phenomenon here on the coast where there are many raccoons in our residential areas. Pretty things though they are, if they decide there is an area of a lawn that is going to make it easy for them to find their food they will come every night and roll up the sod in a neat little roll just the way you put it down.

They will be looking underneath for slugs and worms and other kinds of little bugs that are nice food for them. And this, while it may seem cute, can be very frustrating over a long period of time because the grass never gets a chance to become established. You may have to resort to putting some chicken wire down across the lawn after you have planted it and bang a few stakes in here and there to keep it well anchored down if you have raccoons in your area.

■ LAWN CARE

Once your lawn is established, whether it has been sown from seed or put in by sod, you need to start thinking about maintaining a good lawn—how to keep it nice and green, how to keep it well maintained by mowing on a regular basis, and how to deal with dry periods.

First of all, let us deal with mowing. You need to have a good, sharp lawnmower. There are various lawnmowers on the market. The most common are the rotary mowers, although you do find the odd English-style roller mower around. If you want a really super-looking lawn a roller mower is best. However, the rotary mower is easy to maintain. You can get mowers that are run by gas or by electricity. The old push mower is even making a comeback for today's pocket-size townhouse lawns. How you mow will have a tremendous influence on the growth and development of grass in your lawn. The height of the cut is critical. Proper height varies for different grasses and for different conditions. A lawn, to me, should

4. Steps for laying sod: i) Fertilizing and levelling soil. ii) Securing line for straight edge.

feel like a soft carpet, something that you want to sit on and play on. Kentucky Bluegrass does not tolerate any heights of less then 1 in. (2.5 cm) for very long and really makes for a nice, thick lawn. That is the type of lawn to aim for. With a thicker lawn you stimulate the production of lots of new shoots which keeps it looking green. It also leads to a nice root system and keeps the whole thing really healthy.

Many people hate to mow the lawn, so they let it grow long and then cut it very short. This makes for an awful, brown-looking lawn. To maintain a nice, thick green lawn you have to mow it on a regular basis. There is just no way around it.

If you use a rotary mower that has a collection sack, collect the grass for the compost. But if you feel you are getting an overabundance of grass then with a rotary mower you can cut more often and just let the fine pieces of cut grass fall down among the live blades around the lawn. The dead cuttings will get washed in and used as food for the lawn.

How often should you mow? Grass should be mowed often enough so that only about one-third of the total plant showing above ground is removed, never more than one-half. On average, this means about once a week, but the growth rate in our area is tremendous at certain times of the year and you may need to mow more often. It is very important that you remember to raise the height of your cut during hot, dry periods. This will let the lawn survive better at those times.

It is extremely important to keep the mower blades sharp. It is also a good idea

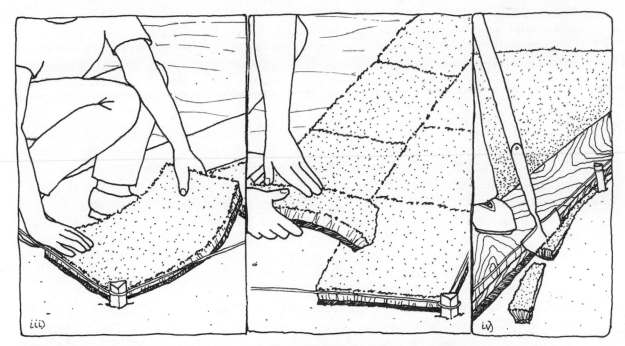

iii) Correct laying method. iv) Using a wooden plank as a guide to trim edge.

to change the direction in which you mow the lawn. This is not as important with a rotary mower, but if you have a roller-type mower, go back and forth one way one time and then diagonally the next time. This will result in a better and more even growth in the grass. Try to avoid mowing the lawn when the grass is soft and wet. Sometimes this is a problem, particularly in the fall, but try not to mow it on a very wet day unless you really have to, unless you have something special going on and want the lawn to look tidy. If not, then leave it until the weather dries out.

■ *Fertilizing Your Lawn* ■

We live in a high rainfall area, and our soil is on the acidic side. Traditionally, this would mean that wherever you want a nice lawn you need to add high-nitrogen fertilizers. But there can be a real problem with adding too much high-nitrogen fertilizer to coastal lawns. Adding nitrogen over a time, particularly if you use inorganic material, will build up the acidity in the soil. I have seen some old lawns run into all kinds of problems because eventually the acid content is so high that the grass begins to deteriorate and slime moulds and other horrible things start to grow in the lawn.

I would say as a general rule that in the spring it is alright to go with high-nitrogen fertilizers, but in the middle of the summer and certainly in the fall, if you are going to feed then try to use a fertilizer with high middle and last numbers. Remember, the middle number means phosphate which produces a good root system, and the last number stands for potash, which promotes a healthy plant. It may not be necessary to feed lawns in the fall if they are good looking lawns. You do see these advertisements all the time, "time for fall feeding of lawns," but think about it before you do it. If your lawn looks good you may decide to leave it for a season.

When applying fertilizer the most important factor to remember is that it should be uniform in distribution. As when sowing the lawn grass seed, one way to achieve this is to divide the fertilizer needed into two parts and apply it in both directions. You can apply it by hand, but you will not get as even distribution as you will if you use a roller or rotary distributor. I prefer the rotary to the roller type because if you set the roller type wrong and have to stop, you can get a great dumping of fertilizer in a row that will be so strong that it will burn the grass completely.

Try to go for a lighter feeding rather than heavy. The "little and often" system seems to work really well for plants in a border, for a lawn or even for house plants. Try not to feed wet grass because fertilizer can cause a lot of burning as it dissolves on the leaf blades. Ideally, you should go out and feed the lawn just before a rain or feed it and then water it in.

Avoid fertilizing during the hot summer months. Slow-growing grass is much more resistant to stresses of heat and drought. If you have a highly maintained lawn and suddenly water is rationed and you cannot water it, then it will turn very brown.

Nitrogen is the key element for vegetative growth and green colour. Phosphate stimulates good root growth and potash improves the tolerance of stresses such as heat, cold and drought. All three elements are essential, but the nitrogen is required in larger amounts because it is used to keep your lawn nice and green.

I suppose I should be ashamed of the little piece of lawn that is in front of my townhouse because it does not get any fertilizer other than in the spring, and in dry seasons in the summer I do not even water it. If I had a perfect lawn, my time-table for feeding it would be as follows.

In early May, I would give it a dressing of 10-6-4—all my applications of fertilizer would be at a handful per square yard (1 m²). If the lawn is a little sad, then I may well give it the same fertilizer again in mid-June and water it in well at that time. Then in early September I would give it an application of something like 6-8-6, the same balance that I use for flowers, vege-tables, trees and shrubs. It is a good all-round fertilizer, and by giving it to a lawn in September it will really build up the root system and get it strong and healthy to deal with whatever sort of awful condi-tions we may have to work with in the fall and winter months. Follow this schedule and you will get a nice, thick-growing lawn with a good, healthy root system. If you grow good thick grass you will have fewer problems with moss and weeds, and you will have a lawn that you can enjoy.

■ *Watering* ■

It never ceases to amaze me, as long as I live on the coast, how after about ten days of dry hot weather in the summer all the grass begins to dry up and it looks as if we are living in California. And, if the drought goes on for a couple of months,

which it can do, lawns can look pretty awful. But you know, after about a week of rain in the fall they all come back. So, I take a "no worry" approach and cer-tainly would not over-water them in the summer.

In dry weather, the first thing in the morning is the best time to water your lawn. You need to wet the soil to a depth of 6 in. (15 cm). Depending on the soil type, this means leaving a good lawn sprinkler on for about an hour. Light, frequent sprinkling encourages shallow rooting and reduces tolerance for heat and drought. Giving it too much water is also undesirable. It is much better to give your lawn a good watering once a week in dry weather for an hour so that the water soaks all the way down to keep those deep roots going. This will help your lawn tolerate the drought for much longer.

■ *Spring Maintenance* ■

In the spring, when the weather warms up you see all the contractors and people going out and raking and spiking their lawns—all that sort of ritualistic spring-time activity. What has it done for them, and what does it actually do for the lawn? Well, the raking of the lawn on the coast usually has to do with removing moss from the lawn. Occasionally, it is done to break up thatch too, but moss is one of the major problems. I have often jokingly said to people when they are so con-cerned about moss in the lawn that they should take a visit to the Nitobe Memorial Japanese Garden out at UBC and have a look at how beautifully and creatively moss is used instead of a lawn in certain areas of that garden.

Moss, you see, has been on this coast a lot longer than any human inhabitant, and it will probably be here a lot longer after we are gone. The soil is very acidic, we live in a semi-rainforest situation, and moss just loves this climate. Fertilizing with high-nitrogen fertilizers raises the acidity in the soil further, which increases moss growth in the lawn because the grass will get weaker, and the moss will take over. So, if you have an area of lawn that has a tremendous problem with moss, cut back on high-nitrogen fertilizers at all times of the year and try to build up the lawn from the roots.

To get rid of the moss, early in the year when the ground dries up, perhaps in March, go out with a hand rake or a mechanical rake and really go to town on the lawn. It will pull out all the old moss and you will get masses of moss mixed up with bits of grass. If you pick out the bits of grass and save the moss, you can use it for lining your hanging baskets. It also can be put on the compost in very shallow layers, mixed with lots of chicken manure or some other high-nitrogen additive to help break it down.

Once you have raked out all the moss then spike the lawn, especially if it is an old lawn. If it is a small area you can do it with golf shoes. For larger lawns use a garden fork or rent a spiked roller that will take out little cores of soil about every 6-12 in. (15-30 cm). This allows you to top dress the lawn with a nice mixture of some good top soil that has perhaps a little bit of sand mixed in with it, certainly some well-rotted manure. Brush the soil in so that it falls down into the holes. This will bring some decent soil to the root system and encourage the growth of good

new roots. Then, just add some fertilizer such as 6-8-6 to encourage this good deep growth, and you should have a rejuvenated lawn.

Since I mentioned thatch I should describe what it is. Thatch is a layer of dead grass leaves or old grass leaves that occurs at the soil level and can build up and prevent enough air from getting into the soil. Grass will begin to rot if the thatch above the soil becomes too thick, and thus becomes highly susceptible to injury in heat or drought and winter cold. The usual causes of thatch are poor drainage, over-watering and over-fertilization. Thatch can be avoided by providing good drainage, judicious irrigation and modest fertilization. Once the excessive thatch is established, mechanical dethatching with a vertical power rake is necessary. Remove thatch either in the spring or in the fall during periods when the temperature is good for regrowth. The dead grass brought to the surface by the machine should be removed and water and fertilizer applied as needed for good growth.

If you have a lot of trees in your yard, in autumn the leaves will fall on the lawn and form a great layer. Try to keep the leaves raked off a lawn on a regular basis. If they are left there they form a great mat that does not rot down quickly. This will damage the grass underneath. It is easiest to run the rotary mower over these leaves and then rake them up or catch them in the catch-basket. Because the leaves are cut up nicely, put them in the compost and they will rot very quickly. Do try to keep the leaves raked off the lawn—this is very important.

If you have an old neglected lawn in the garden when you move into a house, you may need to do some drastic renovation. Fungus problems occur in the lawn where the grass begins to die out, and slime moulds grow in the lawn. In that situation, first test the soil. If it is in poor condition you might need to just plow up the whole area, dig it up, get some fresh top soil and start from scratch. It is very, very difficult to bring old grass back when it has reached a poor state with dead patches in it from various moulds and diseases. There are other problems that can occur in the lawn, and these will be dealt with in more detail in the Pests and Diseases chapter.

■ ALTERNATIVE GROUND COVERS

In a low-maintenance garden, consider planting an alternate ground cover instead of a lawn. I have seen certain plants used most effectively in areas which are difficult to garden. For example, I can think of a wonderful garden on Galiano Island which has very well drained soil and a water shortage problem in the summertime. In it, Wooley thyme has been used most effectively, planted in the gullies in between the rocks. It needs no mowing and it flowers in the spring. The deer do not eat it, which is very important in the Gulf Islands, and when you walk gently around the garden it gives off a most beautiful scent. So, plants like Wooley thyme could be used in specialized areas. For example, if you have a little townhouse garden with a patio that is bricked in, then soften the edges with some rocks and add a little bit of ground cover.

No lawn grasses grow well in the deep shade of cedars, and cedars can be very difficult plants to deal with because not much will grow underneath cedar trees at all. One plant which will is the periwinkle *Vinca minor*. It is a trailing plant with small leaves and small flowers. It is almost weedy but has the most attractive little flowers. Some have blue, some have purple flowers, others have white, depending on what you select. They can tolerate a tremendous amount of shade. If you are going to use this as a ground cover underneath a cedar tree, try to work the top soil a little bit, at least in pockets. Dig out the pockets either in the spring or in the fall before planting the small plants of the periwinkle and work a little bit of leaf mould or some bone meal or something into the hole before planting, just to get it established. It will not grow if you do not get any sunlight at all under the tree, but if you get about one-third sunlight this is a plant that will work.

Another ground cover that works very well under cedar trees is *Pachysandra terminalis*. This little evergreen plant reaches no more in height than 12 in. (30 cm). It has insignificant little white flowers and is sometimes commonly referred to as Japanese Spurge. It works extremely well in the shade, giving an evergreen glossy foliage to look at the year round.

One ground cover plant that thrives in semi-shady bank situations is a little member of the *Rubus* family, *Rubus calycinoides*. The one that I recommend is a plant introduction from the University of British Columbia Botanical Garden that has been given the cultivar name of Emerald Carpet. It really is an amazing little plant, discovered at high elevations in Taiwan, which turns out to be extremely hardy here. It is a low-growing, dense, emerald green carpet that has little flowers in the spring, and in a decent season if there are lots of bees around berries will form on it that are much like salmonberries. It is recommended for open sunny banks, but to my best experience it works well if it gets half a day's sunshine. The leaves are so tough that you can walk around on it without doing a lot of damage. One nice thing about it, as with all ground covers, is that it keeps the weeds down.

If you have a sunny bank to deal with then I recommend one other ground cover from the university's introduction program, the local native plant *Arcostaphylos uwaursi*, or Vancouver Jade. This plant forms a very dense mat of somewhat woody evergreen foliage. It has pretty pink flowers in the spring and, unlike some of the native forms, these flowers are borne above the foliage so they show, and they also have the bonus of a very delightful scent. If these are pollinated you will get little red berries. One of the common names for this plant is also bearberry or kinikinik, that is what the native people used to call it. If it is planted on a bank at about 12-18 in. (30-45 cm) apart it will soon cover the bank. It can tolerate very hot sunny locations on the coast, which makes it good for Gulf Island gardens. Again, it is not like a lawn but is something green to look at that will keep the weeds down and is well worth a place in the garden.

Ajuga reptans is one plant that you can use in very deep shade, not underneath cedar trees but on the north side of a building or perhaps in a shrub border where you want some sort of evergreen basal growth to show off other plants. It is a little plant that comes to us from Europe, and it forms a dense mass of very rich, dark green foliage. There are various forms of it, including some that have a purplish and white variegation to them. In the spring it sends up a spike about 6 in. (15 cm) in height of brilliant blue flowers. When I was a boy it grew in the ditches and fields around home and we used to call it Bugle. It works very well here on the coast for areas that tend to sit moist and yet look messy. When you put it in add a little bit of bone meal or something to spice up the soil, and it will give you a colourful ground cover.

■ THINGS TO REMEMBER

I cannot overemphasize the importance of proper soil preparation when putting in a new lawn from scratch. Also, whether using seed or sod, make sure you choose the correct lawn mix for the type of use you expect from your lawn, and the correct mixture for the sun or shade.

Ground covers require soil preparation. Especially under trees, make sure you give them enough decent soil to get them started. Again, assess the site well and make sure you choose the right plants for the job.

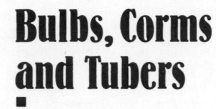

Bulbs, Corms and Tubers

When asked which are my favourite flowers I am hard pressed to answer, as in every season there are blossoms that I find particularly beautiful. However, in a mild climate such as ours, spring bulbs are some of the nicest plants you can grow. They give us something to look forward to as we anticipate the profusion of blooms in the spring. On the coast, bulbs can bloom as early as late January right through until May. Any plants that give that much enjoyment are well worth some garden space.

The best selections of spring bulbs come into garden centres usually about the middle of September and are often around until the end of November. October is the ideal planting month for bulbs, but timing also depends on where you plant them. If you are going to plant bulbs in a mixed flower bed, you do not want to dig up your geraniums or petunias before they have had a chance to finish flowering. In this case you can wait until the middle of November before planting bulbs. However, to take advantage of better weather conditions, I suggest you plant in October.

Choose your bulb site carefully. Contrary to some opinions, bulbs will not grow in deep shade, particularly bulbs that have been in the ground year after year. Bulbs such as daffodils and tulips, which come to us mainly from Holland, are top quality bulbs that have been in the fields until they reach full flowering size. When we get them they are at their peak and may flower in deep shade. However, if it is a permanent planting you want then plant them in an area where they get at least half a day's sunshine, preferably morning sun.

Without exception all bulbs require well-drained soil, which fortunately is common throughout our area. Soil condition can be further enhanced by adding humus. If you are going to plant daffodils and tulips in a mixed border among your annuals, wait until you have pulled out your summer bedding plants before preparing the soil. The bulb site should be in an area where the bulbs are not going to be sitting in water. Dig out a hole 18 in. (45 cm) in circumference and about 12 in. (30 cm) deep and work well-rotted compost or leaf mould into the bottom of it, along with about a tablespoon (15 ml) of bone meal. Get decent-sized bulbs that are of top quality. I strongly recommend that you plant them in clumps. Groupings of ten make a good show. Ten tulip bulbs would fit quite comfortably into an 18 in. (45 cm) hole. Do not let them touch, but set them fairly close together and cover with soil. It is a good idea to mark the spot with bamboo canes or sticks and make a diagram of the border in your log book. Mark the spot and note the variety so you can refer to it when the bulbs begin to bloom in the spring.

Some areas may have a problem with animals. During the winter, voles, or even gophers, will feed on the bulbs. If this is a problem in your area you will need to use some form of protection. When you first dig out a bulb hole, line it with a basket made from fine-mesh chicken wire before adding organic materials and bulbs. This will really out-fox those little critters and keep them away from your bulbs. These baskets are easy and inexpensive to make yourself.

Daffodils are the best bulb to bloom year after year. Many of the tulips tend to die out after their second or third year in the garden, with the exception of the Darwin group. If you are planning on leaving your bulbs in the garden for three or four years and are not going to lift them every spring, it is a good idea to plant them a bit deeper than the recommended 8-12 in. (18-30 cm). This is to your advantage particularly if you have a mixed flower border. If you plant them one-and-a-half trowel lengths deep, then you will not disturb them while planting annual bedding plants in the spring or summer.

If you have only a few bulbs do not try to stretch them out in a long row. When they come up in the spring the effect will be lost. It is much more attractive if you plant them in clusters of five or ten to a clump. This way you will get a fantastic concentration of colour in the spring for you and your neighbours to admire.

Another way I like to see bulbs used is planted naturally in a lawn, particularly underneath a flowering tree. This type of planting is called naturalizing. Because we are so tidy-minded in this country people tend to shy away from planting bulbs in the lawn as they have to leave them to die down naturally. Unfortunately, that means having an untidy lawn because of uneven mowing. However, I think the sacrifice of having long grass is well worth it as the effect is absolutely beautiful. Cluster some crocus or early narcissi in the grass and under the trees...it will look beautiful.

Planting bulbs in a lawn can be a bit of a problem, especially if it is an old lawn and the soil is compacted. With a clean, sharp spade or shovel take out a 12 in. (30 cm) square of sod and dig out the soil underneath as deeply as you possibly can. If the site is near a tree you may run into roots, but try to work around them. Then add bone meal and some compost to the bottom of the hole and plant your bulbs. Do not plant them in a square but in a small clump: the effect will be more natural looking. Put the soil back in, firm it down well and then replace the sod on top. If the soil is a bit dry, water it well. An early blooming bulb like the narcissi Peeping Tom or February Gold will begin to bloom in late February or early March. Once they have finished flowering, they will need to keep their leaves only for approximately six weeks in order to build up the bulb for the following year. You could probably start to mow your lawn, up to the tree trunk line, in the middle of April or early May.

Crocuses do not need as long to die back, and I recommend cluster planting of crocus bulbs as well. Plant them the same way as for narcissi or tulip bulbs but not as deep. You can plant them individually, if you have the time, but I prefer cluster planting as I think it makes for a better showing.

Bulbs can also be used very effectively as feature colour plants in shrub borders. If you have a mixed shrub border of forsythia, rhododendrons, or azaleas, a good idea is to plant clusters of bulbs in between the shrubs. They will show up beautifully against the background of dark foliage.

You may also want to take advantage of a particular viewpoint in your garden, seen from inside your home, by planting a great show of early-blooming bulbs in that site. Nothing lifts the spirit more, on an otherwise dull spring day, than to relax in a favourite chair overlooking a beautiful flush of colour. It also makes you want to get out and work in your garden. It is a wonderful feeling to be excited and raring to go, and this experience can be multiplied when spurred on by a vivid display of early-blooming bulbs.

■ PLANT SELECTIONS

Let me suggest some bulbs that I think are must-haves for this area.

Crocuses. There are so many different types of crocuses. Some of the early species will come out as early as January and February. Those are usually *Crocus chrysanthus* types. There is a yellow-bronze one called E.A. Bowles, which was named for a gentleman from Britain who did extensive work with crocuses. He taught people how to naturalize crocuses among other shrubs so that their colour complemented one another. This is something we should strive for in our own gardens. Other varieties of *C. chrysanthus* are Moonlight and Bluebird. Moonlight is a gorgeous sulphur yellow, and Bluebird is purple-blue with white margins. Another

31

early variety is *C. Thomasinianus*. It is a beautiful thing, very pale lilac with yellow anthers, and is a real joy as it attracts early bees to our gardens. It is also marvellous for naturalizing in lawns. When I was a child I remember a large garden up the road from where I lived. This particular crocus had naturalized there probably for at least thirty or forty years, resulting in a carpet of colour.

The larger, more familiar Dutch flowering forms of crocus bloom a little later. There are many different cultivars and varieties, but one that will be known to many of you is a deep purple one called Remembrance.

Crocuses do not need to be planted very deep...4 in. (10 cm) deep at the most is fine. Something to watch out for with any small bulbs, particularly the crocus, is damage from birds. If you have pheasants in your area, as we do at the University of British Columbia Botanical Garden, you may have a problem keeping your crocuses. Pheasants have a taste for them and will eat the bulbs and flowers. When you plant your crocuses, put some fine-meshed chicken wire or netting across your planting surface and peg it down. This will stop the birds from pecking out your bulbs and will give them a chance to get established.

Daffodils and Narcissi. Daffodils and narcissi are perhaps one of the hardiest and longest living bulbs that you can plant. In older gardens on the coast there are daffodils that have survived for fifty years or more. On the roadside along the causeway in Stanley Park daffodil bulbs were planted many years ago. They receive no care, no additional fertilizer other than the leaves that fall off the deciduous trees, and they put up with much abuse. They are mown by mechanical mowers and some of the poor things get shovelled up during construction work, but despite this they tend to come up year after year, a true test for their hardiness. There are so many daffodils and narcissi that I find it very difficult to pick one variety to recommend. I have mentioned two early narcissi bulbs that I love very much: February Gold and Peeping Tom. Both of these have tubes or corolla that tend to point down with back petals that turn up, a bit like a cyclamen. They are a joy as they come up very early in the season. A later blooming yellow daffodil is Dutch Master. Another older variety I like is Fortune, which has a deep orange cup and yellow perianth. Go to your garden centre and decide for yourself which ones you like best.

Eranthis. There is another wonderful bulb that comes up very early in the year, called *Eranthis hyemalis*, or more commonly, Winter Aconite. It can bloom as early as January if we have a mild winter and looks a bit like a tiny buttercup with a rough collar of bright green leaves just below the flower. Eranthis will grow in semi-shady conditions, reaches a height of about 3-5 in. (9-12 cm) and can be planted about 3 in. (9 cm) deep. Not a true aconite at all but more like a small buttercup, good for naturalizing in shrub borders, it is bright enough to plant in a special focal area.

Hyacinths. Hyacinths are great bulbs. A lot of people grow them as forced indoor plants. However, hyacinths grown outside will give us a tremendous amount of colour and a beautiful fragrance in our gardens. They will bloom, depending on the warmth of the season, in March or April. They are not the sort of bulb to put into a garden and leave for a number of years, like daffodils and tulips, although I have seen them survive for more than one season. Two varieties of which I am particularly fond are Delft Blue and Lord Balfour. Delft Blue has a very pale blue flower and Lord Balfour is light purple. They are both delightful bulbs to put in a border.

Scilla. This is a delightful little plant. Its botanical name is *Scilla sibirica* and it flowers a little later than the crocuses and snowdrops. It usually blooms in March or April with brilliant blue flowers and grows to a height of about 4 in. (10 cm). This one lends itself extremely well to naturalizing in the lawn and for years there has been a wonderful clump of them near the Vancouver School of Theology. Despite the fact that they get mown early in the season, they tend to come back year after year and I would strongly recommend them to you. Blue flowers are my favourite, and this one I particularly admire.

Snowdrops. Because of my English background I have to mention snowdrops (*Galanthus*). There are many different forms of Galanthus, but the most commonly grown in our home gardens is *G. nivalis*. It is a marvellous little bulb for naturalizing in a lawn. As the name suggests, snowdrop flowers are white...they look like small pearl drops...and the foliage colour is silvery-green. The overall height

is about 4-6 in. (10-15 cm). They grow in clumps and begin to bloom as early as January and February.

For me, the snowdrop is one plant that really suggests that spring is just around the corner. They are sometimes a bit difficult to get started from bulbs, so if you have friends who have some in their garden ask if they would like to share them with you. A good time to transplant snowdrops is when they have finished flowering and when they are going to seed but still have leaves. Lift the whole clump at that time, split them up and replant them elsewhere in your garden or swap them with a friend.

Tulips. When it comes to tulips, the choice is endless. I have already suggested that the Darwin's will have a long life in the garden, but there are so many others you could try. There are lovely lily-shaped tulips that have fine pointed petals which do not have the typical cup shape...they form more of a crown-like bloom. One of my favourites is China Pink, which is simply delightful. Parrot tulips, if you can get them, are wonderful as well, with fringed petals that look like parrot feathers and many vivid colours. There is a pink and green one called Fantasy and a scarlet one with red markings called the Red Parrot. Parrot tulips are late blooming, so choose an area in your mixed flower border where they will not get disturbed when you want to plant your bedding plants in the spring. They will keep flowering well into May. I would certainly include some tulips in my garden.

■ BULB MAINTENANCE

Many bulbs are best in their first year of planting, particularly the cultivars of hyacinths and tulips. The reason for this is that they are allowed to come to flower for about three years in the field, then they have their flower heads mown off. As with any bulb this stops them from producing seed. All the nutrients then go into the leaves to build up the bulb. By the time we get the bulbs three or four years later they are keen to blossom and will produce very large flowers. You can help keep your blossoms large by feeding them. The best time of the year to feed bulbs, other than when you first plant them, is later on in the spring when they are just about to bud. That is a good time to liquid feed them with fish or seaweed fertilizer or with liquid 6-8-6.

When they have finished flowering pick off their flower heads so that they will not have a chance to make seed. Then allow their leaves to grow strong and green for at least six to eight weeks. When bulbs have finished flowering many people will tie the leaves in a knot and leave them in the garden. However, this is the worst possible thing you can do. Try not to be overly concerned about having a neat and tidy garden. Let those leaves die back naturally, as it is important that the nutrients built up in the leaves travel down into the bulb to build it up for the following year.

The question now is whether to lift out the bulbs at the end of the flowering season and replant them next year. I tend to favour leaving them in the garden in a naturalized situation. A problem arises if their leaves will be in the way when you want to plant your annuals. However, I strongly recommend that you let the leaves lie on the surface of the soil and plant your bedding plants in between them. If you have planted your bulbs deeply enough, you are not going to disturb them, and as the bedding plants grow they will hide the dried-up leaves. By the time the leaves look untidy, the bedding plants will be large enough that you will not even notice them.

If you feel that you must lift your bulbs from their permanent location in your mixed border to make room for bedding plants, make sure that you lift them out gently. One problem, particularly with tulips, is that they tend to snap off when being dug up. Tulip bulbs are formed differently from most other bulbs, which grow from the pointed area at the top. If

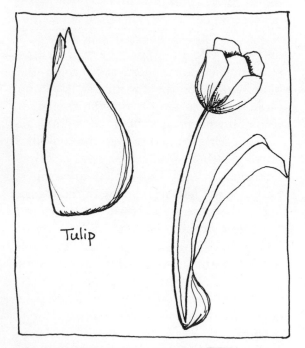

5. *Tulip bulb showing the flat side. The flower grows from the bottom of the bulb.*

you examine a tulip bulb, you will see that the flower stem comes from the base of the bulb and continues up the flat side; this makes the stem very brittle and easy to break off. So, it is better to leave them in place, but if you must dig them up, then here is an idea that works extremely well.

Plants from a nursery usually come in black plastic 8 in. (20 cm) liners with wide drainage holes in the side and bottom. You can plant your bulbs in these during the fall and then just dig out the entire container when you lift them at the end of their growing season. Put four or five bulbs in the pot with good soil, add some bone meal, and simply bury the pot in your garden. Some of the roots will grow out through the drainage holes, but when it comes time to lift your bulbs in the

spring you will find it very easy to dig them out. You can then transfer the pot of bulbs to another area of your garden, perhaps a spare space in your vegetable plot where you could leave them all summer. Be sure to label them so you will remember what varieties you have. Later on, if you need the room in your vegetable garden, lift the pot out and keep them in a shady place behind a garage or shed, some place where they are not going to get soaking wet but also a place that is not too dry so that they dehydrate. You can then replant them easily the following year.

If you go the old-fashioned route of lifting them individually, try to get as much of the root system as possible. Again, in an area of the vegetable garden, dig out a trench about 12 in. (30 cm) deep

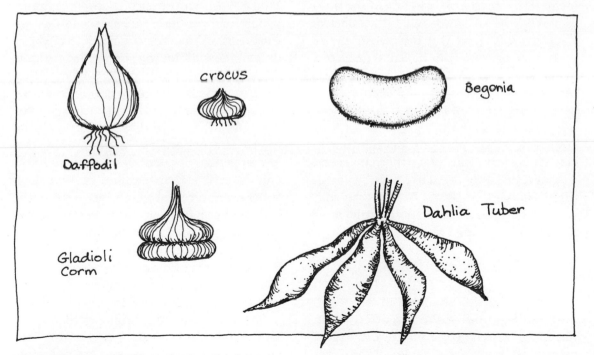

6. A selection of bulbs, corms and tubers.

and lay the bulbs in with the green tops up and label them. When the foliage has died back completely, sometime in July, then lift the bulbs, keeping the varieties separate. Put them in wooden seed flats and leave them on a shelf in a garage or shed. Try not to forget them so that if it gets really hot they are not left to dry out. Make sure there is good air circulation...this is extremely important for the longevity of bulbs.

Major pests and diseases of all plants are dealt with in detail in the Pests and Diseases chapter. However, I want to mention a problem that occurs with bulbs. When storing bulbs or when buying new bulbs there is a tendency, particularly with tulips, for them to flake off their protective layer of skin. Especially if they have been handled a lot, you will find that the outside layer of brown skin will fall away. This can cause bruising of the bulb which can result in rotting. If that occurs I recommend that you dust your bulbs with a fungicide purchased from your local garden centre. The best way to treat bulbs is to lay them inside a paper bag containing some of the bulb dust. Close the bag and shake it vigorously so that you coat the bulbs. Wait for the dust to settle, then carefully place them in a seed flat, or if you dust them in the fall you can plant them right away. Make sure that you wash your hands thoroughly after handling any fungicide.

■ CORMS AND TUBERS

Corms and tubers, often called "summer bulbs," tend to be forgotten when planning a garden. Corms that are most commonly known are gladioli. There are also some wonderful lilies that, by and large, are not used often in the Lower Mainland. There is a gentleman who has hybridized lilies for years in Summerland in the Okanagan Valley. He grows wonderful lilies, and I would like to see more people take advantage of them here. Other plants that fall into the category of summer bulbs are the tuberous begonia and dahlia. Here are some hints about some of the better-known summer bulbs and how you can use them in the garden.

Begonias. Technically, begonias are not a bulb at all but a tuber. These are good plants for coastal regions. They work particularly well in hanging baskets where they get good air circulation. The Butchart Gardens, north of Victoria, have spectacular displays of big, double-flowered begonias. They hang in baskets in a shade house close to the entrance gate. Some people are put off growing begonias as they tend to be very susceptible to powdery mildew. Mildew is a common fungus disease that you more or less have to live with in a high-humidity region such as ours. I recommend that you use begonias not only in hanging baskets but also in mixed flower borders. In the spring, the key to getting a good-sized plant is to go early to your garden centre to select tubers. Tuberous begonias arrive as early as late February or early March. They come in small packages, usually from Holland or some other European source. Select tubers that are at least 3 in. (7.5 cm) or more in diameter; these will result in a large plant.

When you buy tuberous begonias, they look a bit like a squashed potato. The concave side is the top and the rounded area is the bottom. To start them off do not wait to plant them outdoors as they will take far too long to develop. Instead, get a large seed flat of very moist peat moss and start your begonias in that. If you find peat moss difficult to moisten, then work in hot water and you will see that it mixes easily. Put the peat in a bucket, add hot or warm water, then mix it up, and it will take on the moisture much more quickly. Then transfer the peat to a large flat, or put it into individual pots. After the peat moss has cooled down push each of the tubers, round side down, into the surface of the peat. You should be able to get about eight tubers in a regular-sized wooden flat. Keep the flat level and place it somewhere warm, in the kitchen or some other place where you can keep an eye on it. In the warm moisture of the peat the tubers will start to grow at a rapid rate, and you will see lovely red shoots coming from the concave areas. As the tuber develops white roots will spread out into the peat moss. When the tubers have been in the peat moss about three or four weeks and have started to form that root structure, carefully lift them out. Put your fingers underneath and gently lift them out and plant them in individual pots of good potting mix. A good potting mix for tubers would be the same type of soil recommended for tropical plants. Add a bit of 6-8-6 or some other fertilizer and transfer them to a window sill where they will get morning sun and afternoon shade. If started off in March, they will be a fairly good-sized plant when it comes to bedding-out time in May. Then, simply take them out of their pots and plant them in small groupings along with bedding plants or in hanging baskets. They are very pretty things and well worth including as a summer bulb in your garden.

Dahlia. Dahlias are not my favourite flowers, but if you want a spectacular show, they will give you a grand-looking plant with a lot of blossoms and will fill up a large space in a mixed border. Buy them around late February or early March along with the begonia tubers. They arrive in small plastic packages containing one pointed tuber about 6 in. (15 cm) long. At the top end there will be a piece of the old stem from the mother plant and that is where the shoots will develop. To give them a headstart in the flower garden, for the first year start them off with good potting mix indoors or in a greenhouse. Plant the dahlia tuber with the pointed end towards the bottom of the pot and the stem end up nearer the surface. This will give it a chance to get established and make for a nice-sized plant to put out in the garden later in the spring. When planting dahlias be sure to give them lots of space...an area of about 3 ft. (1 m) in diameter. Another thing to remember is that they are hungry plants and love to have well-rotted manure or compost worked into the soil. Even some granular 6-8-6 mixed in while planting out is a good addition, as they need a good start to put down strong roots. Dahlias come into bloom about the middle of the summer and will bloom through until the frost. They will then need to be lifted and brought indoors.

Gladioli. Gladioli corms are most likely borderline hardy in this climate, particularly on the coast and Gulf Islands. If they are planted in well-drained soil on the south or west side of a building, where they will not get waterlogged in the winter, chances are they will come back year after year. Normally, with any of the summer bulbs, they are best lifted in the fall and stored over winter. Gladioli, like the spring bulbs, must have well-drained soil. I recommend, particularly if you have wet soil in your garden, that you add sand to the bottom of the hole when planting your gladioli. Dig out a 12 in. (30 cm) circumference hole about 8 in. (20 cm) deep and mix in something like granular 6-8-6 as opposed to bone meal. This will make the food available to them right away. Plant them in clumps of eight to ten and you will get a wonderful show of colour in the summer. Remember when planting bulbs in clumps to keep to one colour per clump. I think this is much more attractive. If you mix colours they may bloom at different times and the effect will be lost. So always try to plant spring or summer bulbs of the same variety in each clump.

The best time to plant gladioli ranges from March to early May. It is very important that they are in a full sunny location. If there is no sun you will not get any flowers from them at all. I like the smaller varieties, and there are some miniature flower strains that are very nice for cut flowers and look light and dainty in a garden border. However, it is all a matter of taste and if you want to grow gladioli for showing in a summer or fall garden show, then by all means plant the older, larger varieties. To make sure they respond well, feed them on a regular basis to produce top-quality blooms.

Lily. Having said that the lily is a summer-flowering bulb, it is important to mention that they need to be planted in the fall. Lilies have to go out in September or October as they come into bloom at the same time as spring bulbs. Choose your lilies carefully and make sure that you pick out nice fat bulbs, otherwise they will not flower well. You will want to plant them somewhere they can be left permanently for a number of years. Lilies seem to do extremely well if planted in a shrub border, particularly among evergreens like rhododendrons or skimmia, as their dark foliage acts as a backdrop to show off the lily flowers. Lilies need to be planted fairly deep, at least 6-8 in. (15-20 cm), and it is very important for lily bulbs that they do not sit in water for any period of their growing season. When you dig the hole, work in a little leaf mould or compost and then put a layer of sand over that. Cover the bulbs up, and mark their location and variety. This is important because when you weed in the spring you do not want to be hoeing them off or pulling them by mistake.

Again, there are so many to choose from. Two of my favourites are *Lilium Regale* and *Lilium Tigrinum*. *L. Regale* is a beautiful, sweetly scented species that will probably need staking. It grows somewhere between 4-5 ft. (1.2-1.5 m) in height and usually blooms in June or July. It has creamy white blossoms with gorgeous dark markings on the outside and the scent is wonderful. *L. Tigrinum* is also called the Tiger Lily and it blooms a little later on in late July. We have some planted at the Botanical Garden at the University of British Columbia against a backdrop of purple Buddleia shrubs. The colour combination of orange and purple is simply gorgeous. There are many more to choose from and I strongly recommend that you look around your garden centre when the bulbs come in to see if there are a few unusual lily bulbs to include in your home garden.

■ AFTER-SEASON CARE

Of all the summer bulbs I have mentioned, three of them will have to be brought in each year: the gladioli, the begonias, and the dahlias. It is a good idea to wait until the first frost, sometimes as late as the middle of November, before digging them out. I have seen beautiful dahlias in gardens right throughout October and well into November, and it is perfectly alright for the tops to be frozen off. However, once the tops have frozen they will go very black, particularly with the dahlia and begonia foliage. When this happens, the very next day, you should lift them up and cut away the tops. Then wash or hose off the corms and tubers to clean them up and place them in a shed, garage or basement to dry out...some place where they will not freeze. With the gladioli the old corm is the top half and below that there is a new one formed. This newly formed corm is the one that will give you good flowers next year. Also, when digging up gladioli, if they have been happy in your garden, there will be tiny bulbs growing on the underside. These can be removed and planted right away in a seed flat of potting mix. Put them in a greenhouse or cold frame to let them develop, and allow them to grow for a season until they get to be a good size. They could then be planted out

in a row in the vegetable garden, and after three to four years should develop into flowering corms. Otherwise, just take them up and shake them off, keeping only the larger-sized corms.

The begonia tubers should look exactly like they did when you bought them except they will have multiplied and be slightly larger. When they have dried you can fill a deep cardboard box with sawdust or peat and bury your begonia tubers along with your gladioli corms. Put them on a shelf, not in a heated basement but somewhere like a cool shed, where it is not going to freeze and where there is good air circulation. A shelf in the top of your garage is fine. I do not recommend a crawl space underneath a house because often there is a lot of moisture in those areas. If the tubers and corms get too moist they can develop mould and will rot easily. So they need to be somewhere that is frost free but cool, no more than around 5° C (41° F), with good air circulation.

When lifting dahlia tubers, instead of one, they should have anywhere from four to six tubers. To propagate these, split up the tuber clump. The time to divide dahlia tubers is in the fall as at that time they are still soft and green and have plenty of sap in them. The stems of the dahlias tend to get very woody near the base. In the spring the stem would become too woody to allow successful division. Take a very sharp knife and carefully split down a stem and take one or two tubers with it. Never break off tubers as the eyes for the new growth are right up near the base of the stem. Once they are split or if left intact, put them in boxes of peat moss and store in the same conditions as for the tubers and corms of the begonia and gladioli.

One of the keys to successful overwintering for summer-flowering bulbs is to leave them out in the garden as long as possible. This could be as late as November by the time you have dug them up, cleaned and dried them and put them in their boxes for storage. The storage period would then be from December to February, when you could begin to pot them for the following growing season. The shorter the overwintering period, the more success you will have.

If you are successful with your begonia tubers and keep them for more than two or three years, they will get very large, and it is possible to divide them. Divide them anytime before potting them in February or March. With a very sharp knife cut the tuber in half, cutting right across the centre, leaving a piece of the concave part on each section, then dip the cut end of the tuber into a powder fungicide. If you are an organic gardener you might prefer to mix powdered sulphur with crushed charcoal instead of using a fungicide. Grind up the sulphur and charcoal and put it in a paper bag along with your begonia tuber halves and shake. This will seal the cut edge of the tuber and stop it from rotting. It is very important that the knife be clean. Wipe it with some bleach before using to avoid introducing rot into the tuber. Leave the tubers sitting out overnight on a shelf or piece of paper to dry before planting them.

■ THINGS TO REMEMBER

1. Always start out with good quality bulbs.
2. Prepare ground well and make sure it is well drained and in a sunny spot.
3. Use bone meal for fall planting and a general fertilizer for spring planting.
4. Allow spring bulb foliage to die back naturally. Do not tie them in knots.
5. Lift summer bulbs after the first frost.
6. Store all bulbs in a dry, cool, frost-free area.

CHAPTER 4

Summer Annuals

Summer annuals are an invaluable addition to any home landscape. They include all those wonderful plants like petunias, marigolds, nemesia and sweet alyssum. For a small investment in the spring they can provide a tremendous amount of colour throughout the summer months. There are many to choose from and many ways to go about growing them. To grow them from seed, it is a good idea to invest in a greenhouse. It is also possible to grow some of the annuals from seed using a window sill in your home. If you feel you are not successful at growing plants from seed, all local garden centres have a large choice of bedding plants to choose from in the spring.

First consider the selection of seeds. Garden centres normally start to carry seeds as early as February. It is easy to get carried away by all the pretty envelopes and pictures, so try to keep in mind the size of your garden as well as the amount of window sill space you have available for germination.

If you are looking for more unusual seeds it is a good idea to send away for seed catalogues. Seed catalogues are often advertised right after the Christmas holidays and you should have no trouble finding them. It is a fun thing to do in the winter months when you are thinking that nothing is going to grow in your garden. To cheer you up, get some seed catalogues and books that deal specifically with annuals.

Despite moderate temperatures in the winter, our growing season is very slow getting started. In an average year the third week in May is the earliest we can put bedding plants outside. It is sometimes cooler in June than in May and you will have a terrible time getting your bedding plants started if you plant them out earlier. The majority of common annuals develop sufficiently in six weeks to allow them to be planted outside. In this case, the third week of March would be a good time to start sowing seed.

■ GROWING FROM SEED

Growing seed at home can be a challenge. Without proper light, or if you start them off too early, they will become leggy and drawn and be of no use. So, if you want to grow seedlings in your home you must take great care. Potting mix is very important for healthy annuals, and it must be sterilized to make sure that all the weed seeds or fungus diseases are killed. If you use unsterilized soil from your garden you may find dandelions and thistles coming up with your seedling, and they are difficult to tell apart when they are very small.

If you purchase potting mix made at a local garden centre, ask if they have sterilized it. If it has not been sterilized buy a prepackaged starter mix. Prepackaged potting mixes can be found anywhere from large supermarkets to small corner grocery stores. If you cannot find a potting mix then make up your own using equal parts of soil, peat and sand. If using soil from your garden try to get it from an area where it has been cultivated for some time. Take one bucketful of garden soil, screen out the large rocks, and pick out any visible weeds. Add one part peat...in this case it can be fine granulated peat that has been sifted, as you will want a fairly fine mixture for starting off tiny seedlings. Add one part sand, which can be fairly coarse river sand. You do not want any pieces of gravel in it larger than 1/8 in. (3 mm). You could also substitute perlite for sand. However, I am not keen on using perlite in a seeding mix as it tends to float to the surface when it is watered.

Mix the equal parts together and moisten them thoroughly. You are now ready to sterilize your seed mix. Sterilizing soil at home could mean the end of a happy relationship with your partner. Not only do you take over the kitchen oven, but the smell of heated soil can be very unpleasant. Get a large roasting pan with a lid and put the moist soil inside the pan. Preheat your oven to around 177° C (350° F) and bake it for about 35-40 minutes, or until it reaches 82° C (180° F) in the centre. Use a meat thermometer to check the temperature. Once the optimum temperature is reached take it out of the oven, tip it onto a clean surface and let the soil mix cool off. When it is nice and cold add about a tablespoon of superphosphate to the soil and mix it all the way through. Make sure that the soil is still moist, then fill up your pots and you are ready to go.

The best way to fill flower pots is as follows. Put a piece of paper towel or newspaper in the bottom of the pot to stop the soil from going through. Then tip the soil into the pot very lightly. With a straight edge, such as a small board or ruler, run it across the top of the pot rim to take away the excess soil. Then, taking one pot in your hand, use it to level the soil in the others, pressing the soil down lightly. The soil should be about 1/2 in. (1 cm) below the top rim of the pot. It is extremely important that the surface of the mixture be completely level.

While it is important to have sterilized soil it is more important to have sterilized pots. New pots they should be fairly clean, but to make sure wash them in dish-washing liquid. If they are old pots that you have kept from previous seasons, put them in a utility sink filled with hot water, add some bleach and leave them to soak overnight. The next day drain the water, rinse and dry the pots and they will be ready for use. Clay pots also need to be soaked overnight with household bleach or disinfectant, and they will need a good scrubbing before you use them. Clay pots are difficult to get now but I love them. The most useful size for seed sowing is about 4 in. (10 cm) in diameter. From a 4 in. (10 cm) pot you can sow in excess of two to three dozen seeds. Do not be wasteful with your seed: sow only what you have room for as you can save seeds for another year.

Once you have filled your pots and leveled the soil you should have some labels and a waterproof pen handy so that you can write on each label as you sow

your seeds. Write the date and name of the annual on this label right away as it is very easy to get them confused. Another tip is to open seed packages at the bottom. If you open them from the top you usually rip off the name, which makes it difficult to identify them.

Everyone has a favourite way of sowing seeds. Some shake the seed out of the package, but I think that makes it difficult to tell how many seed you have sown, especially if the seeds are dark and blend in with the soil. A former head gardener of mine taught me a way that works very well and you might like to try it. Shake out a small amount of seed onto the palm of your hand. Hold your hand about 8 in. (20 cm) above the pot and gently tap it with your other hand, tilting your palm slightly so that the seeds roll gently onto the soil surface. This is a good way to keep track of how many seeds you are putting in a pot. You will want to sow about two dozen seed per pot. The rest of the seed can be scooped back into its package and kept for another year.

Then take a little dry potting mix in the palm of your hand and, using the same tapping method, lightly cover the seed. Seeds should never be buried any deeper than their own width. There is a tendency, particularly for first-time gardeners, to bury seeds far too deep. If you put a thick layer of soil on top of seeds, they tend to push up little tents of soil when they begin to germinate and can rot easily under these tents. It is important they get into the air very quickly. In the nursery at the University of British Columbia Botanical Garden we use small screens. These are wooden frames, with fine mesh stretched over the frame. A little soil is put in the screen and shaken over the pots. An old kitchen flour sieve will work just as well.

Once you have sown and labeled your seeds you will want to water them in, particularly if the soil has become quite dry. There are many kinds of watering cans available, but try to use one that has fine watering holes or use a spray bottle and gently moisten the surface. A great place to start off your seeds is on top of a refrigerator where it is usually warm. Perhaps there is somewhere else in your house where you think there might be bottom heat. A laundry room is good, as the temperature is usually quite warm. It is also quite alright for them to be in darkness during germination. In fact, I usually put a black plastic bag over the top of my pots. Be sure to check them every day for growth and moisture. You will want to make sure they are kept moist at all times during this period. Just as soon as you see the seedlings start to move and come up, take the pot out and stand it somewhere in the light. Do not place it in direct sunlight. In March the sun is beginning to get stronger, and if

7. *Transplanting seedlings.*

you suddenly put the seedlings in a south-facing window sill the heat through the glass will damage them. A north-facing window sill with indirect sunlight would be fine to start off with. If some of the seedlings have roots running across the surface of the soil, add a little bit more soil to cover them up.

After they have reached - in. (6-10 mm) in height and have their first pair of seed leaves they can be transplanted. You will need bedding baskets which may have been left over from previous years or can be bought from a garden centre. If you are like me you will generally have so many of them saved up over the years you will not know what to do with them all. Make sure that they are clean and fill them with potting mix that has had some fertilizer mixed in. For one household pailful I would add one tablespoon (15 ml) of granular 6-8-6. This should give you good root development and nice strong seedlings. Lift the seedlings very carefully with a kitchen fork or spoon and grab onto the seed leaf between your forefinger and thumb. Make a hole in the mixture with your finger or with a pencil and bury the seedling right up to the seed leaves. The entire stem must be buried, as the stem can form roots during this stage. Label, water them well and place them on an east-facing window sill where they will get good indirect light. Without adequate light they will get very drawn out and leggy.

Among the nicest annuals to grow are sweet peas. Traditionally, they have been grown in rows, but there is nothing wrong with putting clumps of sweet peas in a mixed border. Start your sweet pea seeds off very early. If you have a cold frame you can start sweet pea seeds as early as November. However, most people wait until after the holiday season, perhaps in early February. If you examine the sweet pea seeds you will see an eye on one side where they have broken off from the mother plant and the rest of the seed cap will be either brown or white. Chip the seed on the opposite side from the eye to prepare it for starting. The easiest way to do this is to rub it on a nail file. Once the seed cap has been scrapped, soak them for about two to three hours in a cup of lukewarm water. They will take on moisture more quickly and result in a faster germination period.

Let me recapitulate. You have started to sow your seed in the middle of March and it is now the middle of April. Towards the end of April, if you can, put these plants in a cold frame. (For the construction and use of cold frames, see the Greenhouses, Cold Frames and Cloches chapter.) Provided you can give them temperatures no cooler than around 10° C (50° F) at night and 17° C (63° F) during the day, you should have very nice plants for putting out towards the end of May. It sounds simple, but there are many things that can go wrong. However, I do urge you to try it.

If growing annuals from seed is not for you, then your garden centre should have a large selection of bedding plants available in late April to early May.

■ Steps for Sowing Seed ■

1. Select seeds.
2. Clean pots.
3. Pre-moisten sterilized potting or seeding mix.
4. Lightly fill and level the mix in your pots.
5. Select and sow one variety of seed at a time, making sure not to spill any seeds around the outside of the pot.
6. Lightly cover seeds with mix, then with glass or plastic.
7. Place in a warm place where it is easy to keep an eye on them.
8. Once germination has commenced move to indirect light.
9. Transplant when large enough to handle.

■ PLANTING YOUR ANNUAL BORDER

In a mixed border it is most likely you will be putting your summer annuals where your bulbs were. I prefer to keep my bulbs in so the leaves can die back naturally and then plant my annuals in the spaces between them. You will need to mix in some granular fertilizer before planting, something like 6-8-6 or whatever is your favourite balanced fertilizer. Remember, as a general guideline, to add one handful per square yard (1 m²). To plant your annuals get a good trowel. There are many inexpensive ones on the market but they bend easily. I recommend that, for any gardening tool, you spend a few extra dollars to get a strong tool that will last for many years.

Make sure the soil in the bedding baskets is moist before transplanting annuals. Remove the basket and stand the seedlings on a flat surface. Using an old kitchen knife, cut them apart. If you have a basket containing six plants, run the knife down the middle so that there are three plants on each side. Then make two more cuts across and you will be sure that each plant has an adequate patch of soil. They will also get equal amounts of the root system. This is much better than pulling them apart as so often when you do some get all the soil while others get none.

Dig a hole deep enough to accommodate the root system. Do not plant them any deeper than they were in your seed basket, and please do not plant them in rows. Rows of plants belong only in vegetable gardens. Try to plant them in staggered clumps...they will look more natural that way. A general rule is to give them as much space as the plant is tall. For example, if a petunia grows up to 12 in. (30 cm) in height, plant them one foot (30 cm) apart. Smaller plants can be planted closer together. You want to have them close enough so that, when they develop, their foliage covers up the soil so weeds cannot grow in between them. You

will also get a wonderful solid mass of colour. So, plant them in staggered clumps if you can.

There are some plants that should have their central shoot pinched off at this stage. A few examples are nicotiana (the tobacco plant), snapdragons, zinnias and heliotrope. Heliotrope is one I have in my garden every summer. It tends to send out one long spike, and at this stage you need to pinch out the top. Pinching out is a term that English people use freely which seems to confuse everybody, but it simply means cutting out the top. We call it pinching because we use our thumb and forefinger to break the growing tip off the plant. This forces the buds in the lower leaves to send out new shoots. You will take away the first flower, but instead of getting one flower you will end up with at least eight or more and a nice bushy plant which will be more attractive. Marigolds are also a good example of a

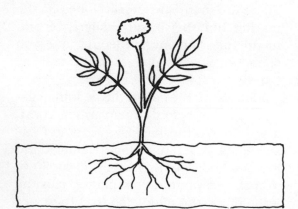
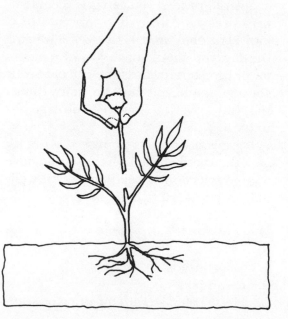

8. *Pinching the flower head from a newly planted marigold...*

plant that needs pinching. When you buy them from a garden centre they will come with one flower on top. Make sure you cut that flower out after planting, otherwise all the energy from your plant will go into making that flower go to seed. That is what an annual plant is, a plant that blooms for one season to produce seed to reproduce for the next year. Once they have produced seed they will not continue to produce flowers. Later in the summer, if you continually pick off the dead flower heads, the plants will have a longer flowering season.

There is another way to use annuals and one that is fun and easy to do in a home garden. I did this as a child and I have often seen very nice annual displays planted in this way. If you have a border that you use only for summer annuals you may want to sow seed directly in the soil. In the spring, as soon as the soil is workable, on one of those nice sunny days in March, sprinkle mushroom manure over the surface of the flower bed. Go over it with a fork or spade and turn it under, then let it sit for a day or two to dry up. Then rake the surface of the soil to level it off. You should try to position the rake low or bend your back a little and move the rake backwards and forwards. Do not rake in one direction pulling everything towards you, as you will end up taking away the good soil. If you move the rake backward and forwards it will break up the lumps of soil. You can rake one day, wait another day until it is a little drier, then rake again, picking off the excess stones and debris. Get down on your knees and look back along the flower bed to make sure it is nice and level. After two or three days walk lightly about on the surface of the soil to settle it down a bit. If you do not do this before sowing your seeds small hills and valleys will form when it rains. If it has been wet and

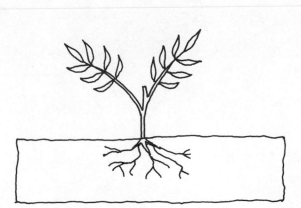
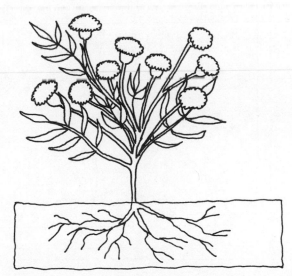

... results in many more flowers.

the soil has not had a chance to dry out, place some boards down and walk on them to level the surface.

Mark the flower bed off using bamboo canes and string. You could mark it off in blocks, but because I am more of a natural gardener I prefer to mark it off in rounds. If the flower bed is oval, say about one yard (1 m) in width and two yards (2 m) long, you can sow up to six to eight different annuals in that area. There are two methods for sowing seed directly into the soil. You can broadcast sow them, which is scattering them over the surface of the soil and raking them in. This is fine but a problem can develop with not being able to recognize seedling plants from weeds. So, even though I am generally against planting things in rows, you could sow your seeds in rows in this case. Start them off at an angle in the first site (see illustration). Make your rows by pushing

the back of the rake down to make a little trench...no deeper than in. (6 mm)...then sprinkle your seeds in and cover them lightly. In your next site make the trench at a different angle so your flower bed will not look too regimented. Now you will be able to weed without pulling out the annuals by mistake. Continue sowing each area, covering them up as you go, being sure to label them and water them in well. A newly raked flower bed is a wonderful litter box for cats, and if you have a problem with this put down chicken wire or twigs on the surface of the soil. It will look messy to start off with but it will keep the cats away. Birds will also come and disturb freshly raked soil and this works to keep them away too. Leave the chicken wire or twigs on until the plants begin to germinate, probably towards the end of April.

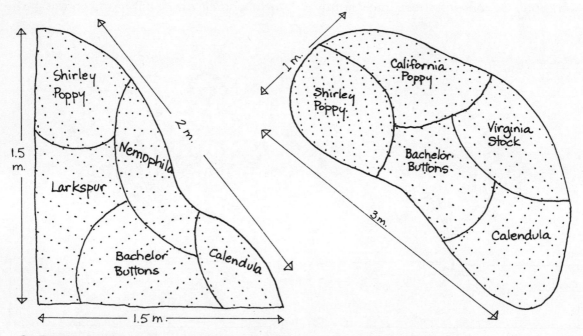

9. *Two annual beds. The dotted lines show seed sowing patterns for contrast.*

■ PLANT SELECTIONS

Let me give you a list of hardy annuals that can be planted in this way. The term *hardy annual* means the seeds can tolerate living in the soil over the winter. They can also tolerate a little frost in the seedling stage and will not die out.

Calendula officinalis (Pot Marigold). *Calendula* is a very pretty plant and you can use the petals of this plant in salads. Once it is in the garden, it will reseed itself and come up year after year. Pot marigolds range in height from about 1-2 ft. (30-60 cm) and will bloom on and off all summer. They have beautiful, dandelion-shaped flowers of orange and yellow and make very nice cut flowers.

Clarkia pulchella. *Clarkia* is a hardy annual. They can become quite tall if sown early in the season, up to about 2 ft. (60 cm). They are a lovely plant with two to three central stems that are somewhat shrub-like and bushy. All along their stems are beautiful double flowers, usually pink, white and purple. They are very nice and well worth garden space.

Eschscholtzia californica (California Poppy). *Eschscholtzia* is another favourite of mine. There are many different forms and they each grow to about 1 ft. (30 cm) in height. The typical California poppy is brilliant orange and a joy to add to your garden. A recently promoted variety called Mission Bells are far from the typical orange flowers. You can get Mission Bells that are magenta, pink or white and they are very pretty plants.

Centaurea cyanus (Bachelor Buttons). Bachelor buttons are very pretty plants with deep blue flowers and look particularly nice planted adjacent to the California poppy. They will grow a lot taller, up to 2 1/2 ft. (75 cm) in height, so plant them in behind your poppies in the middle of the flower bed and they will give a wonderful show for the summer.

Papaver rhoeas (Shirley Poppy). This is the red poppy seen widely in European countries in the spring, especially in Greece and countries around the Mediterranean where it grows profusely along the roadsides. Shirley poppies come in shades of white, pink and red and are a must for your garden. They can be sown directly into the garden in the spring and reach about 1 1/2-2 ft. (45-60 cm) tall.

Nigella damascena ("Love in a Mist"). *Nigella damascena* has very fine foliage, like an asparagus fern, with lovely blue flowers. It will grow to about 1-1 1/2 ft. (30-45 cm) tall. It is very pretty when blooming and has attractive seed pods that can be dried and used in flower arrangements.

You can also sow hardy summer annuals in a mixed border in between your shrubs or perennials. During April, clear the small areas between your other plants and sprinkle some granular 6-8-6 onto the surface of the soil. Then sow your seeds as you would in a larger flower bed. They will give you a lovely splash of colour in your mixed border.

Summer annuals will continue to bloom provided they are cared for by proper feeding and watering. Feed them once a month with a well-balanced fertilizer such as granular 6-8-6 or seaweed or fish fertilizer, but make sure that you do not give them too much nitrogen. It is all right early in the season, but later on if we get a cool wet summer they will produce leaves and no flowers. Use a good balanced fertilizer, higher in the middle and last numbers, to keep the flowers going.

■ SAVING SEED

When you pick the dead flower heads off many annuals you can save the seed. You will get cross-breeding because your neighbours will be growing other forms of the same plants and the bees will be going back and forth between them. So you may not get the exact plant the following year, but for straightforward annuals such as Bachelor buttons, marigolds and poppies I would recommend you save seed for next season. Collect seed towards the end of the summer in August and September. Let some seed pods form, and on a very dry day, about the middle of the day when things are at their driest, gather your seed. Cut the seed heads of one particular plant and put them in a paper bag. Place the bag in a shed or where there is good air circulation and allow them to dry for the next two or three days. You will then notice that if you shake the bag the seeds will separate from the seed pods. Then shake the seed pods onto a sheet of paper and pick out the debris. Funnel the remaining seeds into individual envelopes which have been labeled with the seed name and date you collected it. Immediately put them in an airtight container, such as an old coffee can, seal it and keep it in the crisper drawer of your refrigerator. Do not use the freezer but put it somewhere in the bottom of your refrigerator where it will stay nice and cool. As long as they are kept at a constant temperature many seeds will last for years and years.

■ THINGS TO REMEMBER

1. Always use good quality seed or bedding plants.
2. Choose your site well, making sure it has all the sun possible.
3. Prepare the soil well, adding compost and fertilizer just before planting.
4. Always harden off bedding plants in the spring. Do not put them straight out in the garden from a heated greenhouse.
5. Keep dead heads picked off for long-term blooming.

Perennials

Perennials were some of the earliest plants grown by our ancestors, and when they came to North America they brought perennials with them. Over the years, growing them comes in and out of fashion. Today there seems to be a resurgence across North America, and throughout the western world, towards growing perennials. Many perennials need to be staked, so they will require some maintenance during their growing season. For the average home gardening area I would suggest that you plant perennials in a mixed border. Do not entertain the less showy ones, and if you have to dig some out that you do not care for, do not feel badly about getting rid of them. Try to choose your favourites and develop a border to your liking.

The most important thing to remember is that you cannot dig into a perennial border every year to add organic material, so it is extremely important, from the outset, that you do the best possible job when preparing perennial beds. The best time of year to put one in is the fall. Choose the site with care and think about the location of your border in relation to your house and what you see when you look out each window. I would isolate any area that I see most often and use that for a perennial border. You will want to be able to enjoy the colour from inside and outside your home. Also bear in mind that no flowering plant grows very well underneath large trees. In some areas of the Lower Mainland we have beautiful old evergreen trees, which can cause a problem when we want to grow plants underneath them. Under such trees your plants will not get enough light, and when you add organic material to this area the tree roots will grow up toward it and eventually choke out your perennials. So your perennial bed should be out in the open, somewhere where it gets at least a half a day's sunshine...a full day is better.

Prepare the soil as described in Chapter 1. If possible, double-dig in November for a perennial bed as you are not going to be able to come back year after year and work manure into the soil. Double-digging means taking out not one trench but digging down a further shovel's depth. Work some organic material all the way through the two-spade depth, at least 18-24 in. (45-60 cm) deep. Then when you have dug the border work backwards as before, taking the soil from the first two trenches down to where you are going to finish up so that you have soil to replace at the very end. It will all look very uneven, especially if you have brought up a lot of subsoil. Try not to worry too much about it; let it sit there and the winter rains will settle it down. Some freezing and thawing will break up the soil quite nicely.

Early in the spring when the weather warms up, say in March, get rid of the first crop of small weeds. There are bound to be some weeds coming up, and while you are digging if you run across any major perennial weeds like docks, mare's tail and couch grass do your best to get these roots out. If the odd one or two stay behind, that is alright. Later in the spring you will have an opportunity to reweed the area. At that time it is a good idea to put in about a handful of lime per square yard (m²) over the entire area and work it into the top soil...except in interior alkaline soil areas. By the time April comes around, when you start putting in your perennials, the lime will have broken down, and you will have a wonderful display of flowers for the first season.

The shape and size of your perennial border are important. I particularly like island beds because you can walk all around the outside edges. In this case you would have shorter plants around the edges and taller ones in the middle. A traditional location for a border is along the length of a fence or property line. In this case you would put your taller perennials in the back and shorter ones in the front. Be sure to give some thought before planting your perennials. As a guideline, perennials need to be about 18-24 in. (45-60 cm) apart. Do not plant them in an area where they will not have enough room to grow.

Check out books from the library to research perennial plants. Find out which ones might fit best in your flower bed. In the fall, if you have decided to put in a perennial bed then you will have all winter to do your research. There are marvellous books available on perennial plants, most with very good colour photographs to help you better visualize what plants to use and where to site them.

Once you have researched the plants, write out a plan. Make an outline map of your border and pencil in the various sites. Try to dovetail them into one another like a jigsaw puzzle instead of in square blocks. You will want it to look as free as possible, so make irregular jigsaw-shaped sites. Also, put close together colours that complement one another. In nature all colours seem to go together, but try to keep yellows and oranges in one area, blues and purples in another, and pinks and reds in yet another area. This will make for a more attractive border. Make sure that you make a note of the average height of your perennials. You do not want to plant something 7 ft. (2 m) tall in front of shorter-growing perennials. Save your tallest plants for the back or centre of your border.

Also keep in mind the growth of these plants over the next three to four years. When you first put them in many will look lost, but give them plenty of space to develop over time. Plant growth rate is fairly rapid on the coast, and it will not take long before they fill up the area. In four years time you will want to begin dividing them, so you will have a continuation of young plants for good flower production.

Individual plants will not make much of a show. I suggest that when you are working out your plan for a perennial bed put them in groups of at least three to five plants. Of course, if this is going to be a mixed border, remember to leave space for planting bulbs in the spring or annuals in the summer. You may even want to include plants that would not normally be associated with a mixed border. For example, you could plant a clump of parsley. It looks wonderful and gives a lovely soft foliage edge to a flower border. For summer annual colour near blue perennials, you might also consider putting in some silver foliage plants. Santolina or Cotton lavender is a very pretty thing and its silver foliage complements blue flowers very well. Dusty miller is another silver foliage plant you could use.

There are not many scented perennials. Most of them are very colourful in the height of summer, but they do not generally have much fragrance. Save a space for fragrant plants such as peonies. Peonies bloom early in the season during late spring or early summer. They are delightful and some varieties are sweetly scented. Summer-flowering lilies would be a good addition as well, along with monarda, which is used for the flavouring of Earl Grey tea. Its common name is bee balm and it is available in shades of purple, red and magenta. The foliage, when bruised, gives off a wonderful scent. Then, there are many forms of dianthus. Dianthus, commonly called pinks, go well in the front of a border and give off a lovely scent in the middle of the summer. Dianthus like a fair amount of chalk or lime in the soil, so when you plant them put in a little extra lime and work it into the soil…except in interior gardens where the soil is alkaline.

■ PLANTING PERENNIALS

Planting-out time for perennials can be anywhere from late March through to the end of April. As for any other flower bed make sure the soil has been raked level and pick out any large stones on the surface. Roughly mark out areas, as noted in your planning map, with bamboo canes. Starting at one end of the border, work backwards. If you are planting from pots lay the whole thing out first by setting down your groups. It is a good idea at this time to refresh your memory as to how tall each plant is going to grow. Make a note of it on your labels, stand back and try to visualize what it will look like in a few years. Starting at one end, tap the plants out of their pots and plant them no deeper than they were in their pots. Then push the soil firmly around the root ball and rake it lightly with your fingers or a trowel. If you work backwards, you will leave no footprints or uneven places in the border. If the weather is on the dry side, which it can be during the spring, it is a good idea to water them in well. If you get a perennial plant division from friends, and it is not in a pot, put the roots in a plastic bag so they do not dry out. Whenever you transplant, roots should not be left exposed to the air any longer than two to three minutes. It is also much better to transplant on dull days rather than bright sunny ones when the wind is blowing and things dry out quickly.

During a perennial's first season there are some things to watch for. It is very important in the first year, because they have developed no major root systems, to keep them well watered. So, in a long dry spell in the spring, keep a lookout for moisture content in the soil. Also, make sure to keep down the weeds. This is where a hoe can be very useful. A push hoe, or dutch hoe, with a sharp blade on the front that slides through the soil is good. Push it backwards and forwards, working the soil so you sever the weed

plants just above their roots. Do this on a warm or hot day and the small weed seedlings can be left on the surface to die out. Be careful when you are hoeing as it takes a little practice to perfect the technique. It is very easy, if you have a new hoe with a sharp blade, to chop off your newly planted perennials. I usually hand weed around each perennial plant, then use the hoe for the patches in between.

I learned from my own garden that I tend to overplant. I like to see masses of flowers with no soil showing in between. Because of this I have to pay special attention to the growth rate of all my plants. If I plant a lot of strong-growing annuals in the gaps between my perennials, I make sure that over the summer they do not choke out the perennial plants. You may have to do some severe pruning around your perennials to give them a chance to develop. It is something I do every year in my own garden at home. If you let your petunias run rampant over your blue poppies they will rot underneath the dense growth of petunias. So do not be frightened to cut your annuals back...your perennials will love you for it.

If you put manure into the soil when preparing it earlier on in the season, there should be no need to add other fertilizers throughout the season. Use some bone meal when planting. It will then be useful to the plants over a longer period of time. During the summer stake your plants. I prefer staking plants early in the season...do not wait until they fall over. I have seen so many otherwise attractive perennials bunched up and tied to a stake. The poor things look awful. Be prepared early by knowing how tall the plants are going to grow and give them some form of support early. There are supports you can purchase made from four metal stakes that are pushed into the ground and have two levels of mesh, one level at about 12 in. (30 cm) and the other at about 16 in. (40 cm). This stands over the clump of flowers, which grows up through the mesh to hide the stake. If you do not want to invest in that sort of thing, then you can use what I call pea sticks. Pea sticks are something I remember from my training days in England. I suggest using alder or birch twigs as you can find them locally. Pea sticks are brush wood cut in the winter. Keep them in bundles in your garden so they dry out and do not form leaves. If you are staking peonies, which are at most 2 ft. (75 cm) high, cut your twigs about 2 ft. (60 cm) long, then push them into the ground around the edge of the peony clump. It will look awful when you first put them in, but as the plants grow the leaves will hide them. You will then have a lovely stand of peonies that will not fall over when we get those heavy spring rains.

Apart from that there is not much to do during the summer to take care of perennials. Come fall, with the first frost, you will have a lot of dead material from your perennials. One thing that I cannot over-emphasize is to leave them be and do not cut everything down to the ground in the fall. This can be a very bad mistake as we never know what kind of a winter we are going to get here on the coast. If it is a very cold winter those twigs and dead leaves are nature's blanket and will protect the plant from the cold. The only other way of protecting plants is with snow cover, but we do not get that here as they do in other parts of Canada. In any case it usually does not snow before it freezes, so it does not do us much good. I am a great believer in an untidy garden for the wintertime to help protect it. But if you must cut back your plants, cut them no lower than 18 in. (45 cm). Try to leave all the clusters of dead twigs and leaves on them. If you have some fairly tender plants they will need some protection during the winter. For example, there are agapanthus, which are pretty plants commonly called Blue Lily of the Nile. There is a small form of agapanthus that is somewhat hardy on the coast but needs a bit of protection. For these plants, build a small wire cage and hold it in place with a few bamboo canes. Then, when raking dry leaves in the fall, put some down inside the wire cage to form a blanket over the top. This will really help to protect the roots of the tender plants. The majority of perennials will not need major protection as they are extremely hardy. Peonies, for example, grow all across the country, as do asters. Most of the perennials we have can tolerate a fair amount of frost.

In February, when you notice new growth coming from your perennials prune them back to within 1 in. (2.5 cm) or so from the ground. Prune them close to the ground without damaging the new growth. Then lightly rake through the border, with a hand fork, without doing any major digging. Do not dig down and break up the root systems. If you see the odd perennial weed beginning to establish itself, try to dig it up by lightly aerating the surface of the soil. Sprinkle on something like granular 6-8-6 and gently mix it through. It is also a good idea to top dress your perennial border sometime between February and March with well-rotted compost or manure, particularly if you are growing such plants as delphiniums. I have delphiniums in my garden at home and I give them extra special care every spring. I purchase a bag of well-rotted steer manure from my garden centre and put it on as a mulch around the base of the delphiniums and they seem to love it.

Three or four years later it will be necessary to divide some of your perennial plants. Some of your perennials will have formed very dense clumps. Once they have formed a dense clump of growth at the bottom, when they flower the best flowers are around the outside of the clump and the middle ones tend to be rather bald and stark looking. The Bearded iris (*I. germanica*), for example, will get very dense and the middle rhizomes will not produce any more flowers. In this case, split them up and replant only the outside of the clump.

With the Michaelmas daisy it sometimes takes two people to lift a large clump as they are very strong surface-rooting plants. Lift it in the fall once it has died down and after you have cut it back, around October or November. The traditional way of splitting is to stick two garden forks into the centre of the clump, back-to-back so the tines of the forks are vertical and the handles are a small distance apart at the top. Then push the handles together, being careful not to bang your fingers if the clump suddenly breaks, and pry the clump apart. If it is a large clump you can then divide it in quarters or however many sections you think necessary. Do not save the older inner material as it will not give good flowers. If you share it with friends be sure to give them some of the nice material from the outside. Then replant about five of the sections in a group just as you did when you first planted your perennial bed.

Bearded iris grow with rhizomes, which are fleshy roots, running along the surface of the soil, with leaves and flowers at the ends. When saving the young rhizomes from around the outside of the iris clump, cut the leaves back by half to make it easier to handle, and when planting make sure not to bury them. With Bearded iris you should see the surface of the rhizomes just above the soil; otherwise no flowers will grow.

When you do have the opportunity of going into a perennial flower border once every four years or so to do some major division then you will also have an opportunity to work some more manure into the area. Other than that an annual top dressing of well-rotted compost or manure will help to produce a very successful mixed border.

■PLANT SELECTIONS

Here is a list of some of my favourite perennials that do very well in the Pacific region.

Acanthus mollis. *Acanthus* is a plant that is not common in this part of the world, but in Europe it is naturalized everywhere. I have also seen some very fine specimens in New Zealand. It is a stately perennial plant for local gardens, reaching a height of 3-4 ft. (1-1.2 m) and has wonderful long, spiny leaves. The acanthus leaf inspired the top forms of Corinthian columns in Greek architecture. It takes a lot of space, up to 16 sq.ft.

(1.5 m²), but would be well worth a place in your garden.

Achillea filipendulina. *Achillea* is a handsome border plant. It reaches a height of 4-5 ft. (1.2-1.5 m) which blooms in July and August and needs an area of about 9 sq.ft. (1 m²) to grow in. The variety I like is called Coronation Gold, which has wonderful gold and yellow flowers. The flowers can also be cut and dried and used in the home for winter decoration.

Anchusa azurea. This is one of my all-time favourites, a challenge to grow and not easy to find, although there are some local nurseries that are beginning to specialize in the more unusual perennials. It reaches a height of about 3-5 ft. (1-1.5 m), blooms in the summer and needs an area of about 9 sq.ft. (1 m²). It is a challenge because it needs very well drained soil and plenty of sun to get the most spectacular effect. Even though it is a perennial it is advisable to raise it annually; then you can save seed and start it off in the summer. I have planted a bed of them in the fall and they have bloomed for me the following year, so they can almost be treated like a biannual. One variety to look for is called Royal Blue...it is a knockout and will give you lots of joy in the summertime.

Anemone hybrida. This anemone is the Asian form, and I love it with a passion. It is difficult to know which form to recommend as there are some wonderful pink varieties as well as handsome white ones. Without a doubt some of the best specimens in the Vancouver area are in the VanDusen Botanical Garden. If you have never been to see them when they are in bloom in the late summer, you must make a special trip. I recommend the pink form, particularly one known as Rosea Superba. The flowers are a lovely rose colour and reach a height of 2-3 1/2 ft. (.6-1.2 m). It is a very welcome sight towards the end of summer, blooming during September and October. You will need an area of about 4 sq.ft. (.4 m²) for each plant to develop fully.

Aster amellus. The cultivar of this plant that I love is called King George. It has wonderful blue-violet flowers that usually come into bloom in late August. They grow to an average height of 2 ft. (60 cm) and need about 18-24 in. (45-60 cm) square in which to grow. This is a plant which could go towards the front of a border as it is quite short. Most of the perennial asters are referred to by people from Britain as Michaelmas daisies. There are many forms of the Michaelmas daisy to choose from, and they are well worth including in your border as they give that lovely late summer colour that we all look for.

Astilbe arendsii. This is another one of my favourites and there are many to choose from in shades of pink and white. I recommend a cool white one called Avalanche as it is very pretty. It reaches a height of around 2-3 ft. (.6-1 m) and will bloom somewhere between July and August. It needs about 4 sq.ft. (.4 m²) to develop fully. This plant needs to go in an area of the border that stays shady and has a bit more moisture in the soil. Perhaps on the north side of the border would be best, where it will not get as much strong sunlight, or in an area which gets morning sun and afternoon shade.

Campanula lactiflora. This plant is a very tall-growing member of the *Campanula* group, commonly known as bell flowers. This one reaches a height of 4-5 ft. (1.2-1.5 m). It has beautiful light green foliage and heads of wonderful light-blue flowers that bloom in mid-June. This plant will need to go in the centre or back of your border because it is so tall. They need about 4 sq.ft. (.4 m²) for their full development.

Cimicifuga racemosa. This plant has beautiful fluffy white flowers that bloom in late summer. It reaches a height of about 3 ft. (1 m). A very pretty plant that is light and airy and shows up well against a dark background.

Coreopsis verticillata. The one that I like is a cultivar named Golden Shower. It is a delightful plant that blooms all summer. It grows no taller than 1-1 1/2 ft. (30-45 cm) and has needle-like foliage and brilliant yellow daisy-like flowers. Because it is so compact it needs no staking, and the more cut flowers you take from it the more it will bloom. It blooms on and off from June through to September. This plant needs about 12 in. (30 cm) square to develop. Plant some of these wonderful yellow flowering plants close to a blue flowering plant if possible...it will look beautiful.

Delphinium grandiflorum (Pacific Strain). Among delphiniums, I prefer the large Pacific strain hybrids. As the name implies, they do very well in this part of the world. The flower is a beautiful blue colour growing from a plant anywhere from 4-7 ft. (1.2-2.1 m) tall; they will need staking. As I have mentioned, they are hungry plants that like to have lots of manure worked around their roots. A fascinating thing about delphiniums is that once they have bloomed, if you cut back the flower spike, they usually send up another succession of bloom that will come in the fall. So, their major blooming is in June or July and their second blooming will be at the end of August or early September. They may not produce as large a flower, but they will bloom twice in one season. As they are so tall they will need about 4-9 sq.ft. (.4-1 m²) to have room to grow in, so put them in the centre or near the back of your border.

Echinops ritro. Taplo Blue or Blue Globe thistle is a lovely plant that grows up to 3-5 ft. (1-1.5 m) tall. It has beautiful spiny leaves, dark green on the top and silver-green underneath. They are very erect-growing plants but will still require some staking, particularly if in a windy or high rainfall area. It blooms from July to August and needs about 4 sq.ft. (.4 m²) to develop. Cut some of the beautiful blue globes before the flower opens and hang them upside down to dry for use in dried flower arrangements.

Gypsophila paniculata. *Gypsophila paniculata*, commonly called baby's breath, looks lovely as a cut flower and used in flower arrangements will soften up the bouquet. It reaches a height of about 3 ft. (1 m) tall and blooms any time from June through August; the flowers stay on a long time. The one I recommend is Flore-

Pleno, which simply means double-flowered; it needs about 4-9 sq.ft. (.4-1 m²) to develop. I dot mine throughout the garden as their flowers have a lovely softening effect.

Heuchera sanguinea. There is a form of this plant called Coral Bells which has been around for years. The nice thing about this plant is that it flowers in early summer. It is a good plant to put in the front of your border as it reaches only 1-1 1/2 ft. (30-45 cm) tall and needs only 1 sq.ft. (.1 m²) to develop. It is a very pretty little plant with roundish leaves and wiry stems covered with tiny coral bell-shaped flowers. A very pretty plant and good for cutting.

Iris germanica. These are the wonderful old flag irises that have been around for years. There are so many to choose from I hardly know which one to recommend. There is a beautiful orchid-pink one called Chantilly that looks similar to a large cattleya orchid. They reach a height of about 2 1/2-4 ft. (.8-1.2 m) and will need a fair amount of moisture retention in the soil. They need an area just over 1 sq.ft. (.1 m²) to develop. They bloom for a very short season but have stately foliage that looks nice behind other lighter coloured perennials all summer long.

Liatras pycnostachya. There is a marvellous form of this plant called White Spire. It is a fluffy flower...the one we usually see is purple...which can be found as a cut flower in most corner grocery stores in the Lower Mainland. An unusual flower, it has spiky foliage at the base of the stem and flower. It has very tight buds along the stem which begin to bloom from the top and then work their way down the stem. One of the common names for it is Gay Feather because it looks just like a feather. It needs an area of about 1 sq.ft. (.1 m²) to grow in and grows up to 2-3 ft. (.6-1 m) tall. This perennial blooms usually from August through to October.

Limonium latifolium. *Limonium latifolium* is commonly called sea lavender and is a beautiful thing. It has large leaves approximately 4-6 in. (10-15 cm) across and lovely little wiry stems with a beautiful fluffy top of violet-blue flowers. There is a very nice one called Blue Gown that has light lavender flowers. They grow no more than about 2 ft. (60 cm) tall and will not require staking. Their blooming period is from July to September.

Lobelia cardinalis. When most of us think of lobelia, we think of it as a summer annual. These are the small blue trailing forms that we see so often in hanging baskets and window boxes. *Lobelia cardinalis* is quite different. While the flowers look the same they are a wonderful scarlet colour and the foliage is red rather than green. They have very strong stems. They need an area of your border with moisture and perhaps a bit of shade. It really is gorgeous, reaching 1-3 ft. (30-100 cm) in height, and will bloom from July through to September, requiring about 1 sq.ft. (.1 m²) to develop. It has been hybridized in Canada into many different forms. This red lobelia is certainly a conversation piece and I would like to see more of it grown here on the coast.

59

Lupinus polyphyllus. This includes that wonderful group of plants referred to as Russell lupins and it has many beautiful colours. If you buy them from a producer of plants, a mixture of Russell lupins could get you any colour from orange through to blue, white to pink, and many of them are bi-coloured. Lupins are not grown as widely as they should be here. You see a lot of them in the Atlantic provinces. I have had successful ones in my garden that bloom year after year. Generally, they bloom a little later in the season but can bloom anywhere from June through to July. They reach 2-2 ft. (60-75 cm) high and need about 4 sq.ft. (.4 m²) to develop. When they are not in bloom they have lovely umbrella-like round leaves which look so pretty after a rain as rain drops gather on the edge of the leaves like diamonds. It is a good plant to have and adds texture to your garden.

Lychnis chalcedonica. This plant is commonly called the Maltese cross and has vivid scarlet flowers with large flat heads that look like Maltese crosses. They reach about 2-3 ft. (60-90 cm) tall and bloom from June through to August. It is rarely found in local gardens these days but was quite popular years ago. It is very strong and does not need staking, requiring about 4 sq.ft. (.4 m²) to grow. This plant is a real knockout with its brilliant red flowers.

Macleaya cordata. This can be an enormous plant, and I hesitate to recommend it for small gardens, but it is so beautiful architecturally. It has marvellous leaves that are very deeply indented. The foliage is not green but a buff-pink colour. It will grow in sun or light shade and has a tiny pinkish-coloured flower on its top. However, it is grown mainly for its marvellous leaf design. This plant can grow anywhere from 5-7 ft. (1.5-2.1 m) tall and will be spectacular from July through to September. Try to put a clump in the middle of your perennial bed.

Monarda didyma. The type I like is called Mrs. Perry, named for Frances Perry who was my mentor in England. It has beautiful deep-red flowers that attract hummingbirds to the garden and is the plant used to flavour Earl Grey tea. It will bloom anytime, on and off, from June through to September with brilliant flushes of colour. It reaches about 2-3 ft. (60-90 cm) tall and needs an area of about 4 sq.ft. (.4 m²) to develop. It does not like to dry out so make sure that it is in an area of the border that gets a little more moisture. It could be planted near the astilbe and lobelia.

Oenothera missouriensis. This is one of the many evening primroses. I like this one in particular because it is a good plant for the front of a border. It does not grow to any more than 12 in. (30 cm) in height, has lovely funnel-shaped, brilliant 4 in. (10 cm) yellow flowers, and the stems are often red, which is rather nice looking. It blooms from July through to August. This particular one is well suited to a smaller home garden and needs only about 1 sq.ft. (.1 m²) to grow in.

Peony. There are so many hybrids of peony, but the one I especially like is called Winston Churchill. It is a single variety and has a nicely scented, rosy pink flower with lovely yellow stamens in the centre. It reaches a height of 2 -3 ft. (.8-1.1 m) and needs about 4-9 sq.ft. (.4-1 m²) to develop. It blooms only once in June. Be sure to stake peonies as they tend to fall over in heavy spring rain. Peonies do not like to be disturbed, so once planted they should be fine in that site from seven to ten years before they need to be divided. Once they are divided they tend to sulk and may take a long time before they produce flower spikes, often because they are planted too deeply.

Papaver orientale. These are those wonderful large and hardy perennial poppies. People tend not to grow them as they can get messy and fall over in the spring. However, if you stake them as they are coming up in May and June, you can watch their gorgeous flowers unfold. They look very dainty with their tissue-paper-like flowers and come in many wonderful colours. It is difficult to know which one to recommend but again I am going to suggest one called Mrs. Perry. It is a soft salmon pink with a dark black blotch at the bottom of its petal and a very black centre. You must have at least one of these oriental poppies in your border. It is about 2-3 ft. (60-90 cm) high, blooms in May and needs about 4 sq.ft. (.4 m²) to grow.

Phlomis cashmeriana. The yellow species of these plants is widespread in Europe, particularly in southern Europe and Greece. The common name for them in Europe is Jerusalem sage. They have silvery-grey foliage with rows of yellow pea-like flowers growing up the stems, which can be anywhere from 2-4 ft.

(.6-1.2 m) tall. The one I like has deep-lilac flowers combined with lovely silvery-grey foliage and is beautiful. It blooms from June to July and needs about 9 sq.ft. (1 m²) to develop properly. It also likes a lot of sun, so be sure to put it in a sunny area of your border.

Phygelius capensis. This is a lovely shrub-like plant from South Africa that looks somewhat like a fuchsia and is called Cape fuchsia. It is extremely hardy on the coast. We have had a clump of them in the University of British Columbia Botanical Alpine Garden since the garden opened in 1974. Even after our coldest winters it comes back to bloom the following season. It is so beautiful and reaches a height of 4 ft. (1.2 m). I have read that they generally bloom in August, but the one at the Botanical Garden tends to have blossoms starting in July and goes on blooming right through until the frost.

Physostegia virginiana. This is an interesting native of Virginia commonly called obedient plant. When you push the flowers around on the top of the stem they tend to stay where you have pushed them. They are a lovely plant to have in a border and reach about 2-3 ft. (60-90 cm) in height and bloom August to September. They require about 2 sq.ft. (.2 m²) in which to grow. The best cultivar, called Vivid, has bright rose-purple flowers. Try to find a Vivid at your garden centre in the spring.

Platycodon grandiflorum. This plant is fairly new to the perennial market. Commonly called the balloon flower, it is very much like a campanula. When it is just coming into bloom the buds burst into a ball-shaped 2 in. (5 cm) flower which is purple-blue. Their stems are about 1-2 ft. (30-60 cm) in height and tend to fall over, so it will need staking. It blooms from August through September and needs about 4 sq.ft. (.4 m²) to develop.

Scabiosa caucasica. These beautiful plants are very pretty and have pale blue flowers about 2 in. (5 cm) across. One cultivar called Wanda is a good choice. It reaches 1 1/2-2 ft. (45-60 cm) tall and is good for cut flowers. They bloom from June to September, and if you keep the flowers cut they will send up more spikes. They need about 1/2 sq.ft. (.15 m²) to develop and like lime in the soil. It is important that they have well-drained soil with about half a handful of lime sprinkled around them each spring.

Sidalcea malviflora. This is a pretty plant that looks like a cluster of dwarf hollyhocks with typical mallow-like flowers. The flowers, which bloom in the height of summer, during July and August, are not as large as a hollyhock but are very pretty. They are borne on spikes 2 1/2-3 ft. (75-90 cm) tall and need about 4 sq.ft. (.4 m²) to develop. There are many to choose from but the type called Sussex Beauty is gorgeous. It has satin pink flowers.

Stokesia leavis. Sometimes commonly referred to as Stokes aster, this is a marvellous plant for the front of your border. It has a wonderful colour and looks like a China aster with rich lavender flowers about 2 in. (5 cm) across; it reaches 1-1 1/2 ft. (30-45 cm) in height. The cultivar called Blue Moon is delightful and worth a place in your perennial border.

If you would like more information on perennial plants refer to the suggested reading list at the back of this book. There are many more perennial plants suitable for a home garden in British Columbia and I have recommended only a few of my favourites.

One of the joys of gardening is that you alone choose the plants that you are going to grow. And, the endless hours of planning are rewarding enough. But when it comes to planting and watching the results develop over the years, the enjoyment is tenfold. You will always want to grow more and more lovely plants as you discover them.

■ THINGS TO REMEMBER

1. Plan and prepare a perennial border well.
2. Make sure that it is well located away from the shade of trees or a tall building.
3. Remember that the initial soil preparation will have to last for the next four years or longer.
4. Support perennials in their developing stages—do not wait until they fall over.

Shrubs
■

Many people these days want a low-maintenance garden, and it is true that if you choose carefully the types of shrubs that you put in, along with some ground covers, you could have a fairly low maintenance yard. However, any garden takes a certain amount of work, and I believe that if you love and enjoy it then you can be persuaded to grow a complete garden as well. In this part of the world, you can have colour from shrubs on a year-round basis.

Shrubs are extremely useful for forming a screen, as opposed to having a straight hedge, if you want to put up some sort of boundary around your yard. Whether they are standing free or against a fence, with a little bit of care and thought you could position one or two very colourful shrubs that are not going to get too tall, that will not be too difficult to maintain.

There are winter-flowing shrubs. There are spring-flowering shrubs that give wonderful fall colour. There are shrubs that have interesting seeds and berries. So really, the sky is the limit. While shrubs will grow close to trees, the competition from those large evergreens that are native to our coastal areas is enormous. You will get the best results and all-around enjoyment from shrubs if they are put in a bed on their own, with a lot of light...at least eight hours of sunshine a day. Being out in the open they will not be influenced to grow away from a building or from a tree. A nice open space is important for a healthy, well-formed shrub.

Soil is important too. If you are starting from scratch and planting a shrub, by all means try to get some compost and well-rotted manure worked in to at least two spades' depth. Leaf mould is also very important. At the University of British Columbia Asia Garden we have had great success with our rhododendrons by adding a layer of about 12-24 in. (30-60 cm) of leaf mould on top of the scant old-growth forest soil and planting the rhododendrons or other shrubs right in it. You could modify this technique a bit in your home garden situation. If you feel the hard pan is too difficult to tackle, then by all means raise your bed up with a couple of railroad ties and work in some leaf mould, then plant your shrubs.

We are very fortunate on the coast that we can plant shrubs almost any time of the year. However, if you are doing traditional lifting and moving of shrubs...supposing some people you know in the area have sold their house and offer you that wonderful camellia that you have always admired...the best time to move that plant would be in the fall or early spring. At that time, when they are resting and dormant, shrubs can take to the move much more easily. The same goes for purchasing shrubs. Most garden centre stock within the city will be grown in containers, so essentially it can be bought at any time of the year. Some suburban nurseries will have field-grown shrubs which they will lift for you and wrap the roots in the traditional way in soil and burlap. The best time for planting these would be in the fall or in the spring.

Those are just guidelines, and in an area such as ours where we get a tremendous amount of rain, you can move shrubs at just about any time of the year. I had some dear friends who gardened on the North Shore for years and years and they were always having discussions, perhaps mini-arguments, about where plants should be and where they should not be, and then they would come to some compromise and move their shrubs whether it was March or August. But they always chose a time when it was rainy weather, and I think that is the absolute key. It is very important that once you have planted shrubs or trees you give them adequate water supplies for the rest of the season following the time of their move and perhaps early into the next season, especially if the move is made in the summer.

When you buy a plant you want it to be a particular colour or form. Many times people call me and say that they have a wisteria that they bought five years ago, and it has never bloomed. It is possible, with some plants, that they have actually been grown from seed. When shrubby plants are grown from seed, the chances of them being crossed with others are very strong and you will not necessarily get that wonderful dark purple wisteria that you saw in somebody else's garden, or in a picture in a book. You might get quite a weedy form or you may get a form that just does not flower very well at all.

The same goes for rhododendrons. You can buy rhododendrons in April and May in garden centres when they are in full bloom. They are very tiny at that stage, but they will have flowers on them. And if you buy one with flowers on, you will know for certain that it is going to come that colour for you every year afterwards. So, there is a lot to be said for selecting container-grown shrubs, if it is bloom that you are after, when they are in bloom.

When I first moved to Vancouver there were still a lot of the old houses around, and I can remember one down at the foot of Denman Street in the West End that had two rhododendrons outside the front door that had grown up above the bedroom window. It was a two-storey house and you had to walk in underneath them. I suspect those rhododendrons were fifty to seventy-five years old. What I am trying to emphasize is that you may be taken with a pretty little plant when it is in the nursery pot in the garden centre, but read about it before you plant it and find out how large it is likely to grow. This way you will not end up putting the poor thing in a narrow border between the front garden path and the garden fence, so that when it grows up it becomes a constant problem because you walk into it all the time. Another classic mistake is to put a foundation plant underneath a view window, then before you know where you are it has grown up and obscured the view. There are smaller species and cultivars to choose from, so do not just choose plants for their colour. Read about them first and you will avoid the disappointment of pruning or ruining the shrub later on.

When you have selected a few shrubs and have decided it is time to go ahead and plant your shrub border, it is very important to draw up some sort of a plan before you start. Before you go to buy the shrubs, do a little bit of reading to find out the mature height and width of the species you have chosen. This is very important.

Commercial landscapers will sometimes plant small shrubs far too close together. Now, this is fine if it is done deliberately...many of the so-called filler shrubs are disposable things that you can dig out later and get rid of or give to neighbours. But if it is prime shrubs that you are planting, the ones that you expect to be in your garden for at least the next ten to fifteen years, then try to make sure that you give them the right amount of space in between to develop. You can always fill in those bare spaces with other seasonal plants such as annuals or even some perennials with a little careful choosing on your part. So, make very sure that you are putting the plants in the right place.

When it comes time to dig the hole, assess the size of the root area of the plant. If it is in a container this is easy to do. If it is balled in burlap you will want to have a good look at it. If it is something that is coming from a neighbour's garden and you are not sure how large the root system is going to be, then dig the hole twice as large as you think you will need. One yard (1 m) in diameter and 12 in. (30 cm) deep is a useful size of hole. Even if the soil has been well worked at some time with manure, still put some leaf mould in the bottom of the hole.

When you bring the shrub into place, if it is balled and wrapped in burlap then take off the burlap very carefully. It is a good idea to stand the shrub down into the prepared hole before you remove the burlap because sometimes all the soil or some of the soil in among the roots will fall away. If this is the case, it is quite alright to untie the burlap and just lay it out flat in the bottom of the hole. You do not want great lumps of burlap being buried with your shrub, so cut away the extra around the outside with some scissors or your garden knife. The remaining burlap will eventually rot and not cause a problem.

However, it is important that you undo the burlap. I have been called out to places and seen gardens where shrubs are planted in a hurry and have been just left balled up in burlap. If the burlap is tied tightly around the trunk, as the tree grows, the twine grows into the trunk and the whole plant can die as a result. So, it is extremely important to untie any burlap from the stem or trunk so that it will not restrict the development of the shrub at a later stage.

Fill in the soil around the shrub. If it is on the dry side, then use your foot to tamp the soil in and around. If you are planting at a very wet time, then remember the problem of soil compaction. If the soil is wet, it is probably better to just fill the soil in, even though it is wet, water it well and then let the water settle down the soil. You can firm it with your feet at a later date. If it is dry and workable, it is much better that you put the shrub in, and work some soil in as you go. Mix some leaf mould compost in with it and then just tamp it in with your foot lightly so that the shrub cannot easily be pulled up again.

It is very important, before filling the hole, to make sure that the original surface of the soil around the shrub's basal branches is just a wee bit lower than the actual soil surface around it. When I say a wee bit, I mean 1-2 in. (2.5-5 cm), so that when planted it ends up in a sort of saucer. It is much better for the shrub to be in a shallow saucer than up on a hill, where it cannot be watered properly. So, have it in a saucer and then water it in, and if it needs to be watered over the year then there will be somewhere for the water to collect and filter down to the roots.

If the soil contains a lot of organic material, then fertilizer is not important, but you cannot go wrong by putting a handful of good old bone meal or even 6-8-6 in the bottom of the hole, depending on the time of year. If planting in the fall, add bone meal, which will bring nutrients to the plant in the spring. If planting in the spring, use 6-8-6 or some other balanced fertilizer at that time because it will be readily available to the shrub two to three weeks after planting.

■ TRANSPLANTING SHRUBS

When transplanting a shrub from another garden in the area, chances are that if the plant is more than four or five years old it will have a fairly large root system and you will break quite a few of the roots as you dig the plant. So prune the top back by two-thirds, which will make it somewhat easier to handle.

Have the hole ready for it to go into when you bring it to your garden. Remember, if it is going to be transported very far, it is important to wrap the roots either in black plastic or some damp burlap to keep them moist. This is very important because if the roots dry up the poor shrub will go through a lot of trauma.

If transplanting a flowering shrub in the fall when it is covered with flower buds, one of the best things you can do for that plant is to remove all those buds. If the plant has gone through a certain amount of trauma, which it will have from being moved, it will do everything in its power to bring those flower buds to fruition. This will further stress the plant, so rather than let that happen, pick off all the flower buds. Also, prune some of the straggly branches back by about one-third to help cut down on the overall water loss from the leaf area since its supplier, the root system, has been reduced quite drastically.

If you do this, you will not get any flowers for the first year, but the shrub will do very well the following season.

■ CONTAINER PLANTS

Since container plants can be bought at any time of the year, they can be planted at any time of the year, as long as you are going to be around to give them the after care and watering that they will need. If you are not really sure where you are going to plant them you might keep them in a holding area. Stand them on a bed of sawdust and water and feed them through the hottest, driest weather and then plant them when the weather breaks. Try to dig your hole at least twice as wide as the container and a little bit deeper, work some manure into the bottom, and you should have no problems.

■ PRUNING SHRUBS

Once shrubs are established they will need pruning. Following are some general guidelines for the type of pruning that needs to be carried out on many of the shrubs we grow.

Spring-flowering shrubs, such as forsythia and Japanese quince, bloom best on new wood that was produced the previous year. A great mistake with forsythia is to try to grow it clipped into a round ball, or some other shape. All the new shoots that start to come out after flowering will get cut right off, so that there is only a very small speckling of young growth that will give you any flower at all. Forsythia should be allowed to grow as a free-form bush. The best time to give it a good pruning is in the spring. If you like to do flower arranging you can take the entire cut branch that is covered with blossoms and use it for your decorations in the house, in the church, or wherever you want to use it.

You may have taken away a great clump of blossoms, but you will get one or two very good strong new shoots coming from the base which will give lots of colour for the following year. So, with spring-flowering shrubs that flower best on the previous year's wood, the idea is to get them to produce a fair amount of new wood annually.

In addition to forsythia, here are some shrubs that require heavy pruning. *Chaenomeles*, the flowering quince that we call japonica, definitely responds well to harsh pruning after flowering time. *Spirea arguta*, the bridal wreath spirea, needs cutting back right after flowering. With *Jasmimum nudiflorum*, the winter-flowering jasmine, you will get many more blossoms if you cut a lot of the old wood out right after it has finished flowering.

Some other shrubs need renewal pruning. They do not bloom on the first year's growth but seem to do well on the second and third year's growth. Then, once the wood gets any older, the blossoms get fewer. With such shrubs you should take out one or two of the oldest branches, usually in the spring. Look very closely at the main branches coming out from the base of the shrub. You will be able to tell by the colour of their bark which are the youngest and which are the oldest. The oldest will be quite woody. This is where a pruning saw comes in very handy, one with a pointed end. Reach in and cut out the two oldest branches, right to the very base, or as close to the base as possible without damaging adjacent stems.

This seems like a drastic move, but what it does is encourage two or three new shoots to come from the bottom, which will then keep the floral show going three or four years later. So while you do not cut everything away every year, you cut out at least one or two of the old branches to keep some new ones coming along. Renewal pruning is best for lilac, for *Viburnum farreri*, the winter-flowering viburnum, *Philadelphus*, which is the mock orange, and for *Deutzia*, another one of those late spring, early summer flowering shrubs which is very attractive. Of course, this pruning is only done on mature shrubs. The first few years of any shrub's life it should be left with just the tips pruned back now and again to promote bushy growth until the plant reaches mature size.

Hydrangeas fall into a category all their own. These are the wonderful blue hydrangeas, not the P.G.'s (*Paniculata grandiflora*) that you see in other parts of the country, but the beautiful blue hydrangeas that you see in all the old established front gardens around the Vancouver area. They usually bloom right through to late summer. The thing to know about them is that they tend to get untidy looking after they finish flowering. Usually the panicles are a lovely blue colour, or sometimes they are a bit on the pink or purple side with some greenish colour coming into them right through until the fall. Then the leaves drop off and dead brown heads are left. Leave these on through the winter as added protection against a severe cold spell. In the spring, sometime around February when the weather starts to warm up again, if you go and have a look underneath these dead

10. Typical pruning of spring-flowering and summer-flowering shrubs.

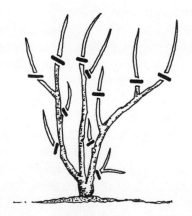

First year.

heads, the first two shoots just below them will have started to grow out. It is these that are going to give you flowers in the coming season. Cut off the dead head at this time to let the shoots develop. If a bush is enormous, falling over the path and hitting you every time you walk by, then cut some of the branches right out to reduce the problem. When I say cut right out, I mean go to the centre and cut them close to where they are coming from...that will encourage new shoots to come up from the base. You have to understand that if you cut all the hydrangea growth away from the top, which I have seen people do, you will miss out on flowers for at least one year and sometimes up to two years. So, at that time in the spring, remove the dead heads from the strongest shoots, and if you feel an old bush needs thinning out then go in, here and there, and cut out the weaker shoots

down to the base. That way you will still be assured of some colour for the coming season.

■ PROPAGATION

Of all the groups of plants that we deal with shrubs are some of the easiest to propagate in the home garden. All you need is a cold frame and a decent rooting mix of peat and sand. The majority of the shrubs that we have in our home gardens are best rooted from semi-hardwood cuttings, and these are usually ready any time from late July through August. It depends a lot on the season. If we have a late spring and plants are late maturing, then take cuttings a little later in the year.

To take a shrub cutting, look for the growth that has occurred off the older stems in this current season. There will be, all over the place, little strong side

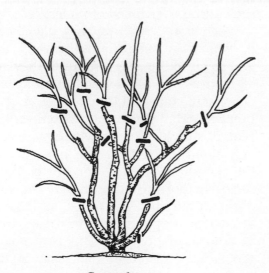

Second year.

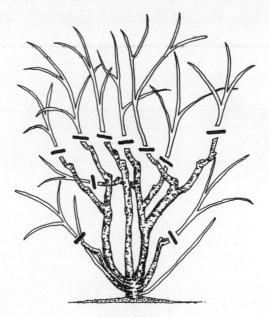

Third year.

shoots coming from the older branches that at that time of the year will be anywhere from 6-8 in. (15-20 cm) in length.

11. *Removing a side shoot of viburnum (above). A cutting showing the heel (below).*

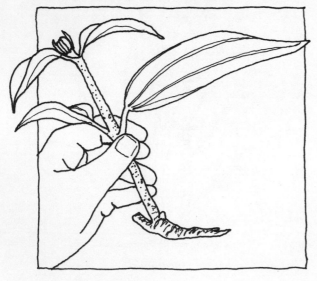

Pull off this new growth with a downward motion, holding the old branch in one hand and the new growth in the other. Pull it down so that it strips away part of the old wood with it. This is called a *heel cutting*. It takes part of the main stem with it, with a little sliver of skin or bark off the trunk. Gather several of these together. If you do not find that sort of material suitable you can try some tip cuttings of some of the other plants. Get a plastic bag for gathering the cuttings and labels for labeling as you go around, and put the cuttings in bundles with an elastic band or twine around them.

Take them all back into your work area, whether it be a potting shed, a bench in your garage or perhaps just a kitchen counter, lay them out and pinch the tops of the cuttings so that they are reduced to about 6 in. (15 cm) length. With a very sharp razor blade trim the heel at the bottom so that it is not left jagged, but leave part of the old heel on the stem, and then remove two or three of the lower leaves so that the bottom half of the cutting is stripped of its leaves.

When you have prepared all of one particular kind then bundle them up again and go on to the next kind until they are all ready. Then go back out into the garden where your cold frame is set up. For propagation of shrubs at this time of the year it should be somewhere that gets only about half a day's sunshine, not all the late afternoon hot sun, but perhaps the early morning sun. Prepare the cold frame with a nice deep mix, 6 in. (15 cm) at least, of two parts of perlite or two parts of sand to one of peat. This is a typical propagating mix. Dip the bases of the cuttings in a rooting hormone, usually strength number 2, which is for semi-hardwood cuttings, before sticking them in rows in the bed.

Stick the cuttings in firmly so that they are at least half-buried and firm them in well with your fingers. Then, if it is a cold frame with a built-in top, put the top on. If it is a crude one that you have built yourself from some boards and plastic, just put the plastic over the top and keep it closed. Usually these cuttings will start to root within a couple of months from the time you put them in, but they are best left in their propagating area until the following spring as long as it is in a protected spot. It is much better not to disturb them until the following February, if this is possible.

This method is probably the easiest way to propagate most of the common shrubs that we grow in local gardens. However, there are some that tend to be more difficult to deal with. Magnolias or camellias are not necessarily easy to root from cuttings, even in a greenhouse situation, unless you have a really good misting system with bottom heat and controlled temperature. There are two methods of dealing with these plants. You can lay them in the ground or you can air layer them. Let me deal with *air layering* first. For this you will need sphagnum moss, which you will have to collect yourself. If you buy moss from a garden centre it will not be sphagnum moss. If you know an area where there is a bog, then gather some of the light green moss from there because it holds many times

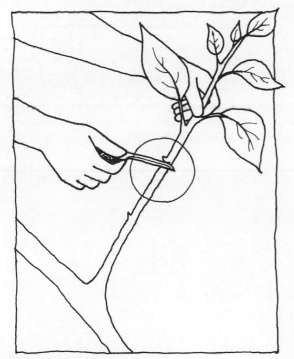

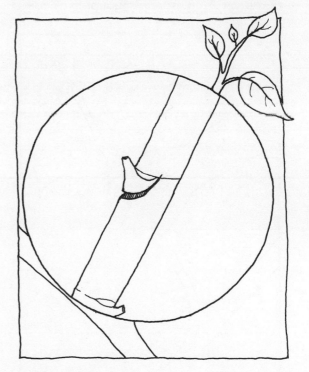

12. Air layering:
i) Making a cut underneath a leaf joint.

ii) Close-up of the cut showing correct position.

its weight in water for long periods of time, which is desirable when you are doing air layering. You will also need a strip of plastic, either heavy gauge or supermarket bags cut down each side and opened up like an elongated bandage. Whichever you use, it should be clear so that you can see through. You will also need a couple of twist ties handy in your pocket to secure the whole thing in place and a little bit of rooting hormone, usually the same strength as for your hardwood cuttings, but consult with your garden centre.

The time of year to do air layering is at the end of July or early August. Select a strong new shoot. Go back to where it has started to go woody, not on the old branch itself which is hard, but at the base of the new piece. Here, remove four or five leaves

so that the branch is essentially bare and bald. Then, directly underneath one of the leaf joints, about midway up this bald patch, with a very sharp knife make a cut, below the leaf joint but up behind it, about half-way through the branch at a 45° angle. Go up behind the bud and bend it very carefully so that you can open up a little "v" and in that "v" put some rooting hormone with a little bit of moss. Push it in so that it holds that gap open like an injury.

Next, take two handfuls of good wet moss and wrap it tightly around the cut. Then wrap it with the plastic so that it looks a bit like a Christmas cracker, sealing it at both ends with twist ties. Then just go away and leave it. The moss should stay moist for a long time. Have a look in September or October and you may see

iii) Wrapping the cut in wet moss.

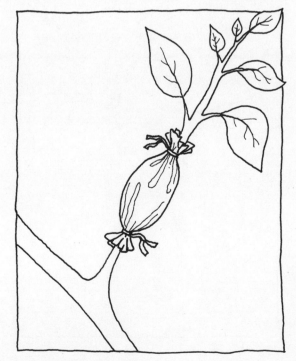

iv) Completed air layer enclosed in plastic and secured with twist ties.

some roots starting to form. You certainly will see them in February. The following spring, about March, you can cut off the branch below the root-filled moss and plant it as a new plant.

If some of the branches of your camellia or magnolia are close to the ground and you do not feel that you want to do air layer propagation, bend one of the branches down and make a bit of an injury in the bark with a sharp knife. Strip off the bark to a length of at least 2 in. (5 cm) on the underside of the branch that is going to be buried in the ground and put the stripped segment into the soil. Put something heavy on top of it such as a rock or a brick, or even make a wire hoop and push it down to hold the branch into the ground, and then cover it with soil. Chances are that a year later it will have rooted.

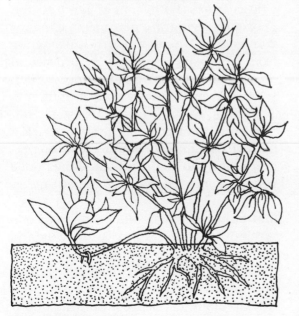

13. *Ground layering.*
Shows lower branch secured below soil.

■ SHRUB SELECTIONS

■ *Winter-Blooming Shrubs* ■

We have such an unusual winter compared with the rest of the country. True, in the odd year we can get hit with snow and frost, but it does not go on for the great lengths of time it does in the prairies, for example. And so, in our winter there are many shrubs that will bloom. I think they deserve to be placed in the garden where they can be seen from the house, so that you can get total enjoyment from them whether you are in the garden or in the house during the winter months.

Cornus mas. A member of the dogwood family, *Cornus mas* is sometimes called the Cornelian Cherry because it is followed by little fruits that look somewhat like tiny cherries. In all the books it is referred to as a small tree which grows no more than 30 ft. (9 m) in height with a spread of 6.5 ft. (2 m). However, it can be kept to a manageable size by pruning. It usually blooms in late January/early February in this area, and on the leafless branches little clusters of bright yellow flowers appear. From a distance it looks like foam, that is the best way to describe it. As with many of the winter-flowering shrubs, it is best planted against a background of dark evergreens so that it shows up well. If you want a delicate show of colour in the winter, I would strongly recommend this for your garden in our area.

Hamamelis (Witch Hazel). This plant starts to bloom as early as late January, and by early February it is in full bloom. There are two common forms. *Hamamelis japonica* forms a small tree or a large bush about 20 ft. (6 m) in height. The flowers are very yellow with narrow waving petals a few centimeters long, and they have a red calyx at the base. The lovely thing about these blossoms, as with all winter-flowering shrubs, is that they are borne on the bare trees. An added bonus with this plant is that the hazel-like leaves appear after the flowers and give good fall colour, so two times a year it is delightful to look at.

H. mollis has been hybridized in recent years into some good garden forms. *Pallida* has the palest lemon yellow flowers and is very sweetly scented. It is possible that when you are searching for these plants you will find *H. virginiana*. This is the plant that is used for manufacturing witch hazel. The only difference is that it blooms in the fall rather than in the spring and will show tiny yellow flowers all in among yellow leaves in the fall. As the leaves drop off the flowers are left behind, which is very pretty too.

Jasmimum nudiflorum. *Jasmimum nudiflorum* is a wonderful little shrub because it starts to flower on its leafless branches as early as November and will go right through until March. It is probably best used as a kind of a climber, although it does not really climb. You have to prop it up on the wires to get it to go up the wall. We have used it in our winter garden as a ground cover, just letting it ramble all over the place, a little difficult to weed in amongst. I have seen it used most effectively at the library at the University of British Columbia where it is planted in some window boxes above the basement windows. In February these little shrubs trail down, hanging in front of the library windows, full of yellow flowers...a sight for sore eyes. It blooms best on first-year wood, so right after the flowering, prune all the flowering bits back to within one or two leaf joints of the woody stems. It can be as large or as small as you want it to be. When I lived in an apartment I grew one in a barrel.

Lonicera. *Lonicera* is a bush honeysuckle, and the one that I recommend is *L. purpusii*. It is a little deciduous shrub that does not reach any more than about 6.5 ft. (2 m) and is not terribly attractive to look at. It has the typical bushy appearance of the bush honeysuckles that are grown widely on the prairies. But the beauty of this is its little, insignificant white flowers that bloom in January and February, giving off a perfume that makes you wonder where on earth it is coming from. You walk around your garden and do not notice it in bloom, but you smell it. While it is not a showy plant I think it is something to place near a doorway...not in a prominent position, perhaps back a bit with other plants in front of it...so that every time you go in and out of the house you get a marvellous whiff of perfume.

Mahonia japonica. *Mahonia japonica* is a relative of the Oregon Grape which is abundant in the woodlands around here. It is a very pretty shrub, reaching a height of about 5 ft. (1.5 m), with rosettes of prickly, holly-like leaves. Starting about the end of November or early December through until February, wonderful spikes of little yellow flowers bloom, looking like

74

yellow Lily of the Valley and smelling as sweet. Because of its prickly nature it is something that you might not want to put near your entrance gate or near a path where you are going to bump into it all the time. Up against a border fence, it is a very good evergreen background plant, and it is such a joy to have little yellow flowers at that time of the year. There is a form at the UBC Botanical Garden called "Arthur Menzies," and if you see this in your garden centre, get it.

Rhododendrons. There are several species of rhododendrons that are sold in garden centres. One, *Rhododendron barbatum*, blooms early in the year. It is a wonderful rhododendron that comes from the Himalayas. It grows to a maximum of about 6.5-10 ft. (2-3 m) in height and has a typical rhododendron bush shape, with large evergreen leaves and what look like hairy barbs close in to the flower head and the stem. They are not really barbs at all, but this is how it gets its name. The beauty of this plant is its incredible red flowers that can start as early as late January and will definitely be in bloom by February to early March. Even though it is unusual and difficult to get, if you have space for it I would strongly recommend it.

Viburnum. To end up the winter section, I would like to mention two *Viburnum farreri*. The form that I would strongly recommend is *bodnantense*, which was originally developed at Bodnant Gardens in North Wales. Gerald Farrer collected the viburnums on one of his trips to Asia. During the summer months they are not very attractive shrubs to look at, but

throughout the winter, as early as October right through until March, they are covered with little clusters of very sweetly scented, pinkish-tinged white flowers. Cut a little branch of it and bring it into the house. Everybody will wonder where on earth you got this exotic-smelling plant. It looks extremely well if planted against a dark background of cedar trees or pine trees. If you could only have one flowering shrub that bloomed in the winter, this would be the one that I would go for, simply because of the length of its blooming period.

V. tinus is a shorter evergreen form, perhaps 5 ft. (1.5 m) at maximum height, which is quite borderline hardy. The beauty of this form is that the flowers are not as sweetly scented. They grow in little flat umbels, pink and white. Because it is evergreen and keeps its blue berries from the previous season during the winter when it is in bloom, you have blue berries, white blossoms and evergreen foliage, something that is very pretty to look at in the dull winter months.

■ *Spring- and Summer-Flowering* ■ *Shrubs*

You may not need as many spring- and summer-flowering shrubs, simply because there will be lots of other colour in your garden.

Buddleia. *Buddleia* are the so-called Butterfly Bushes. They bloom in the summer and respond well to being cut back early in the year, so that new growth comes up and will bloom beautifully in the summertime. They do encourage butterflies to the garden, which is a very nice thing. We have few butterflies in the Lower Mainland, but you will see the odd Monarch coming through and they will certainly find your Butterfly Bush.

Many buddleia can be somewhat weedy. In fact, there is one that has escaped and is naturalized all around the Lower Mainland. One that I particularly like and would recommend is called Royal Red. It is not really a red at all. The flowers are deep reddish-purple, a very strong colour, unusual and very sweetly scented.

Chaenomeles. There are quite a few *Chaenomeles*, but probably the most common are from a cross called Superba. For years they have been called japonica, and I should clarify here that japonica simply means that a plant is from Japan, and so there is *Camellia japonica* and *Fatsia japonica* and so on. Chaenomeles are not true quince but are sometimes called Japanese quince, and they do produce fruit from which you can make a rather tasteless jelly. If you have a friend who has a particularly good form of this shrub in her garden, ask if you can take a cutting because it is difficult to buy one that will yield good, brilliant red flowers. There is a form I remember from my childhood called Knap Hill Scarlet which really had the most vivid colour. Chaenomeles is a thorny plant and can easily get out of hand if it is not pruned properly, so make sure that you keep all the old dead wood cut out if you possibly can. It takes up about the same space as the forsythia.

Deutzia. There are various species of *Deutzia* to choose from. The one that I really like is the cross rosea. It is a hybrid

deciduous shrub which reaches about 6 ft. (2 m), with broader petals in small flowers. The nicest thing about them is that they grow in little florets or clusters, white to blush pink, which usually bloom in summer. This is a useful sort of plant for the in-between time, after the rhododendrons and the forsythia finish and before there is a lot of other colour. It cuts well for flower arrangements and is very pretty.

Exochorda giraldii. This hardy shrub blooms in late spring. It is a wonderful plant that is not grown widely enough in our home gardens here. It has the common name of Pearl Bush because before its white flowers open, the little racemes have round buds that look just like pearls. It is a deciduous shrub and can get to be quite out of hand in that it will spread over an area of 10 ft. (3 m). But in the right place and with careful pruning, which can be carried out right after it has finished flowering, it can be a controlled, spectacular shrub when in full bloom.

Forsythia. Most of the garden forms that we grow are from a cross called Intermedia. These are the more upright-growing forms. One of the best known, called *F. Spectabilis*, has large yellow flowers. There are many others to choose from. I suggested in the pruning section that forsythia should be allowed to grow in much more of a free-form fashion, and they do tend to take up rather a lot of room. They will grow to 10 ft. (3 m) or more in height but respond very well to pruning. Forsythia, for that very first early flush of colour in the garden when your daffodils are out in April, is a must.

Hydrangea. The hydrangea we grow most widely is *H. macrophylla*. There are many forms to choose from, but the one that I like most of all is the lace-capped type, called Blue Wave. It can reach a height of about 6.5 ft. (2 m) with about a 6 foot (2 m) spread and has brilliant blue flowers or bracts around the outside and tiny lacy flowers in the middle. I have seen it planted with a clematis running through it. The clematis was a reddish, magenta colour called Ville de Lyon. The combination was quite stunning.

Hydrangeas are good because they can tolerate shady conditions, so they could go towards the far end of a border or towards the back, as long as you do not obscure them with tall plants in front. They like moist soil. Where I grew up in England the soil was primarily alkaline or limy, if you will, and all hydrangeas were pink. Everybody wanted blue ones, so they used to put lots of rusty nails or acidic fertilizer around them to turn them blue. On our coast, the opposite is true, and if you want a pink one put lots of lime around it.

Philadelphus. There is a native *Philadelphus* that David Douglas, an early plant collector, took back to Scotland with him when he first came and collected plants from British Columbia. From that parent, we have many cultivars to choose. One that I particularly like is called Avalanche. It has small fragrant flowers which weigh it down in arching branches, usually in mid-summer. A very pretty plant, it is sweetly scented and smells like oranges. It does get to be quite tall, so you will need to plant it where it has at least a 10 foot (3 m) span.

Tamarix. I love *tamarix*. The one I recommend is *T. tetrandra* which blooms in late spring. It has spikes of bright pink flowers packed on shorter spikes, and as you stand back the whole bush has a light, airy feeling because there are no leaves, but rather tiny leaflets, and it almost looks like a feathery fountain of pink flowers. I have only seen one or two in gardens in the Lower Mainland and they do extremely well here. So try to put a tamarix in your garden if you can.

Weigela. There are many, many different cultivars of *Weigela*, but most of them come from the species *W. florida*. The one most grown is called Bristol Ruby, which has deep-red, free-flowering blossoms all along the branches. Usually they start to flower about the middle of the summer and will go on and on right through until the fall. The flowers themselves are somewhat like forsythia, although this is not true taxonomically. The little tubular flowers are usually pink or red. If you go to a garden centre, take the time to pick out one in a container so that you know exactly the colour that you are getting. The nice thing about weigela is that it does not take up a tremendous amount of room. It is about half the size of the forsythia, and if you prune it well, you can keep it in balance.

■ *Fall-Flowering Shrubs* ■

Two or three shrubs that give very good berry colour in the fall are an asset to any home garden.

Callicarpa. *Callicarpa* is commonly called the Beauty Berry. The species *C. bodinieri* is a wonderful plant that comes to us from China. It reaches a height of just over 10 ft. (3 m), although I have only seen it 6.5 ft. (2 m) tall in the Vancouver area. The most stunning thing about it is that it has brilliant purple berries in the fall. The first time I saw this plant from a distance I thought it was blossom because you do not associate purple berries with the fall. While it is self-pollinating, if there are two bushes you will get much better berries. I have it growing with Clematis orientalis through it, and the orientalis seed pods are white and fluffy against this purple bush in the fall. It really is a knockout.

Euonymus. Any mention of fall colour cannot go by without *Euonymus*, the common name for which is spindle tree. There are two that I should like to mention. First is *E. eropaea*, the original spindle tree from Europe, although it is not really a tree but a small shrub reaching a height of about 10 ft. (3 m). The wonderful thing about this plant is that it has pinkish berries, hanging in clusters down from the branches in the fall among very beautiful fall coloured foliage. As they open they have orange seeds inside, which is a gorgeous sight.

Closely related to it is the Burning Bush (*E. alata*), which has marvellous winged branches which look pretty when the leaves have fallen off in the fall. For about three weeks in the fall the red of this is unbeatable, and we do not get much red on the West Coast, so I strongly recommend it.

Pernettya. *Pernettya* is a very pretty, very short shrub that comes from South America. It has purple-berried forms, pink-berried forms and white-berried forms. We have one at UBC called the Pearl which stays lower than 3 ft. (1 m) in height, has evergreen prickly leaves and is covered with gorgeous white berries which stay on throughout the winter.

Carefully chosen shrubs can give colourful and year-round interest while screening and giving you privacy in your home garden. In spring and summer, shrubs can provide colourful and sweet-smelling flowers. In fall and winter, they boast good leaf colour and showy berries which will attract birds to your garden. Do not forget those winter-flowering shrubs for coastal gardens.

■ THINGS TO REMEMBER

1. Read up on the subject first and visit local gardens where shrubs are labeled to get a better idea of what they look like.
2. Prepare the ground or planting area deeply, adding fertilizer.
3. Always leave shrubs in pots or containers until ready to plant. If they are bare-root, keep the roots covered to prevent drying.
4. Water newly planted shrubs well during dry spells in their first season in the garden.
5. Adopt a regular pruning program to keep shrubs in control, and to promote flowering on an annual basis.
6. Top dress annually with well-rotted manure or compost.

Trees and Climbers

Ornamental trees can be useful in the home garden for blocking out such eyesores as a hydro pole or perhaps to shield a neighbour's house to give you a little more privacy. But you have to be very careful about the size and the siting of a tree. More so than shrubs, trees can grow to take over a large space in your garden. So if you have seen a tree and you think, ah, that is for me, before you buy it I urge you to read up about its mature height, about its root system, and how it may possibly end up engulfing your whole garden. The siting of the tree in your garden is also important. For example, if you want to plant a small tree in a mixed flower border where you already have perennials and bulbs and are going to be putting in annuals, this will be fine for the first few years. But eventually the tree roots will take over. When you give your flowers their annual feeding, this will bring tree roots up to the surface and make it pretty well impossible for you to have a successful flower garden underneath the tree.

A tree in a lawn can be very pretty if it is planted in the right situation so that it can be viewed from all around. It could be off centre, or it could be in a corner of your lawn. You will find that grass will be able to tolerate the competition of the tree a lot better than would a flower border. This, of course, applies only to deciduous trees. If you are going to put in an evergreen, eventually nothing will grow underneath when it reaches a mature height.

In a small home garden, if you decide to have an area that blocks off a hydro pole, then make it a shrub and tree border. If the shrubs and the trees are put in at the same time, early on in their life the shrubs will have a chance to establish themselves while the tree is doing the same and there will not be tremendous competition. Down the road, something that is planted close to the tree may not do as well underneath it, but a combination of trees and shrubs in a border is a very good way to go.

Trees can be planted either in the fall or in the spring. It is possible, just because of the traditional way garden centres operate, that you will get a better selection in the spring. If you can drive out into the country, you will find growers that have some unusual plants and trees. They would be willing to lift one for you in the fall, if that is when you want to put it in, or likewise, in the spring. If the tree is going to be balled and wrapped in burlap I would rather plant it in the fall. Containerized, I would rather plant it in the spring.

As with any new plant in the garden, soil preparation is extremely important. Try to dig the hole twice the size of the root area of your tree and twice the depth. Work plenty of well-rotted compost, leaf mould and mushroom manure into the base of the hole. If planting the tree in the fall, work in a handful of bone meal at the bottom of the hole because it will take most of the winter to break down. If planting in the spring, use one of the superphosphate fertilizers and work that into the bottom of the hole. This will encourage new roots to develop and give the tree a chance to get established within that first growing season.

As with all other gardening it is important when choosing where to dig the hole and plant your tree that the site be well drained. If the area sits wet during the winter time then you will have no success at all growing anything there. You cannot plant a tree in an area where water sits. Sometimes gardeners make this mistake because they live in a garden area for a year or two and notice a wet spot where nothing else will grow, then think "well, maybe a tree will do." Well, it will not. Nothing likes to be waterlogged for a great length of time, particularly during the winter months. So, the site for your tree must be a well-drained spot.

Whatever tree you select at a garden centre will probably be three to four years old and will already have formed a stem and a little top. It is very important to stake it well when first putting it in. If it is a bare-root tree or one that has been lifted from the field, knock a stake in down through the root system at the time of planting, using a good sturdy wooden stake. Use treated lumber so it will not rot too quickly and plastic ties that are like a little belt that fits around the stem. These ties can be expanded so that they do not restrict the development of the trunk: this is important. Often people will just use ordinary cord or twine to tie a tree, and in the early stages they will tie it too tightly with only a little bit of space between the stake and the trunk. As the poor tree grows the string or wire will cut into the trunk and can eventually cause a serious fracture, so that in a heavy wind the tree will snap right off. This is not a desirable way to grow a tree.

It is important not to plant your tree in the soil any deeper than it was in its original pot or field. Draw a mark on the stem as a guide to the soil level. Hold the tree in the hole first. You may need to fill in the hole a bit more to achieve the proper soil level. Sit your tree in the bottom of the hole and then stand back, take a level board or rod, and run it from one side of the hole to the other to make sure that the soil level is exactly the same.

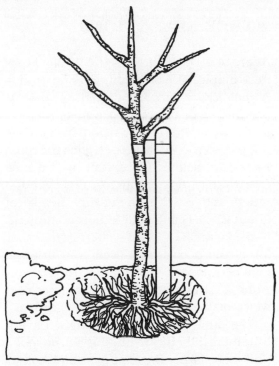

14. *Correct placement of a tree against a good strong stake.*

Many ornamental trees are grafted early on in their years. Take care not to bury the graft because it will root out. Some nursery trees are grafted onto root stocks, and quite often the root stock will grow, even when planted properly, and you can end up with many problems. I will deal with these later when I discuss pruning.

Site your tree so that it is level. If it is a bare-root, shake it up and down gently as you add soil to the hole so that the soil falls in between the roots. If it is wrapped in burlap, loosen the burlap. If it looks like the whole root ball is going to fall apart then just untie it and lay the burlap flat around the bottom of the hole and fill in the soil around it. If it was in a pot or a container, do not break up the root system at all. Just tap the pot off and set the tree in place and then gradually put your soil around the root area, using your foot to tamp it in lightly and settle it as you go. When you finish planting, if it is looking like it is not going to rain for a while then definitely give the tree a good watering. All newly planted trees, no matter what they are, should always be kept well watered during drought periods in their first growing season. A lot of grief can come once a tree is planted. You think, "oh well, it is established" within a month or so, but it takes at least a year for a tree to get established in your garden.

When selecting trees for your garden, think about all the benefits they can bring. First of all you will want them to be an interesting shape. You may think that all trees are just roundish on the top. That is true, but some of them have very attractive branches. You want to choose something that is going to give you good spring colour, whether it is lovely early foliage or just blossoms in the spring. The leaves should also be taken into consideration. Their texture can be very pleasing if you choose a tree carefully. Fall colour is something else to think about. Is it going to give a good colour in this climate? Remember that the predominant colour is gold to brown in our natural trees in British Columbia. If you want a bit of real colour like you see back east, good reds or oranges, choose a tree that will give you that type of colour as well. Lastly, look for berries and for interesting seed pods so that you have something to enjoy about your tree in every season.

■ PRUNING TREES

Deciduous trees for the first few years of their life will probably not need much pruning. If there are some very low branches that get in the way, encourage the upper ones to develop by pruning the leading shoots back by one third and all the side shoots back to within two or three buds. Try to encourage the branches to grow open and outward. You do not want any cross branches going back in across the centre of your tree. Your tree needs good air circulation. It is important to prune deciduous trees either right after the leaves have dropped or early in the year, no later than mid-February, because many trees will bleed when the sap starts to run if you prune them later than that. Try to prune them when they are most dormant.

Some ornamental trees such as cherries and plums, if they are a standard tree, will have a trunk of an ordinary wild cherry at the bottom and will be grafted at chest or eye level. This is where the new

tree comes from. From the trunk, branches may come up that will be very strong and will grow quite quickly in the first season. You may get one branch coming up that has white single flowers on it, and you may think in the early stages that this is unique and pretty and leave it there. Believe me, that wild cherry is going to take over. If you see this happening, do not cut the branch off while it is blooming but mark that branch, and when pruning in the following fall take it out as close to the stem as possible with a pruning saw and seal the cut with some pruning paint. Then, in the spring if you see more buds coming out from that area just simply rub them off, just break off any buds that are coming on the stem to prevent the graft from taking over: it will spoil the tree.

■ TREE SELECTIONS

Acer. *Acer palmatum* is the lovely Japanese maple. The one that I recommend is *A. palmatum atropurpureum* because it has the most interesting crimson leaves all the way through the summer. It comes out red, stays red, and then goes the most wonderful scarlet in the fall. It is a nice tree that is not going to take over too much and reaches a mature height of about 23 ft. (7 m), so it is not too difficult to deal with. The stem structure is rather lovely too because it sweeps in oriental fashion and you can cloud prune it if you want to. It is a very pretty little tree and well worth space in your home garden.

The other one that you might have a little more difficulty in finding is *A. griseum*. This is the Paper Bark maple which comes from Asia. Its bark will peel in long flakes during the later part of the season so that in the wintertime you get beautiful, almost orange-brown bark. It looks a bit like our local arbutus but is even more attractive. The foliage is pretty in the summertime, but in the winter when the sun is low and shining through from behind the tree, all the lovely highlights of the coloured bark show on the stem. In maturity *Acer griseum* can reach 30 ft. (9 m).

Amelanchier canadensis. Another tree that is not used much in West Coast gardens is *Amelanchier canadensis*, which simply means that it is a Canadian native. It makes a delightful small tree with green leaves and white, apple-like blossoms in the spring, followed by small red berries. It will turn a lovely red in the fall. It is a nice tree because it only varies from between 20-30 ft. (6-9 m) in height and can be pruned, but does not need a lot of pruning. Perhaps it would be nice to have something native to Canada in your garden.

Betula. I recommend *Betula papyrifera*, the Paper or Canoe birch. Back east you see wonderful birch trees, but the very white stemmed birches have a tough time on the coast because we do not have the dry air that they have in the east in wintertime. Betula does tend to get quite tall, reaching more than 33 ft. (10 m) in height, but it can be pruned, and if you have the right spot for it, a nice paper bark birch would be a good addition to your garden.

Cornus. The native dogwood is a *Cornus nuttallii*. The cultivar that I would recommend for gardens on the coast is the one that was adopted as Vancouver's Centennial tree, Eddy's White Wonder, hybridized in British Columbia by the late Henry Eddy. He crossed the eastern dogwood, *C. florida*, and our own native *C. nuttallii* and came up with a very nice small tree, really a very manageable size for the home garden, growing to no more than about 23 ft. (7 m) in height. It has lovely big four-petalled blossoms that come out in the spring. This hybrid seems less susceptible to the dogwood leaf blotch that is currently troublesome.

Another excellent cultivar is *C. kousa*. It tends to be a more spreading tree, reaching about 23 ft. (7 m) in height and up to 23 ft. (7 m) across. It flowers in May, a little later than the other dogwoods, and has masses of blossoms all along the tops of its branches. From a distance it looks like snow. They come out green, turn white and then go a reddish colour. It also has a good fall foliage. In a small garden it will take over if you mix it in with your shrubs, so make sure that you have the right site for it.

Halesia carolina. *Halesia carolina* (as in the state of Carolina) is native to that part of North America. Its common name is the Snowdrop tree, and when you see it in bloom the reason will become very apparent. In the spring, the naked leafless branches will be covered with white, snowdrop-like flowers. The leaves, which come in later, are green, oval and toothed...quite interesting. It is a tree that loves to be in an open situation and loves well-drained soil. It does not go a terribly exciting colour in the fall but is spectacular in the spring and makes a nice small tree ranging from 23-30 ft. (7-9 m).

Laburnum anagryoides. I am very fond of *Laburnum*. It is a tree that has had a lot of bad publicity because the seeds are known to be poisonous. I think teaching children and adults to be aware and not to eat the seeds is not an impossible task. I grew up in a yard where there was a most wonderful laburnum tree which was spectacular when in bloom. There are some cultivars, one called *L. watereri*, which has particularly long flower trusses when blooming in May to June. These long pendulous trusses of flowers hanging down with yellow pea-like flowers give them the common name of Golden Chain tree. Laburnum is small, growing to between 16.5-23 ft. (5-7 m) in height.

Magnolia. There are so many *Magnolias* to choose from, but the one that I recommend is *M. kobus*. It can tend to get a bit large and unwieldy at the top. In the spring magnolias look like the idealized trees that you see on hand-painted birthday cards because they are absolutely covered with lovely little white flowers that smell good too. I believe it to be a good tree for a small home garden even though it has the ability of reaching 30 ft. (9 m) in height and spreading 30 ft. (9 m) across. It responds well to pruning, which in the case of the magnolia should be done right after it has finished flowering.

Malus. *Malus* are the ornamental flowering crab apples. They get bad publicity because they are terribly affected by apple scab fungus. Now there are some species that have been hybridized at the Agriculture Canada research station in Ottawa that are said to be less susceptible to the scab. There are so many cultivars to choose

from, but the one that I particularly love is called John Downie. I like it because it has very pretty apple-like blossoms in the spring, but in the fall it is covered with marvellous golden conical-shaped crab apples that will stay on quite awhile after the leaves have dropped and when ripe will encourage many interesting birds to come through your garden. Malus will reach about 23 ft. (7 m) in height.

Prunus. *Prunus* covers all the ornamental plums, cherries, almonds, peaches and laurels. They do have a problem locally with fungus problems, but that is not to say that you should not grow some in your garden. The one that I recommend, even though it is very common in this part of the world is *P. cerasifera atropurpurea*...what a mouthful! It is commonly called the purple leaved plum and is used all along the boulevards throughout the city of Vancouver. It makes a very fine small home garden tree, reaching no more than about 26 ft. (8 m) in height. The foliage is pretty, and the blossom is delightful. It is always one of the earliest to come out as soon as the weather warms up. I have seen them in bloom in late February/early March, followed by lovely purple-coloured leaves which stay on throughout the summer. If it has been a good season when they were in bloom then purple plums form on the tree as well, which incidentally are edible.

Sorbus. *Sorbus* covers the whole group of the Mountain ashes. The berries of the Scottish form, the Rowan, are brilliant orange in the fall, and when they start to ferment the robins eat them and get drunk and fall about all over the boulevards. A beautiful cultivar named Pink Pagoda has been introduced recently onto the market from the University of British Columbia Botanical Garden. It is a form of *S. hupehensis* which comes to us from China and has the most beautiful coral-pink berries that stay on the tree long after the foliage has disappeared. It will not reach any more than about 30 ft. (9 m) in height.

Stewartia pseudocamellia. One small home garden tree that needs to be promoted and grown much more widely is the *Stewartia pseudocamellia*. It gets its name simply because the flowers resemble camellia blossoms. The beauty of this tree is that it has so much to offer. Its small leaves are very pretty and its flowers come in that in-between time of June to August when other flowering trees have finished and before the summer flowers come along. Later, they set very pretty seed pods which are large and green to start and then dry to a beautiful brown colour and stay on the tree long after the fall foliage is gone. The fall foliage is spectacular. It makes the tree look like it is on fire, ranging through oranges to yellows to reds, and is the most beautiful sight. On the coast it will not reach much more than 30 ft. (9 m) in a home garden.

Even though I am not a great lover of evergreens I will mention a couple here.

Holly. *Holly* is nice to have in a home garden because it is useful for cutting berries for Christmas decorations. The so-called English holly or Oregon holly that is grown in this area is *Ilex aquifolium* and is the one that gives you the lovely berries at Christmas time. The thing to remember is that you must have a male and female tree in order to get berries. A good place to see a great selection of hollies is in the VanDusen Botanical Garden in Vancouver, so you might want to go there before deciding on which holly to put into your home garden. As a general rule, holly ranges somewhere between 23-30 ft. (7-9 m) in height.

Thuja (Ornamental cedar). In this area we have so many evergreen trees around that it really is much nicer to plant deciduous trees to give variety in your garden, but if you want a quick-growing evergreen to really block out an unsightly view for you, then choose one of the *Thujas*. Our native one is *T. occidentalis*, the great big cedar, The one that is usually used for hedging is *T. pyramidalis*, but you really will have to go to a local nursery and decide which is the one for you. There are some with gold variegated foliage, some with blue-green foliage...something to suit every taste. Thuja grows so fast in a coastal region such as this it can put on up to 24 in. (60 cm) of new growth each season. I would appeal to you that once it reaches the height that you want it to be, the most comfortable and manageable size, go out there in the middle of the summer and cut out the top on an annual basis. If you leave it, eventually you will have to cut the poor tree in half and it will look awful...it will take away that nice conical shape. So do some pruning on your evergreens in August after all the new growth is done for that year, and keep them to within the size that you want them to be.

■ CLIMBING PLANTS

Climbing plants are so versatile and yet, I feel, underused, possibly because they ramble about and therefore do not appeal to the tidy minds of North American gardeners. At the UBC Botanical Garden there is a fine display of climbing plants in the Arbor Garden, where they are trained up and over a beautiful covered walkway which is interesting to walk through on a year-round basis and cool during the hot days of the summer. Another great use for climbers is to let them ramble up over dead tree stumps or even up into cedars and other evergreens that surround your garden area. And, they can be trained up the outside walls of your home. Planting time for climbers can be in the spring or in the fall. They need to have well-prepared situations just like any other plant that you put in your garden. Do not plant them right up against a wall or right up against a tree stump. Go at least 12-18 in. (30-45 cm) away and prepare your area well, digging it at least 12-18 in. (30-45 cm) deep and as much wide, so that you have room for some well-rotted leaves and good compost to be worked in. As with other plants, add bone meal in the fall or in the spring add some superphosphate to get the roots going.

One of the important things to take into consideration when planting climbers to go up the outside of your house is that very often the eaves jut out and there is a rain shadow which may cause plants to dry out in the summer. Put even more organic material into an area like that. Clematis, for example, do not like their roots to be hot: they must be cool. Plant the clematis root on the north or east side of the house and bring the vine around to a west or south side. Plant them so that their roots are in the shade and they can be brought around onto the sunny sides of your house and you will have much better success. Also, I would not recommend planting ivy on a stucco wall because it clings onto the wall and can ruin the stucco. Other plants that are not self-supporting will need some kind of trellis. Build a trellis so that it can be easily detached from the wall and laid down when you want to paint your house. Little things like this are easy to overlook, but it can be quite devastating if you have a wonderful Tender Jasmine that blooms so beautifully in the summer and then decide to have the house painted. It would be a shame to have to chop the whole thing down to the root, so try to make a trellis that is bolted to the wall of your house in some fashion that allows you to take it down and lift it away from the wall when the time comes to do house maintenance.

Also, if you are planting climbers to cover an old tree stump or a dead tree, or even to grow up into a live tree, plant them far enough away so that they can find some open ground without a lot of tree roots to give them a decent start in life. You will need some sort of device to get the climber to the tree once you have planted it. This could be done by putting in a 6.5 foot (2 m) bamboo cane at an angle up towards the tree and gradually tying the climber onto that until it reaches the tree and has a chance to cling.

Often when giving classes I talk about letting climbers go up into trees, and people ask "Is it going to kill the tree?" Let me assure you, it will take an awfully long time for the type of vines that I am recommending to kill the grand old evergreens that have been around on the coast for a couple of centuries. I would not worry about that at all; I would just use them as a wonderful structure. There is no prettier sight than a wisteria in full bloom all the way down from the top of a hemlock or a Douglas-fir. It will just knock your eyes out. It looks so much prettier than just being restricted to a little trellis in a home garden.

Here are some of the plants you could use.

Campsis radicans. *Campsis radicans* is an extremely hardy and vigorous climber that belongs to a predominantly tropical family *Bignonacea*. It has pointed compound leaves that somewhat resemble those of the ash tree. In the summer, during August to September, it has wonderful brilliant-orange funnel-shaped flowers that attract hummingbirds like crazy. If you want something that looks subtropical then by all means go for campsis, but it must be in a good sunny location to perform well.

Clematis. You could write an entire book about *Clematis*. One species that I love, even though it is quite common, is *C. montana*, which comes from the mountains of Asia. In the spring, it is covered with pinkish or white blossoms that look like the flowers of little wood anemones. It can take off and put out a tremendous amount of growth, and if it gets out of hand the time to prune *C. montana* is immediately after it has finished flowering. You can cut it back quite drastically because after that it will send out lots of new runners. If you have it climbing up in a tree then you will not need to do any pruning at all. It likes cool roots and enjoys a handful of lime sprinkled around these roots every spring.

Another clematis is the winter-flowering *C. armandii*. This is an evergreen clematis with very long, dark-green leaves. Quite a vigorous climber in this part of the world, it does extremely well. It needs to be on a sheltered wall but is not too happy on a north wall. The one that I have at home is called Apple Blossom. It has beautiful pink blossoms that start to bloom in February and their scent is wonderful. I have it trained up along the front of my townhouse so that I can look out into the garden and see it surrounded by beautiful trusses of pink flowers early in the spring. *C. armandii* is a very good choice for a climber in your winter garden.

Jasmine. I am very fond of all the *Jasmines*. There is a white one called *Jasminum officinalis* which resembles the little winter-flowering jasmine shrub, except its very sweetly scented white blossoms never come out in great masses but appear on and off all summer. It needs a sheltered location on a south- or west-facing wall. The scent is delightful, reminiscent of the tropics, and if you plant this to grow up and around a window that tends to be open a lot, such as your kitchen window, you will get the lovely scent of it drifting in throughout the day in the summertime. It needs little pruning except a bit of renewal pruning. When it gets old, cut out some of the old branches down close to the ground to encourage new ones to come up.

Passiflora coerulea. *Passiflora* is the Passion Flower, and an almost hardy form of it is *coerulea*. If we get a terrible freeze or frost you will need to give it some sort of protection. Build a little chicken wire cage around the base of the climber and fill it with dry leaves as they fall in autumn, and that will be all the protection that it needs as long as it is planted on a south- or west-facing wall. It also works well in barrels in sheltered patios or balcony gardens. The wonderful Passion Flower blossom is a grey-green in colour, and then when it opens up it reveals beautiful blues and greens and oranges and yellows...quite a spectacular plant.

Rosa. There are so many wonderful climbing roses. One that I remember so much from when I was a child in England is called Albertine. There was an old cottage in the village with an enormous old apple tree that had been there for years and years. A rose had been planted to climb up through this tree, and every June the entire top of the tree was covered with beautiful coppery-pink flowers of the rose called Albertine. Climbing roses work well on trellises, and you can grow them up posts in your mixed flower border. Prune them in February when you prune your hybrid tea roses. Just cut back all the side shoots to within two or three buds of the main stem, and perhaps every fourth year or so cut out one of the very old climbing branches almost down to the ground to encourage some new growth. The sky is the limit with climbing roses.

Vitis. *Vitis* belongs to a group of grape vines. *Vitis quinquefolia*, sometimes referred to as Boston Ivy or Virginia Creeper, grows on the Empress Hotel in Victoria and on the Sylvia Hotel in Vancouver. It turns the most gorgeous red colour in the fall. One I recommend that is not as easy to find in this area is *V. coignetiae*. Its common name in the old country was the glory vine. It has largish leaves which are very grape-like in their shape. A rapid climber, it climbs extremely well by its own little tendrils and will go up into an evergreen. Its beauty lies in its fall colour. The leaves will range from pink, orange, yellow, to red. If you have a big old tree stump that you want to cover or an evergreen this spectacular vine is one for you.

Wisteria. One of the most beautiful vines is *wisteria*. Locally, you will most often find *Wisteria floribunda* or a form of it. At a garden centre choose one in a container when it is in bloom because wisteria are often grown from seed and can vary in colour. Some bloom a lot and others bloom very little. Wisteria usually blooms in May to June with beautiful, sweetly scented, violet-blue, pea-like flowers hanging down in great clusters, almost like the laburnum tree. Once they finish flowering they will start to send out lots of long new shoots all along the vine. If you have an established wisteria that is blooming poorly, these new shoots should be trimmed back to within two leaves of where they came from in July. This very often will harden the wood and cause it to form flower buds. If you have one that was a poor choice right from the beginning and has never flowered well, chances are that it never will. All you can do is to give it a couple of feedings each year of potash and perhaps do a bit of root pruning. Wisteria can be used either to climb along the house or up into a tree, and it will give off a lovely fragrance in the latter part of spring and early part of summer.

All climbers require some sun and some shelter, but not everyone has a wall or a good open location. So, I would like to recommend three climbing plants that will work well in the shade.

Hydrangea petiolaris. *Hydrangea petiolaris* is a real winner. It is a deciduous climber that clings onto a wall much like ivy, so you need to think a little carefully about it before planting it on a stucco wall. Perhaps it is better on a fence. It certainly works well on the north side of a cedar tree in a deeply shaded area, or on a hemlock. It is a beautiful vine. The leaves drop and reveal lovely yellowish-brown stems which are attractive all winter. Its white flowers are like the lace-capped hydrangea, with flowers all around the outside and tiny flowers in the middle. The bracts will stay on for a long time and turn green with age. Because it thrives in the shade it is a very useful vine for difficult areas.

Lonicera. One of the most common red forms of *Lonicera*, or honeysuckle, that is grown in this region is Dropmore Scarlet. It is very pretty, but I like the old-fashioned honeysuckles called *L. periclymenum belgica*. This is the very sweetly scented honeysuckle that some of us remember from our childhood. It blooms on and off throughout the summer, although the main part of the bloom comes in early summer. It starts in June and will go on right through to August. The vine itself is deciduous and will have red berries on it. It is a pretty plant and because it tolerates the shade it is well worth adding to your home garden.

Polyganum aubertii. The Russian Lace vine or Silver Lace vine *Polyganum aubertii* can become quite a weedy thing, but it is marvellous in the shade. It has beautiful white lacy flowers which bloom from August through October. It is a deciduous vine, but the leaves are heart shaped and very pretty. I have seen it used well climbing up into a dark evergreen because the white flowers show up so beautifully. If trained on a north-facing wall it will do well for you too.

The benefits of trees and climbers are similar to those of shrubs. A tree placed properly can provide privacy. Climbing plants climbing through trees can add interest over the long term, and if they are planted on a trellis can provide seasonal privacy or hide an otherwise ugly fence or wall. Careful selection of both can add interesting flowers, berries or foliage texture and colour to your home garden, no matter where you live.

■ THINGS TO REMEMBER

1. Careful selection of the right tree or climber is most important: these plants will be with you a long time.
2. Correct siting and staking are important.
3. Good soil preparation is essential, adding well-rotted manure or compost where needed.

4. Keep well watered during dry spells during the first year.
5. Follow an annual feeding and pruning program. This will keep the tree or climber healthy and under control in its early years.

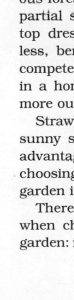

Berries, Bushes and Canes

No home garden, no matter how small, should be without delicious summer berries such as strawberries, raspberries and blueberries. Here on the West Coast we have the ideal climate for growing not only those familiar berries but also some of the less known or perhaps forgotten berries like black currants, red currants and loganberries.

All the bush and cane fruits require similar siting and soil conditions. In nature we will find raspberries and wild currants growing on the edge of deciduous forests where they get the benefit of partial shade plus a wonderful annual top dressing of fallen leaves. Nonetheless, berry bushes should not have to compete with trees, especially evergreens, in a home garden situation. A location more out in the open is desirable.

Strawberries in nature grow on open sunny slopes where they can take full advantage of the summer sun. When choosing a site for them in your home garden it should be in full sun.

There is one common requirement when choosing a site for fruit in your garden: it should be in an area of good air circulation as this will help deter fungus diseases. Ideally, the site should not be in a low hollow where cold frosty air can collect during freezing in the winter. In the United Kingdom these were always referred to as frost pockets.

Preparing the soil is extremely important for all fruits, simply because they are going to grow in the same location for a number of years. Deep digging of the soil is essential. Because berry crops are not

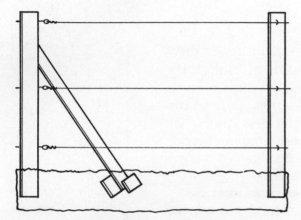

15. *Correct support system for raspberries.*

too deeply rooted, good organic matter such as well-rotted manure or compost should be concentrated more in the top 12 in. (30 cm) or so. Deeper digging is important for good drainage.

Since all the berry bushes and canes need to be planted in late fall or early spring let us deal with them first, and leave the strawberries till last.

Try to get your site preparation done early in the fall. Remember, if you will not be planting until the spring, digging in fresh manure at this time is perfectly alright, as the winter rain will leach out

any harmful salts by the time for spring planting. Always make a supreme effort while digging to remove all perennial weeds such as morning glory or couch grass because if some are left behind they will be impossible to remove from the centres of your established berry bushes.

Raspberries. When selecting your plants from the garden centre in the spring choose healthy looking canes. Often they are sold in tight little bunches, tied then wrapped in a plastic bag containing sawdust or peat. On the bag there is usually a picture of what the fruit looks like, along with its name. Always insist on slipping the bag off right then and there in the garden centre, as so often the canes have been in the bags a long time and some may have died. Purchase carefully and thoughtfully.

Prepare the ground well ahead of time. Mark out rows, preferably running north-south. This way the one row will not shade the other too much. Space the canes singly 12 in. (45 cm) apart and plant them so that the soil level is just below the first dormant bud. Make sure that the roots are well spread out and not left in a bunch. Raspberries should not be planted too deeply or they will not send up the much-needed suckers.

If you feel space is too limited in your garden for long rows, raspberries can be planted three canes to a single supporting pole. Two or three of these plants about 1 yd. (1 m) apart is quite sufficient for the needs of a small family.

It is important to put up some kind of support wires for the rows. In fact it is better to put up the support system first and plant later. Always use treated lumber and space the support posts at 10 ft. (3 m) intervals. Use 7.5 ft. (2.25 m) posts driven 18 in. (45 cm) into the ground.

The wires stretched between the posts should be spaced with the first one 18 in. (45 cm) from the ground and the second one 18 in. (45 cm) above it, with the topmost one 6 in. (15 cm) from the top of the pole.

In the first year the newly planted canes should be topped back to just above three

ing of 6-8-6 at the rate of a handful per square yard (1 m²).

You can expect fruit the first year. As soon as it is finished cut out the fruiting canes and start to tie in. If there are any excess or weak canes remove them also, as well as any that might be coming up away from the row.

Once the raspberries are established, top dress them in the fall with freshly fallen leaves, which then break down to

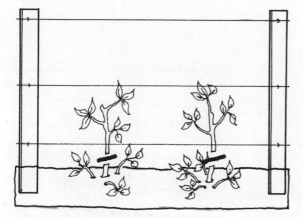

In the first season prune immediately after spring planting.

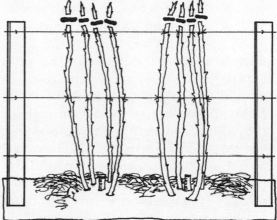

First season's new growth correctly tied-in during November or December. In February or March cut the tips back to within six inches of the top wire.

or four buds. Then, as the new canes develop, cut the old canes out completely. By July some decent-sized new canes should have developed. All should be saved and tied in about 8 in. (20 cm) apart. For the first two seasons this will be the case, but after that you will be able to thin out weaker ones and just tie in the strongest. In February or March, depending on the weather, cut the tips of the canes back to within 6 in. (15 cm) of the top wire. Then mulch the rows with well-rotted manure or compost to a depth of about 4 in. (10 cm). Sprinkle a top dress-

give that much-needed mulch in the spring. Every year remove the old canes immediately after they have finished fruiting and tie in the strongest 4 in. (10 cm) apart.

These methods refer only to the traditional summer-fruiting raspberries. My recommended varieties of summer bearers would be Haida, which has a bright, uniform, tasty fruit and is very winter hardy; Chilcotin, which has wonderful uniform tasty berries and tends to produce over a longer period of time, and Boyne, especially for home gardens as its delicious berries tend to ripen quickly and go a darkish red. The first two varieties were developed especially for commercial growers who need the fruit to last longer for shipping.

Fall-bearing raspberries are fun to grow in milder regions as they produce delicious fruit right up until frost. I have picked raspberries as late as early November.

They should be planted in the same way as the summer bearers, with similar supports, and all the same care and feeding. But rather than prune them after fruiting, leave the canes on until February. Then cut them all down to ground level before you top dress them. New canes will grow rapidly throughout the spring and early summer and can be tied in to fruit in the fall. Ideally, I would suggest two rows or patches of raspberries for your home garden: one regular summer-bearing and the other fall-bearing.

Two good fall-bearing varieties are Heritage, which is very vigorous producing many delicious fruits, and Amity, a newer and slightly earlier bearer with fruit that can be difficult to pick.

Black Currants. Black currants are a fruit which used to be grown more widely. They make tasty preserves because of their tartness, and if you have room I encourage you to grow a bush or two in your garden.

All currants are hungry plants and need an annual top dressing of some decent manure or compost. They also spread quite a bit when mature...up to one yard (1 m) for a small garden is probably enough. Prepare the ground well,

as for raspberries. Select a couple of good-looking bushes from your garden centre. They may either be bare-root and packed in sawdust in a plastic bag, or growing in a gallon-sized nursery pot from a local grower. Either way, look for a healthy plant with good balanced growth, and branches of equal vigour all around.

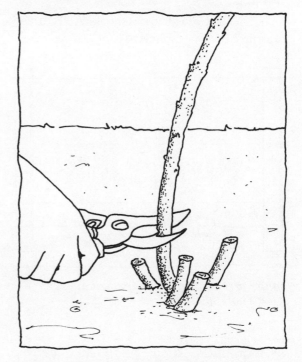

16. *Pruning a newly planted black currant bush.*

Dig the hole twice the size of the root system and plant the bushes 2 in. (5 cm) deeper than the soil line shows on the bare stems, or the soil level in a nursery container. This will encourage the production of strong basal shoots later. For the pot-grown plant, leave the roots intact and tamp soil in around them. With bare-root stock, spread the roots out evenly and shake them up and down a bit to distribute the soil in between them. Then tamp the soil carefully but firmly. At this stage you may add some general fertilizer, such as 6-8-6, at a handful per square yard (1 m²). Then cut the newly planted bush back to within 4 in. (10 cm) of the soil level. This will encourage strong new shoots to come up throughout the

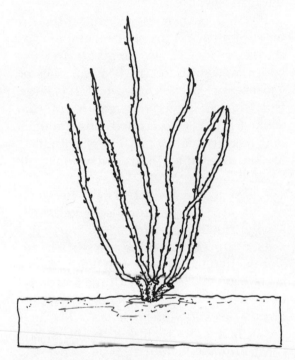

Resulting new growth.

summer. These shoots will carry your first crop of fruit the following year.

As with raspberries, top dress currant bushes each spring with well-rotted manure or compost to a depth of 4 in. (10 cm). In the third year it is quite acceptable to prune the black currants either at fruiting time or immediately after harvest. Years ago when I was an apprentice gardener we always cut off the entire

branches of black currant fruit when harvesting; it makes the task much easier and resulted in strong new shoots being sent up ready to produce fruit the following season.

It is important to note that this crop requires well drained yet moist soil conditions. They should not be allowed to go through fruit production time without watering.

A couple of good varieties are Wellington, which produces large fruit in abundance, and Baldwin, which is of United Kingdom origin and difficult to find, although some of the nurseries in the Fraser Valley carry it.

Red Currants. Red currants are not as widely grown as they should be. All the techniques in their culture apply exactly as for black currants. The major difference is the pruning, since red currants fruit on two-year-old and older wood. Most definitely, do *not* prune them at harvest time. If when you purchase the plants they do not seem very hardy cut them down to about 6 in. (15 cm). A good basal branch structure will start which will form the framework of your bushes for years to come. In the following November or December remove the weaker shoots or any growing on an angle towards the centre of the bush. Tip back the remaining shoots by about 4 in. (10 cm). This should encourage them to form fruiting spurs in the following month. Over the next couple of winters continue to shape the bush, pruning the leader shoots by one-third and the side spurs by two-thirds, much like pruning an apple tree.

Red Lake is the only variety found locally in garden centres. It produces tart-tasting fruit which makes for delicious pies.

Gooseberries. Gooseberries were once grown commercially in the Fraser Valley and you can still find a few in local markets in early summer. One reason why they are not so popular is because they have ferocious thorns which can cause grief, both when harvesting and when pruning. But the fact that they produce delicious fruit for pies and other wonderful desserts and preserves should make the prickles a minor problem. Careful pruning can make for a nice open bush for easier harvesting.

Planting time is early spring, when the majority of plants come into garden centres. Most likely gooseberries will be bare-root packed in sawdust in a small plastic bag with a picture of the fruit on the outside. Dig the hole larger than the root area and spread the roots, making sure that the soil gets distributed among them. Try to plant them no deeper than the soil line shows on the stem. It is important to keep the branches of gooseberries up away from the soil. Otherwise, slugs and other ground pests will eat the fruit before you do. Try to keep about 6 in. (15 cm) of bare stem between the soil and the branch structure. This may mean removing some strong-looking basal branches the first year. Gooseberry bushes reach a mature size of approximately 3 ft. (1 m) across, so allow for this when spacing.

If there are some decent-looking branches left, trim them back by half to an upward but outward facing bud. This will allow the framework to grow away from the ground and away from the centre of the bush. You will probably get some fruit in the second year, but do not expect a lot until the third year. Always prune in November or January, leaving lots of room for your hands between the branches. This will also improve air circulation, discouraging fungus diseases such as powdery mildew. It also allows for easier fruit harvesting.

Prune gooseberries by cutting the tip by one-third and the side shoots by two-thirds or shorter, forming side fruiting spurs of 3-4 buds. The best varieties of gooseberries are Pixwell, which has large fruit that is sweet enough to eat uncooked if left on the bush long enough, and Oregon Champion, which is well suited to the area since it was developed in Oregon.

A pest problem which is most tiresome in this area is the so-called gooseberry sawfly. The flies lay their eggs early in the season around flowering time. Then the worms hatch out and can literally eat every leaf on the bush within a few days. Malathion™ is the recommended spray, but do not spray any bushes while they are in bloom as it will kill the bees. For those of you who hate to spray, you could try enclosing your bushes in Remay™ cloth while the fly is around. (If you do spray follow the instructions in the B.C. Ministry of Agriculture pesticide book listed in the reading list.)

Blueberries. Blueberries are a commercial crop in British Columbia, and because of our acidic soil conditions and ample rainfall they love it here. If anything they can tolerate a fairly poorly drained soil since essentially they are bog lovers. If you have well-drained soil additional peat can be added when preparing the planting site.

Blueberries are always sold as two- or three-year-old plants in nursery containers, never as bare-root stock. They should be planted in rows, about 6.5 ft. (2 m) apart all around. This allows for easy access for picking. Since blueberries are natural branchers, they should not need much pruning during their first two years. But in the third winter some thinning should be required, especially cutting away inward-growing branches. One of the oldest branches should be cut down to almost ground level, which will encourage some nice new growth from the base. This is referred to as renewal pruning (discussed in more detail in the chapter on flowering shrubs). Annual spring mulching is also required, and if your soil is a bit on the light side you might include some peat with the well-rotted manure and compost to improve the humus content of your soil.

Since these are bog-loving plants it is essential that they be kept well watered during their fruit-developing months. It may seem strange to mention watering for coastal gardens, especially if you are a new gardener to the area. But it is possible to get six weeks or more without rain during April-May, and because our soil tends to be so porous an added application of water is required. Annual feeding should be done in the spring with a fertilizer such as 6-8-6 applied at a handful per square yard (1 m²). Good varieties of blueberry are Blue Crop, which is a vigorous and very prolific mid-season bearer, and Northland, which is a lower, smaller spreading bush but has by far the best-tasting fruit.

Blackberries. When travelling around the Lower Mainland during August and early September it is not uncommon to see people scrambling all among and over bushes with little pails full of blackberries. Closer examination of the pickers' arms will reveal a scratch or two. They are collecting wild blackberries, which some people would refer to as a noxious weed. However, there have been developments in the hybridization of these plants, and there is now a very good thornless variety on the market which is often just sold as Thornless blackberry. Personally, I do not think the flavour equals that of the wild ones.

The key to growing blackberries in a controlled fashion is having the space to do it, along with the proper supports. Against a fence or wall is ideal, preferably west or southwest facing. Put treated lumber posts 6.5 ft. (2 m) apart. They should be well buried in the soil to a depth of about 18 in. (45 cm) with 6.5 ft. (2 m) above ground. Some people advocate having support wires every 18 in. (45 cm) apart, but I like the two-wire system. String the first wire 3 ft. (1 m) above the ground (this way you do not have to bend far when picking) and the other 3 ft. (1 m) above it.

Plants are sold in bundles at the garden centre much like raspberries. Check to see that they are good quality. Plant them in pairs. This is where the question of adequate space arises. Ideally, you would have three posts, giving 13 ft. (4 m) of wire to work with. I would then plant two plants at each outside post. When planting, spread the roots well. The depth at which you plant is not critical as blackberries are essentially weed plants.

97

Cut the newly planted canes back to about 18 in. (45 cm). Throughout the summer they will send out at least three new shoots each, which will spread rapidly. When the shoots are long enough tie them in to a post or wire if you have the time. Out at the UBC Botanical Garden we leave them to run on the ground and then selectively tie them in during August or September. In the first season you might tie in all the new shoots, just halving them out and tying them in bunches along the two support wires. These will carry fruit the following season, then should be cut out to the ground in late summer. Six of the strongest and longest new shoots should be tied in again, three on each support wire.

While the thornless varieties are nice to grow because they are easy to deal with I would like to suggest a rather thorny one for flavour. Black Satin has large, delicious berries which make superb preserves.

Loganberries. Loganberries require the same planting and cultivation methods as do blackberries. If you had to decide whether to grow them or the blackberries, I would go for logans, because they really have a superb flavour.

Boysenberries. Boysenberries are also very nice to grow. They are a bit like an enormous blackberry and require the same cultural conditions.

Tayberry. My all-time favourite among the rampant climbing berries is the tayberry, which is hybrid between the blackberry and the raspberry. As you might imagine the flavour is delicious. In all honesty, if I only had room for one climbing berry it would be this one.

In summary, for all the bush, cane and climbing berries there are one or two key points to their success in your home garden.

Plant them in a sunny spot with well-prepared soil. Top dress annually in the early spring with about 4-5 in. (10-13 cm) of good organic material such as compost or well-rotted manure. Keep them well watered during dry times, especially when they are in flower or forming fruit. Mulch will help maintain the moisture in the soil. Try to feed them annually in the spring with all-purpose fertilizer.

If you tend to get more leaves than flowers and fruit I would strongly recommend applying a high potash fertilizer in February. This is the main element used by plants for flower and fruit production.

Lastly, since all of these fruits are surface rooted, when cleaning out any weeds between the bushes do not dig deeply or use a rototiller as it will sever roots. Just hand weed them out carefully.

All the climbing berries...blackberry, loganberry, boysenberry and tayberry...have a tendency to tip-layer themselves. This means that any runners that sit on the ground will root at the tips and if left will become weedy and run rampant like the wild berries. Normally, you can just dig them out carefully and cut them off and discard them. However, this is an easy way to propagate them for giving to friends.

Strawberries. Much work has been done in the hybridization of strawberries. There are ever-bearing types, alpine types and even some that are suitable for growing in hanging baskets. No matter what size of garden you have it is possible to grow strawberries.

First and foremost when selecting a site for growing strawberries in your garden make sure it is in full sunlight, preferably for the better part of the day. If there is any shade it should only be for the early part of the day. In nature strawberries grow usually on a dry rocky bank of almost silty soil. In a garden, the soil should be well drained...not waterlogged at any time of the year. To produce full-sized, good-quality berries, some well-rotted manure or mushroom manure should be worked into the soil two spades deep. The strawberry bed will not be disturbed or dug over again for at least three years, so while digging get out all the perennial weeds.

If you are using plants purchased from a garden centre, then planting will take place in the spring. If, on the other hand, you are getting some plants from a friend or from established plants elsewhere in your home garden, they will be in the form of runners which are ready for transplanting in July. The soil preparation should be the same no matter what the time of year.

Again, I would caution that when buying bundles of plants from a garden centre you should open up the one you have selected to make sure all the plants inside are good and healthy.

Plant your strawberries in rows in the prepared site, 18 in. (45 cm) apart in the row and 39 in. (1 m) between rows for ease of picking and maintenance. Before planting, sprinkle a general fertilizer such as 6-8-6 at a handful per square yard (1 m^2). Then, mark your rows and plant individual plants with a hand trowel, planting them to the depth of the roots only. Do not bury the leaves or crown of the strawberry plant.

With spring planting you really should pick off the flower buds as they appear in the first season, the theory being that allowing them to fruit the first year will weaken the plant. However I, like most of you I am sure, could not bear to do that. If you do allow them to fruit that first year, just an extra shot of fertilizer after fruiting will build the plants up quickly, especially if you use one of the liquid kelp or seaweed fertilizers.

Keep the plants well watered in the first season. Try to water in the morning so that water does not sit on the leaves overnight which will encourage mildew problems.

Strawberries got their name from the fact that traditionally straw was put under the plants as the blossoms developed to stop the soil from splashing up and cov-

17. *Planting strawberry plants.*

ering the berries. Straw is still fine to use if you can get it, but plastic can be used, although I hate to recommend anything that takes so long to break down. One idea I saw in a community garden in Montreal was the recycling of paper and aluminum plates. A cut was made from one side of the plate to the centre and a small hole cut in the centre, just large enough to fit snugly around the plant. Then the plate was put around and under the plant. It worked like a charm. Does this mean we could now call them Plateberries?

In subsequent years when the strawberries have finished fruiting older leaves will look a little yellow, and there will be masses of runners coming out from around each plant. These runners will have rooted in, so it will take some careful digging to clean them out. If possible, in the first three years pick or pull off runners as they develop before they get a chance to

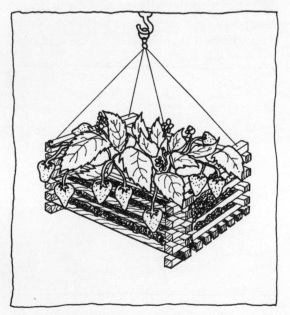

18. *Strawberries in a hanging basket.*

root. After the plants have finished fruiting pick off all the old leaves and top dress between the rows with a shallow 2 in. (5 cm) layer of well-rotted manure or compost.

It used to be that some of the runners should be saved and planted elsewhere in the garden, so that you always had a new row coming along. Now it is considered best to discard them annually, and then in the third season to plant up a new area.

You can put a plastic tunnel cloche over a couple of the rows early in the season to encourage your strawberries to ripen early. Or, if you have a moveable cold frame you could put it over a patch.

Netting of some sort will be required to keep the birds off the ripe berries. There are various kinds of nets available from your local garden supply shop.

It is possible to grow the ever-bearing type of strawberry from seed. If you like a challenge, there is one for you. For first-time gardeners it is much easier to buy plants. Having said that it is possible to grow strawberries in hanging baskets, here is just a quick word on how. First, the basket must be a decent size, otherwise it will dry out too quickly. I like baskets made from 2 x 2 in. (5 x 5 cm) rough cedar, built log cabin style (see illustration). Ideally, they should be 18 x 12 in. (45 x 30 cm) and at least 8 in. (20 cm) deep. The gaps are then filled with moss to stop the soil from falling through.

Fill the basket with a good potting mix in March or April and plant it up with six strawberry plants, keeping it well watered and fed with some liquid fertilizer. The berries will hang over the edge of the basket and ripen, looking almost too pretty to eat, and they will be the envy of your

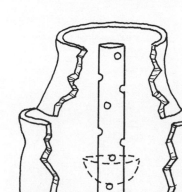

19. *The correct way to prepare a strawberry jar for planting.*

neighbours. Another novel and attractive way to grow them on your townhouse patio or apartment balcony is in a Mexican strawberry barrel. These terra cotta planters are nice but not reliable in the winter as they will freeze and crack. However, you can protect them with either chicken wire or leaves, or with an old coat.

Put drainage in the bottom of the pot, such as old broken pots or scrunched up plastic ones, or styrofoam cups. Fill with good potting soil to the first level of holes, then place your plants in from the inside, gently pushing their tops out through the holes. At this stage add a piece of plastic drainage pipe with holes in it down through the centre, so that it is level with the top of the pot, to act as a water conductor (see

illustration). Then continue to plant till the pot is full, and plant a couple of plants at the top. Water it well and keep it in the sun, turning the pot once a week so that all the plants get equal sunlight. Once the pot is covered with fruit, it will look too good to eat.

Some recommended varieties of strawberries are Totem, a variety that has been around for a long time in this area and has a good flavour, and Burlington, which is not as well known but is delicious.

Summing up, strawberries need lots of sunlight, annual feeding and definitely a good cleaning up after fruiting. The average productive life for a strawberry plant is three to four years, but remember, you can always propagate new plants from the runners.

■ THINGS TO REMEMBER

1. Select a sunny site in your garden; avoid frost pockets.
2. Prepare the soil well, digging in copious amounts of compost or well-rotted manure.
3. Always purchase good plant stock. Make sure you check it well at your garden centre. Open bundled canes and strawberries to inspect them.
4. Top dress and feed annually.

Fruit Trees

Home growing of fruit trees is becoming popular again, especially with the advent of the new dwarf root stocks for apple. There really is nothing like your own fruit from your own garden. But fruit trees can be susceptible to pests and diseases, and if they are not planted in the correct place they will not produce well for you. Fruit trees take a little work but in the end are well worth the effort.

Whether you can accommodate fruit trees and how many you can grow will depend on the size of your garden. Fruit trees need to be in a good open location. By that I mean well away from any large trees or any buildings because these will hinder the development of individual fruit trees. I remember some years ago, when we first put in the fruit tree garden out at the UBC Botanical Garden, there was a whole row of Douglas-firs along the south border. Even though they were at least 30-50 ft. (10-15 m) away and we were growing small bush trees, it soon became evident that the fruit trees were growing away from these large evergreens, so they had to be taken out. It is very important that you have an open growing area.

If fruit trees are grown out in the open, with good air circulation, they will experience fewer problems with fungus diseases. However, I should point out that with the humid climate that we have to deal with on the coast, they will always encounter problems with powdery mildew and scab.

The other thing about fruit trees is that they cannot stand to be grown in a water-logged soil. If you live in a lower-lying area near a river, you may need to raise up the bed in which you plan to grow fruit trees. You should know your garden well, and you should never choose a spot where water tends to sit during the heavy winter rains. In all honesty I think it is best if you can have a special place dedicated to fruit tree growing alone. This can take up quite a lot of space, so it is acceptable to have one or two trees dotted around your lawn, but I would not recommend that you plant an apple tree in the middle of a flower bed or in the middle of a vegetable patch. Eventually, it will cause too much shade and there will be tremendous competition among the roots, and nothing will grow successfully underneath the tree. Make sure that fruit trees have a space of their own.

Preparing the site in readiness for planting should be the same whether you have chosen an apple, pear or cherry, though each tree may have a few special requirements. Dig out a hole at least a yard (1 m) in diameter and dig down a foot (30 cm). Then work lots of well-rotted manure and other organic material into the bottom of the hole, so in effect you have double dug. Once you have put the manure in and turned it underneath, leave the hole open until you are ready to plant your tree. Do

your planning well in advance: get the trees, decide where they are to go, then dig the holes, then transplant your trees.

Because of our mild coastal climate fruit trees can be planted in the fall, during October and perhaps early November. If you cannot do it then, wait until February. There have always been arguments as to which is the best time to plant. I prefer fall planting, particularly in a mild climate, but the argument against it is that if you plant in the spring and the tree starts to grow, then it will not have any setbacks from the cold. Fall or spring, it is up to you.

When you are getting ready to plant your fruit tree in the hole, make sure that you have a decent stake available to support the tree from any wind (see tree planting illustration in Chapter 7). Get something like a nice fence post and knock it into the ground so that it is very secure in the centre of the hole, then plant the tree, then fill with soil. You will know that the post is going to be a good support and, because you put it in place first, you will know that the stake has not interfered with any of the tree's roots. To secure the tree to the stake, use plastic or rubber tree ties that are not going to hurt the trunk of the tree. If you tie with string or wire, you tend to forget about it and leave it on, and as the trunk of the tree swells, the wire or string will grow into the trunk and can actually cause the trunk of the tree to break off at that point. If you use specially designed rubber or plastic belts, they can expand as the tree grows and will not damage your tree.

If you buy new fruit trees as bare-root stock from a garden centre, make sure that you wrap the roots in some damp sacking then put them inside black plastic garbage bags for transporting home. If you are not going to be able to plant them right away then heel them into the garden. Just dig out a hole and plant them in so that the roots do not dry out. If they are in a container this is not necessary. Many garden centres will sell trees in fibre pots containing a sawdust mixture. Never leave any bare-root plants, whether they are trees or anything else, out of the ground any longer than a few minutes. Winds will dry off all the root tips, which is where the active root initials are, the active feeder roots, and once they have gone the tree has to work at making a whole new set before it can get on with growing. So never let the roots dry out.

Also, when you are planting your tree make sure that you do not plant it any deeper than it was originally. Most fruit trees are grafted down near the ground level, and you will be able to see the grafting on the stem...it shows up as a bump. That is where the variety you want to grow has been grafted onto a root stock selected by the grower. If you plant so that the bump is below the ground, the tree itself will try to root out of its own stem...it will take over and take on the vigour of its natural tendencies. If it has been grafted selectively onto a root stock that will keep it nice and dwarf and small and within balance for your garden, then the whole benefit of this is lost. So always make sure that the graft is well above the surface of the soil, yet the roots of the tree are below the surface and nicely spread out in the hole.

There is something else to watch out for. When fruit trees have been lifted and bundled, the roots may have been straightened out and tied up in the bundles so that they are all bending towards one side. When you have your stake in position and have brought the soil level up in the hole to make it right, place your tree in the hole and spread the roots out as they would be normally. Then, as you fill the soil in around it, just lightly shake the tree up and down so that some loose soil can go between the roots and allow them to spread evenly as they would in nature. Once you have filled in the hole, tamp it in lightly with your foot and water it well. But remember, if you do this in the fall and there is a lot of rain, do not stamp down too hard around the tree because you can cause soil compaction.

It is advisable to leave the area around the tree uncultivated and unplanted for the first two or three years so that the tree will not suffer any competition from grass roots or bedding plants. There is nothing wrong with leaving it clear. Just keep the weeds cleared out, and then you will be able to add fertilizer when needed for the next two or three years.

Fruit trees, unless you want to grow them specially trained as espaliered trees on a fence or on a wall, should need no pruning at all in the first season that you plant them. However, for future reference, the best time to prune fruit trees is when they are dormant, when they have lost their leaves. Anytime from November through until the end of January is a good time for pruning all of your fruit trees. As I deal with each specific variety, I will elaborate on its pruning requirements.

Apples. Let us start off with "A" for apples. The ideal soil for apples is often referred to as a medium-well-drained loamy soil, not heavy and wet. On many parts of the coast our soil is basically glacial till and that means that it drains very quickly. It is important if you have very well drained soil that when you are preparing the hole for planting you dig in lots of good organic matter, be it well-rotted manure or compost, something that will really give the soil good moisture retention. Otherwise, during a summer hot spell when the fruit is developing and the water runs through the soil so quickly that there is no moisture retention, the fruit will drop off or just will not mature properly. If you live where the soil is fairly heavy, such as the heart of the Fraser Valley, then you need not be as mindful of this.

Apples like a slightly acidic soil, much like vegetables, with a recommended pH somewhere around 6.7, but they are tolerant of a wide range of soils. Apples are almost always grafted onto a root stock. This is because apple roots can sometimes be terribly vigorous and can make the tree grow all out of proportion to the rest of the garden, and they can be susceptible to certain root problems or root diseases. Over the years much research work has been carried out at East Malling in Kent, England, into the vigour of root stocks and into developing good root stocks for apples to grow on. The resulting smaller or dwarf varieties are becoming very popular in North America now, because of the smaller size of modern gardens. People are moving into townhouses with very small garden spaces and require a fruit tree that is manageable for the home gardener.

Only a few root stocks are commonly available locally as apple trees for a small home garden. M7 is a semi-dwarfing tree that can be controlled by training and pruning; you can reckon that it will end up 16.5 ft. (5 m) wide, which is suitable for a home garden. M9, on the other hand, is very dwarfing. It is one of the most dwarfing root stocks and is widely used for making a tree somewhere between 6.5-10 ft. (2-3 m) in height and spread. It bears fruit early, usually from the third year onward, and sometimes it will actually have fruit on it in the second year. It does require good soil conditions and will not tolerate neglect or competition from other plants around it. It is also not a strong tree, so it requires staking or supports throughout its life. M9 is a great choice for an espaliered fruit tree, but for a regular home garden, a dwarf open bush-type tree or a pyramid-type tree is ideal.

M27 is another extremely dwarfing root stock which is now being brought into this country. It is very useful for townhouse growing because it enables one to grow a fruit tree in a half barrel on a patio. It needs staking throughout its life. A little M27 in the UBC Botanical Garden had fifty apples in its third year, and it has had fifty or more apples on it every year since. If you have only a small space, your choice should be M27.

For a regular little bush-type tree, or what is called a dwarf pyramid tree, let the central leader go up and feather out the side branches so that there is room for the air to circulate, for you to get your hands in to pick the fruit, and also to let the sun in to ripen the fruit. The best way to start is when you buy your tree. Most likely it will be a three-year-old tree, so it will already have some form to it. When making your selection, try to choose a tree that has branches at an equal distance around the outside of the tree, so that you will have a nice, uniform-looking tree. And choose one that has a fairly strong leader. If you plant it either in October, November or March, once it is safely staked and the soil is all in place, go around and do some pruning. Reduce the top leader by cutting it back one-third from the top. Try to cut it above a strong bud, at a 45° angle away from the bud so that you have a slanting cut behind it. On each side shoot, try to cut it back by two-thirds, taking two-thirds of the branch away. Again, make sure that you make your cut above an outward-facing bud because you want the branches to form out to give a rounded tree-like shape.

By August the original laterals, the ones that you have cut, will have extended, and there will be a new central leader growing on up. This should be tied to the stake as it grows, and the side branches should grow out evenly. In the winter of the second year, again reduce the central leader by one-third. With the side branches at this point, decide which are going to be the main branches and cut back the three or four leaders of these main branches by one-third. Any shoots that are coming from them lower down, cut back by two-thirds so that you are within two or three buds of the main stem. I know it sounds complicated but if you look at the little illustration below, I think it will help and give you an idea how. Following this method you will train your tree to have open growth. Do subsequent pruning every winter for the rest of the tree's life, trying to keep it nice and open.

In the early years of a tree's life it is a good idea every spring, after you have finished your pruning in February, to top dress around the base of the tree with a mulch of well-rotted manure. This will certainly help to produce some very good fruit for you.

Now how about some apple varieties? Gravenstein is an old variety that has been used around this area for many years. It is a good early cooking apple, and as it gets older it is not a bad eater as well. It makes good pies early in the season. The only thing against the Gravenstein is that it is terribly susceptible to apple scab, and even if you follow a very careful spraying program you will never really get this problem under control. My advice would be that if you have only room for a few fruit trees then avoid the Gravenstein.

Golden Delicious is a very popular cultivar for this area. It is not the best-flavoured apple in the world, but it is a very encouraging one to grow because it is a heavy bearer and will bear early fruit which is excellent quality for eating, for use as a dessert apple and for processing. It makes good apple sauce. The medium-sized, tapered apple is golden yellow, occasionally with rosy streaks on it, and its flesh is green-coloured and has a delicate flavour. It will ripen as early as the end of September and will keep well in cold storage until February.

King is another apple that I really like. It is not easy to find in garden centres but is well worth hunting for. The fruit is large to very large and roundish with a smooth skin, sometimes with russet dots on it or a fine yellow colour washed with orange-red shading. The flesh is yellowish, crisp and aromatic and is very good tasting. It is in season from late September through to December. The King is a very good apple for use in baking.

The Spartan apple is a great one. It was actually hybridized and developed by the Ministry of Agriculture research station up in Summerland, British Columbia. It works very well for that dry climate, but it will also work well on the coast. The fruit is usually ready for picking in October and is a great cooking apple which will keep well in cold storage until January.

If you want to consider something a little out of the ordinary, a very good cooking apple for this area, and I mention

this because of my United Kingdom roots, is the Bramleys Seedling. It is a large cooking apple, very roundish-flat to look at. It is bright green and the flesh is extremely white, firm and quite acid—it makes marvellous pies and baked apples. It can be harvested in October and is good for keeping from November through to February. Because of the similarities in climate with its home it does extremely well here.

If there are no other apple trees within the neighbourhood to cross-pollinate you will not get a good crop. Therefore, if you have room I would strongly recommend that you grow a Hyslop crab apple in your

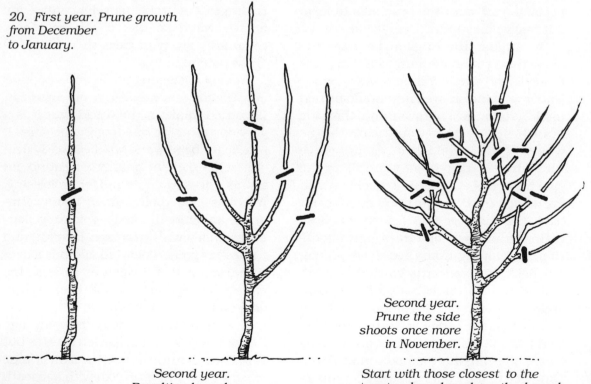

20. First year. Prune growth from December to January.

Second year. Resulting branch growth. Prune again in January.

Second year. Prune the side shoots once more in November.

Start with those closest to the tree trunk and work up the branch. Leave the top central shoot intact.

garden. It has very pretty blossoms in the spring, as do all the apples. Later on it produces tart, wonderful little crab apples, dark red with a purplish bloom on them, that will stay on the tree right until the leaves have dropped. These are the best apples for making crab apple jelly. But Hyslop, you see, is a good cross-pollinator for just about every other apple that we can grow in our gardens in this area. So, if you feel that there are no other pollinators around, definitely make room for a Hyslop.

Cherries. The first thing I would like to say about cherries is that usually the birds get them before you do. So if it is a first-year garden, perhaps they are not the best fruit to start out with. Cherries are also extremely vigorous. There is no such thing as a dwarfing root stock of a cherry—it will take up a lot of room. A good idea is to grow them in a fan shape against a fence or between some wires and posts so that you can control them fairly well. This also makes it easier to put a net over the whole thing to at least try to keep the birds away.

Cherries grow in any good, well-drained soil, and they must be really dug deep. The pH should be between 6.7 and 7.5. They will not prosper in light sandy soil,

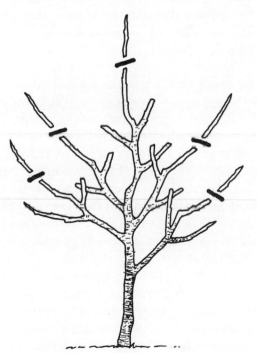

Third year. Prune the leader shoots in January.

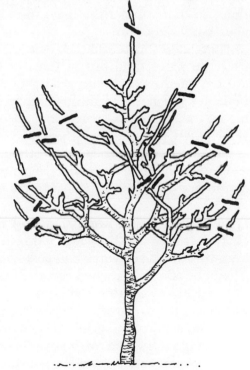

Fourth year. Minimal pruning of leader shoots in January promotes the development of fruiting spurs.

so it is important that you add in lots of organic matter, as for the apple trees. If you decide that you are going to grow them on posts and wires make sure that you put in some decent heavy posts about every 6.5 ft. (2 m); the wires between these posts should be about 12 in. (30 cm) apart. Plant your tree in the centre of this structure. In the spring, or in this area even as early as February, cut the whole top of the tree back down to just below the lowest wire so that you have two nice side branches coming out which can be trained up the wires to form the first part of your fan. They should be further cut back to about 12 in. (30 cm) to encourage side shoots to develop from them so that you get the main frame of your fan for later on.

These side shoots will then develop all over the place, and out of that 12 in. (30 cm) stem you should get up to five branches which will be adequate for training up the rest of your wires. In the third year, when pruning, cut them back to about 18 in. (45 cm), encouraging them to send out a further two shoots. This will continue to develop the framework of the fan.

It is important every spring to top dress cherries, and it is extremely important, if they are growing on wires and posts near a fence or house, that you keep them well watered in dry weather. Otherwise you will lose your fruit very easily. With the exception of one variety, all cherries need cross-pollinators. The two cultivars that I would recommend for this area are the Compact Stella, a self-pollinator which gives a very good crop of fruit, and the Mazzar, which bears a not very large, bright red fruit which is very sweet to tart.

If you have the two of them then you will have no problem with cross-pollination. But do remember that they take up a lot of room.

Figs. There are many people with European roots living in the Lower Mainland, and there certainly is a large Greek population. When you drive around and look at the gardens, especially if you are new to the city, you might be surprised to notice so many large fig trees growing in backyards. Obviously, many of those varieties have been brought with people from their homelands, but there is no reason why you should not try a fig in your garden. I think it gives it a nice Mediterranean or Californian feeling. If you choose the right spot for it you can keep it controlled, and a fig can be a most enjoyable plant.

Figs can tolerate a wide range of soils but must be well drained, so they adapt well to the soil in our part of the world. They also appreciate having organic material worked into the site. They are rather surface rooted, so you do not need to go terribly deep. It is most important that they be grown against a south- or west-facing wall, so that they get reflected heat. The best way to prepare the site is to dig out a trough about 6.5 ft. (2 m) in length and about two spades wide and two spades deep. Then work in a lot of leaf mould and well-rotted manure. This allows the fig to have a lovely surface area for its roots to grow through. It will have a tap root, but certainly the surface roots will appreciate that trench that you have prepared for them. Figs should probably be planted in the spring, when plants will be, if bought in a container, up to 39 in.

(1 m) in height and perhaps have one single stem.

Figs respond well to pruning, and rather than have the one tall stem growing up, as soon as you have planted the tree cut the stem back to within 12 in. (30 cm) of the soil level. This will encourage it, while it is making its new roots, to send out many shoots from the base that you can tie in a fan form onto the wall so that they get the maximum amount of sun on each branch.

With luck you will get one crop of figs per season. In tropical areas of the world, figs produce three crops in a season. You will find that they will try to send out fruit at all times of the year. I have been told by many people who grow figs that you should pick off any unripened or immature fruits that are still on in the fall. This makes the fig produce more flowers early in the season in the spring. Fig trees have minuscule flowers—you hardly notice them at all—that start to develop as early as April, and their fruit will ripen in August and September.

One recommended variety for this area is called Brown Turkey, but check around some of the garden centres or specialty shops. If you see other varieties for sale, then by all means incorporate them in your garden.

Peaches. Peaches are not a very good choice of plant for this part of the world. They would need to have a south- or west-facing wall or fence, like the fig, to get all the protection from the cold eastern and northern winds and as much sun as possible. Peaches bloom very early, and even if they are self-pollinating need to be hand-pollinated. Because they are a stone fruit they like a little bit of lime worked into the soil. Peaches are not usually a long-lived tree in this area. They suffer from a fungus disease called peach leaf curl, though if you plant a peach close to the house, under the eaves where it will not get splashed by the rain, peach leaf curl is less likely to be a problem.

Peaches like a soil that has a pH of about 6.7 to 7. Quite surprisingly it is a very hardy plant. It loves to have a cold winter and intense summer heat, which we do not always get on the coast. However, peaches are fun to try and by all means put one in your garden if you have the space for it. Try not to work the soil too deeply. About 18 in. (45 cm) of the surface soil worked in with some good manure is sufficient. Possibly the best time to plant is during March or April. If it is a container-grown tree it can generally be planted at any time.

As soon as you have planted it, apply a mulch of well-rotted manure or compost or even mushroom manure for about 18 in. (45 cm) around the root area. This will really help the tree in its first year and is something you need to continue to do on an annual basis.

Pruning should be almost the same as for the cherry. You want to form a nice fan. One of the better varieties to grow in this area, although sometimes hard to find, is Haven. Not Red Haven which you see all over the place, but Haven. Haven is one of the older, whiter-fleshed peaches. It yields yellow-white-fleshed, very sweet peaches and really does give you top-quality juicy fruit.

Another one to try is Renton, but in all honesty if you want a very good peach, try Haven.

Pears. Pears require the same soil conditions as apples, but unfortunately pears are not one of the better crops for this region because of their flowering time. They always bloom early in the season, and often that is when we get cold, wet, rainy weather and there are no bees around to pollinate the pears. This is not to say that you should not try to grow a pear because occasionally you will get a decent crop. Make sure that they are planted in an area that gets plenty of sunlight and where the bees are most likely to find them.

Pears are grafted onto root stocks. The one most commonly used is Quince C, which is a moderately vigorous root stock. It will make a pear tree anywhere from 10-16.5 ft (3-5 m) in height. It is suitable for highly fertile soils and vigorous varieties, but not where the conditions are poor. Most pear trees that you will find in a garden centre are on Quince C, although there is a Quince A that is used, which is a slightly more vigorous form. If you feel that there is a problem with poor soil in your garden then by all means go for one that is on the Quince A stock.

For the pear, the same sort of pruning and planting techniques should be followed as for the apple. The only difference with pears, something you find out quite quickly, is that they tend with their new growth to always send the shoots vertically into the air so that they are all very close together. They do not spread out and make a nice open tree. When these new branches which form early on in the season start to grow straight up in the air, put several stakes around the perimeter of the tree about one yard (1 m) away from it. Then bring a branch down when it is

almost mature but while you can still bend it and tie it with twine to a stake so that the tree opens up. Leave it tied for a whole season. This way the branches will form and harden and remain open. This is the only way that you are going to get a pear tree to open, and if you do this in its first year or two you will get a nice open network of branches. Once this has happened, the subsequent pruning is the same as for the apple.

The variety that is most commonly cultivated is the Bartlett pear. It is a marvellous one for canning. When I was young we called it the William pear. It ripens in early September and is a good home garden variety. It will set fruit without a pollinator, but because pears bloom so early it might be a good idea to go out with a little brush and pollinate the blossoms on a warm sunny day in the spring when they are open so that you do get some decent fruit. Its fruit is medium-sized, fleshy white and very juicy—just a delicious thing to have—so by all means if you can only have one pear, then have a Bartlett. But if you have room for others, there is a lovely pear called Anjou. It is late to mid season in ripening and will store well. It bears a fine-flavoured, medium to light russety fruit with a short neck.

In fruit markets you find very sweet and juicy big pears that are brought in from the Orient, wrapped individually in netting bags. The Twentieth Century Oriental pear will not reach anywhere near the size of those big russety pears that you buy in the markets, but it is extremely juicy and so good to eat. You can just pick and eat them right from the tree from late September to early October.

If you have room for a Twentieth Century Oriental pear, by all means get one for your garden.

Plums. Plums can grow very well in this area; in recent years there have been some excellent crops. Soil preparation for planting should be similar to that described at the start of this chapter, but plums do like to have a certain amount of lime in the soil. So when preparing your hole that is 3 ft. (1 m) across, sprinkle in a handful of lime around the bottom where the roots are going to develop.

Another thing that you might be pleased to know, if you dislike the laborious business of digging holes, is that it is a good idea not to dig too deeply for a plum. If you give it too much good soil down below, it will send several suckers up from its roots. I am sure that you have

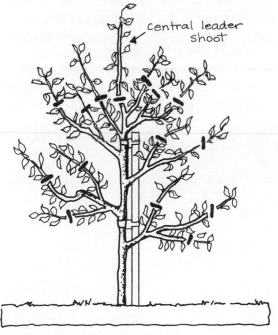

21. *Pruning a plum tree in July.*

seen this in old home gardens where there is a plum tree in the lawn which tries to send up suckers up all over the place. If you do not dig too deeply this will not happen to you.

Plums are not grafted onto any root stock, they are on their own roots, and so they tend to get to be quite vigorous trees, growing to a diameter anywhere from 16.5-33 ft. (5-10 m), so give them lots of space. As a rule they are not self-pollinating, so it is good to have at least one or two others in the vicinity or at least be sure that your neighbours have a plum tree in their garden. Ornamental plum trees can be used for pollinating purposes too.

Once planted and staked, as with any other tree, in late winter, perhaps February, cut back the stem of a plum tree to about 3 ft. (1 m) from the base. That is for a dwarf or bush tree. If it is going to be standard, that means it has a stem already, then cut about 6.5 ft. (2 m) from the base just to stop it at the top. Then cut back the remaining laterals, or side branches, by one-half.

Later on, in July, shorten the new growth of branch leaders to about 4 in. (10 cm). Prune at downward-facing buds because you do not want the tree to go on growing up and up—the plum has a tendency to grow its branches vertically from the ground. Cutting it to downward-facing buds will shorten the current season's laterals on the branches, leaving the central leader to continue. In March of the second year shorten the central leader by two-thirds of the previous summer's growth and keep doing this until your tree has reached about 10 ft. (3 m) in height. In subsequent seasons shorten the central leader to 1 in. (2.5 cm)

113

annually during May. This keeps the tree at its desired height. In July shorten the current season's growth of each branch leader to 4 in. (10 cm), about eight leaves from its point of origin. This will keep your tree nice and bushy. Also at this time remember that you do not want to save every one of the side branches. It is very important that there is room to get your hand through, to allow for good air circulation and to allow the sun to get in—this will cut down on disease problems. One of the best varieties for this region is called Bradshaw, which is just a regular plum with very good-flavoured fruit. If you only have room for one then choose Italian Greta, which is self-pollinating. It is a medium-sized tree with fruit which ripen a very typically purple plum colour and are sweet and delicious for eating. They are the sort of plums that you want to run out and steal from the tree when they are ripe. They are also good for canning and for freezing. Italian Greta plum is the one for any home gardener in this region—you will not be disappointed. One last thing about plums

is that they tend, in good season, to form too many fruits. Too many will set on the branch, and you will need to thin them out to about 6 in. (15 cm) apart to get a decent crop off the tree. If you leave too many fruits on the tree they will just be very small.

Quince. There is great confusion about the quince. Many people refer to that pretty red flower that blooms in the spring as a Japanese quince, or japonica. This is not a true quince at all. One true quince which has no cultivar name can be found in specialty nurseries listed under its proper name of *Cydonia oblonga*. It is a very ancient fruit. There are records of it in southern England, Crete and other Mediterranean countries, and it is found in temperate climates such as Romania and Bulgaria. This quince is a most beautiful tree. It has very large leaves and rather large and solitary apple-like blossoms in the spring. The marvellous golden-yellow, fleshy fruits are about the size of a pear. These are too sour to pick and eat as you would a pear or an apple, but when

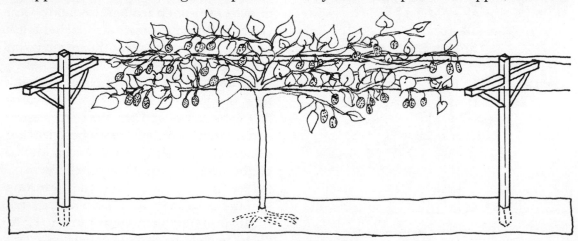

22. *Mature kiwi vine on support structure.*

cooked and sweetened they make the best preserves and jams.

One of the reasons that I like them is that, because they are so tart in flavour, if you are using a cooking apple that is really rather bland to make a pie or some apple sauce, incorporating one quince with it really jazzes up the whole flavour and makes it absolutely delicious. The fruit should be left on the tree as long as possible and not harvested until perhaps late October or early November, even when all the leaves have dropped off, because this allows them to develop a full flavour. Then they can be stored as with other fruits and used throughout the winter. Because it is so closely related to the apple and pear, it should be planted in exactly the same fashion. When pruning it in the dormant season, try for a globular shape with an open centre because it will bear its fruit on the tips and spurs of the previous year's growth. Do not cut back every tip or you will not get decent fruit. If you have space in your garden, try to grow a good old-fashioned quince.

Kiwi. One last fruit that I would like to put into this chapter, but which is not really a tree fruit at all, is the kiwi fruit. The kiwi is really a vine that comes to us from China. Its original botanical name is *Actinidia chinensis*, but the improved variety which bears nicer fruit is called *A. deliciosa*. When I was a boy we used to call them Chinese gooseberries, and the only reason that the kiwi fruits are called by that name is because New Zealand adopted and patented them as a commercial product for their island.

I would recommend that you plant one in your garden, but if left untouched they can put on 10-13 ft. (3-4 m) of new growth every year and can take over your entire garden. If you want to grow them for fruit, you will need a male and a female plant. Build a wooden structure and let the plants grow up a single post to a height of about 10 ft. (3 m) and then prune back the laterals and train them out over the edges of wires so that you keep them very much controlled.

■ PRUNING ESTABLISHED FRUIT TREES

If you move onto some property that has some established fruit trees that have been there for years and years, very often they will have been neglected and not pruned properly. I think pruning is one of the most therapeutic things you can do in the garden. It is a great thing to do if you are a bit mad at the world and want to go take out your frustrations. But, on the other hand, you must do it with a certain amount of care. To carry out any good pruning on any tree or shrub it is important that you have a decent pair of pruning shears. I prefer the ones that have a pointed cutting edge so that you can reach down into the centre branches and really cut in awkward places. Some of the older cutting types that have a flat blade to cut against are not the best because they will squeeze the wood. It is much better to have a blade that cuts on both sides so that you get a good clean cut.

The other tool that you will need for pruning larger and established trees is a pruning saw. A pruning saw has a curved blade with teeth that only cut when you pull the saw towards you. This makes it very useful to use when you are up on a ladder or climbing up in the centre of the tree, because you can reach away and then pull towards you and make sure that you can make a good clean cut when taking out a branch.

With a very old tree that has been neglected, it is quite alright to go out sometime in November or December and cut out a lot of the old branches right back to their source so that you open it up to let some air through. Then, with the branches that are left along the side, try to stick to the rule of cutting back the leader shoot by one-third, and reducing the side shoots by two-thirds. My old head gardener who trained me many years ago in England told me that, when pruning a large fruit tree, you should stand underneath it afterwards and throw your

hat. All head gardeners, in the old days, wore Trilby hats. He said that when you have finished pruning the tree, take your hat off and try to throw it up between the branches. If it did not get caught up, then you have opened it enough to allow good air circulation and let the light in.

It is possible to get terribly carried away when pruning. Some people are frightened to death to do pruning, and they just snip off a few of the other branches and call that a pruning job. Others get carried away, get up the ladder, stand there and saw and saw and saw. When they have finished there is hardly any tree left. So it is very important when pruning a tree to assess the situation, to decide the shape that you want in your mind's eye. Stand back and have a good look, go

23. *Pruning an established fruit tree.*

up and cut the first branch that you think you should cut out, and once you have cut it stand back and see how much it has opened the tree. If you keep doing this as you go along, then you will end up with a nice uniform but opened tree. Certainly, do not be afraid to prune and make sure that you do some decent training so that you end up with a well-shaped tree. There are many books that give good illustrations of how best to prune different trees for different effects.

The obvious benefits of growing your own fruit trees is the fruit you get to eat. However, they can also provide seasonal privacy once the foliage has developed. Quite honestly, some of the prettiest spring blossoms to my mind are those of apples and cherries. I strongly recommend some fruit trees for all home gardens.

■ THINGS TO REMEMBER

1. Select your site well, making sure that it gets a lot of sun, is not water-logged and is away from the shade of evergreen trees and tall buildings.
2. Prepare the planting hole well with additions of compost or old manure.
3. Place the stake in the hole before planting and secure it with a proper tie afterwards. Check annually to make sure it does not grow into the trunk.
4. Prune and train annually.

Vegetables

Whether or not the benefit is psychological, there is a lot to be said for growing your own vegetables. I really do believe that they taste better, and just the fun of having grown them makes it all so exciting. When you have friends over to dinner . . . and you can say "yes, we grew the beans ourselves" or "aren't our potatoes good," it really gives a tremendous feeling of achievement.

However, there are a few things about vegetable gardening that need to be looked into before you embark on such a project. First of all the site is important. Vegetables need good light and good air circulation. By good light I mean that they should not be close to tall trees or a large building, or anywhere where light is going to be restricted. Ideally, they should get sunlight all day, but if you can only give them half a day's sun then I would definitely favour an area that gets full morning sun and full afternoon shade.

Air circulation is another very important consideration. If your vegetables are tucked up against a building where there might be a lot of stagnant air, particularly on those early days of summer, you will encounter problems with such diseases as powdery mildews, a fungus disease that looks like a chalky white powder all over the surface of the leaves. Vegetables such as peas are especially prone to it. Good air circulation will help reduce the likelihood of disease problems.

Once you have chosen a site for your vegetable garden, then follow all the guidelines outlined in the Soils and Fertilizers chapter and really make sure that you add some good, well-rotted manure to the soil. It is extremely important to add good organic material to the soil.

Vegetables are very hungry things. They take a tremendous amount of basic fertilizers from your soil. All the leaf vegetables take much nitrogen, all the root vegetables take up phosphates, and the potash will go for their flowers and fruit. So, it is extremely important that these nutrients be renewed or added to the soil on an annual basis.

In combination with organic material I use some inorganic fertilizer. For the longest time I have used the balanced all-purpose granular fertilizer 6-8-6. However, if you are truly organic in growing and do not want to use inorganic fertilizers then think about the different requirements of your vegetables. Consider whether they are essentially a leaf or stem or root crop, and you can usually find some form of organic material that will help grow these vegetables well.

To further illustrate this point, a good first-year crop for any vegetable garden is potatoes. They seem to be a good ground cleaner. By that I mean that they are a large enough crop that you can see any major weeds that come up in between them. And they grow extremely well on freshly manured ground. So, they are well suited to the first year.

Where I trained in England years ago we had an enormous compost pile, and some of the best potatoes that ever grew in the garden grew right on the well-rotted compost. They usually came from potatoes that had been discarded or perhaps even potato peels that had been thrown out. We got terrific early potatoes...those little ones that are so good with peas and roast lamb first off in the summer...marvellous to eat.

While potatoes can certainly tolerate manure, watch out for other root crops. Fresh manures can cause a tremendous amount of problems for root vegetables such as parsnips, carrots or beets. For example, if parsnips and carrots are put in where too much fresh manure is used, they will suffer very poor or distorted root development and lots of forking and breaking up of the root, not those nice conical carrots and parsnips that you really desire.

Other vegetables have their own particular tolerances and intolerances. Beets cannot tolerate very much nitrogen. The members of the *leguminosae* family, legumes as we call them...the beans, the bush beans, the scarlet runners and so forth...do not need added nitrogen at all. They grow little nitrogen-producing nodules on their roots, in which bacteria form all the nitrogen they need. That is why alfalfa, which is related and has the same nodules on its root, is often used as a green manure crop because it is a way of introducing nitrogen to the soil. So, be careful not to put any high-nitrogen fertilizer where you are going to grow peas and beans.

Cabbages, broccoli, brussels sprouts, cauliflowers, any of the group usually referred to as brassicas, really respond well to lime. So, you can see that thought has to go into the types of manures to put in for the types of vegetables you wish to grow in your garden.

There is always the tendency for a first-year gardener to overdo the manure and the fertilizer. If you have a vegetable garden that is going into an area that had been lawn for a number of years, just the very fact of turning over that lawn and adding some manure should be sufficient for you to grow a good crop of vegetables the first year. Dig up the lawn in the fall and put manure in at that time. Then all you need add at the time of seed sowing and planting vegetables, which would be later on in April the following year, would be your choice of granular fertilizer, at a rate of about a handful to the square yard (1 m²).

Remember, more is not always better. You can burn and distort your crops by putting in too much nitrogen. The plants may look wonderful...you will get fabulous leaves...but because of excess nitrogen, very poor root development. If you have grown radishes that have not formed radishes but have gone straight to seed, or carrots that have just formed dumpy little buttons on the bottom yet have strong tops, this is usually caused by over-fertilizing. So, while the fertilizer is important, do not overdo it.

24. *Crop rotation. Shows the best position for the crops in your garden over a three year cycle.*

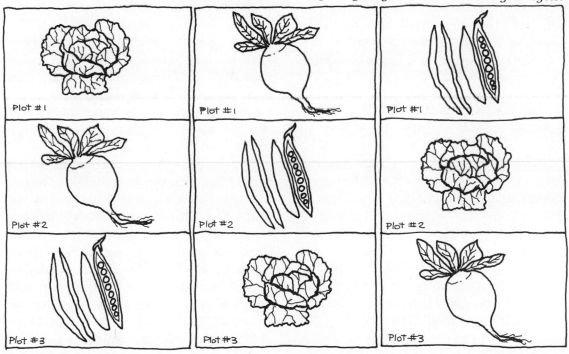

Year one.   *Year two.*   *Year three.*

121

■ CROP ROTATION

It is extremely important that you do not grow the same crops in the same garden plots year after year after year. First, they will take the same component of the fertilizer out of the ground and impoverish the soil in that area. If you grow root crops in the same place every time, they will take all the phosphate out of the soil. Likewise the leaf vegetables such as spinach and greens will take the nitrogen out of the soil. So, it is very important to move things around, perhaps on a three-year crop rotation. The accompanying illustration will help you to decide which vegetables to grow where.

In addition, if you grow the same crop in the same place all the time a particular root disease or pest drawn to that plant will make its home very nicely in the same soil and affect the crop year after year. Rotating crops is an effective way of cutting down on pest and disease problems in your garden.

■ GROWING VEGETABLES FROM SEED

Many vegetables can be seeded directly outside or started out in a cold frame or greenhouse. This is all part of the fun of growing your own vegetables...putting in the seeds, watching those little things come up. Corn always amazes me. One little corn seed can produce a plant that is over 6.5 ft. (2 m) in height and can give you some wonderful corn for your barbecues on those high summer days.

Seed catalogues are a very good way to find out what seeds are available to you. It is a fun project for those grey days of

January and February when you are sitting around and cannot do any gardening. You can sit and you can plan your garden, deciding what vegetables to grow and where to put them in your garden. Try to keep a little log book. (I tell everybody to keep a log book but I never do it myself.) If you keep a log book recording when you sowed and when you planted anything in your garden on a regular basis, after about five years, it will be the best gardening guide for your home garden that you could ever have because you will know about your local conditions, you will know where you sowed plants and if they worked out, and you will know which crops did best for you and which ones to avoid. Start your log book in January when you are thinking about what to grow for the summer.

Garden centres do not carry just one company's seeds but all kinds of imported seeds from overseas, and seeds from throughout the United States and Canada, even locally grown seeds. They usually get their seed stock in about the middle of February, so that there is plenty of time for you to plan your vegetable garden.

If you are new to the area you might not know what varieties do well. For example, if you have just moved here from the prairies or other areas with good hot summers you might want to grow something like beefsteak tomatoes. Well, beefsteak tomatoes on the coast are usually a dead loss unless you can plant them in a very hot spot in a pot against a south-west-facing wall. Many of the larger, faster growing varieties of vegetables that you had if you lived in areas that enjoy hot summers may not do well, so check around and see which varieties are good for the area. Ask your neighbours to give you some help. The UBC Botanical Garden offers a garden information service, as does the VanDusen Botanical Garden and the Center for Urban Horticulture at the University of Washington. Both of these places would be willing to recommend varieties for your first-year garden.

When you buy your seeds do not be tempted to buy the cheapest. Seeds are becoming increasingly expensive every season, I know. It seems that the price goes up and you get fewer seeds per package, but make sure that you are getting good quality seed. Try to grow something a little different. Experiment a bit. This is part of the fun of gardening. When you buy your seeds or when your order first comes through the mail, if you are not yet ready to sow put the seeds in the bottom of your fridge. Remember, the crisper drawer of your fridge is a great place for storing seeds because it has a constant temperature.

When ordering seeds from a catalogue, for both flowers and vegetables, you will find that some hybrids are referred to as an F_1. You will see a large F and a little 1 just a little lower in the line. These hybrids result from a complex breeding process in which two true breeding plants are crossed to produce a hybrid generation, known as the "first filial" or F_1 general. The advantage of growing F_1's is that they are often more vigorous than their parents and have more uniform characteristics. The selection and careful crossing over a number of years means that F_1's are invariably more expensive than conventional varieties, but you should never save seed from F_1 hybrids because

the next generation of plants will have lost its uniformity. F_1 hybrids do not suit everyone's vegetable requirements, but they are good if you like to grow vegetables for show and want to have them all mature at the same time, or want to have absolutely uniform tomatoes or uniform zucchinis.

The conventional varieties of vegetables have been grown successfully for years. Scarlet Runner pole beans are a good example. Conventional varieties mature over a longer period and often they are preferred by gardeners, particularly if they want to save their own seed. If you get a good crop out of an established variety of something like a pea that you have grown for years, by all means save seeds but make sure when you are saving it in the fall that you take it from one of the best plants of the lot, one that is the healthiest and has produced the best crop. Otherwise there is a danger of the whole variety breaking down.

Once you have bought all your seed and have it there in front of you, you will become restless and want to get on with sowing it early. But do not be tempted on the first warm day in February to sow little tomatoes in pots on your window sill because they will come up very quickly as they respond to the heat of the room. They will grow too fast and become very leggy, and you will not be able to plant them out until the third week of May. It is very important that you not start your seeds off too early.

■ SOIL PREPARATION

Before you begin to sow your seeds inside, you ought to make preparations to sow them out in the garden. You will have dug your soil in the fall or early spring and left it roughly turned over, not finely raked, and in a rather lumpy condition. With those nice drying winds that we sometimes have in March to April you will notice that as the sun hits the ground it dries off the surface and the lumps begin to crumble. It is on one of those days that you want to get out in your sunny backyard with a rake and start to work the soil backwards and forwards, working it down into a nice fine tilth. That means that it all breaks apart very easily, and that you have removed the big rocks and other debris.

Remember that when you are raking, do not just rake from one end to the other, pulling everything towards you, but push your rake backwards and forwards. In fact, for the first raking, it is not a bad idea to use a cultivator. Press those large tines down into the surface of the soil, breaking it up. Just push it backwards and forwards, backwards and forwards. You need not get this all done in one day. You can go out on the first sunny day and spend a half hour working on your soil. Break it down a little, and then the next day or two days later, whenever the sun shines again, you can go and work on it with the rake to really work it down.

Just before sowing your seeds, if you want to use an inorganic fertilizer such as 6-8-6 or another balanced fertilizer, go out and sprinkle it onto the ground at about two handfuls to the square yard (1 m^2). It is very important to emphasize that you should not walk around on a garden if it is still very wet. Sometimes if we get a long wet spring and you want to get started you may be tempted to work

on it before it is time. If so, then try to work out where the rows are going to be and put down boards to walk on between the rows.

Compacted soil will result in many problems unless you are growing onions. They happen to like soil that is fairly well firmed, but most other vegetables like the lightness of soil with some air in it. So do be careful not to compress the soil by walking on it too much before it is dried out. Once it has dried, then go ahead and sow your seeds.

■ SOWING YOUR VEGETABLES

Direct sowing of small seeds such as lettuce and carrots is usually done early in the season, and there is always a temptation to start things really early, but if you watch the garden and notice when the weeds start to germinate freely, then you will know when you can put in some of the cool crops. This is the time to sow such crops as spinach, carrots and lettuce. Work out how much space these crops need, and mark the rows with some little twigs or canes. Then take a good garden line or some straight edge that you can lay down as a guide for making your seed drill. Different people have different ways of making drills. I usually use the back side of the rake, the flat side, and just push it down along the row, making a very small depression yet in a nice straight row.

The next thing to remember is that there is a tendency to oversow everything. Thinning is something that we all usually have to do. It is so easy to get carried away and put in every seed that is in a package. Think about it and sow them very thinly along the row. For example, lettuce will need to end up being about 12 in. (30 cm) apart, so space them accordingly. Of course, with lettuce you can use the young greens for early salads, but think about it and sow very thinly. Remember, if it does not seem that you have put in enough, that usually means that you have sown far more than an average family can use.

Once your first row is sown, carefully cover the seeds very lightly. I usually go along squeezing the soil together over the top of them with my thumb and finger so that they are just covered. Then, with the rake head horizontal to the surface, I tamp it up and down on top of the row to just nicely firm the soil in and give a good level surface. Then the most important thing is to put a label at the end of the row and use a good waterproof pen or a pencil on a wooden label, something that will be durable, so that you know what vegetable you put in, what variety it is, and the date it was sown. If you have brought your log book and have a plan of your garden, mark it in there too, so you have a double record of what you have sown.

Because our summers are often very slow in getting started, it is a good idea to plan on starting some of the warm season crops indoors on your window sill or in a greenhouse or cold frame. Crops such as corn, pole beans, perhaps some of the bush beans, and certainly squash, zucchini and tomato all need to be started off indoors so that there are established plants to put out in the last week of May or the first week of June. Otherwise, if you plant in a very cold season, your plants will take forever to get started because they

need the heat of the summer. Start them off indoors and you will be able to put a decent-sized plant right into your garden.

Soak larger seeds that you are going to start indoors for two to three hours before you sow them. This takes me back to school days. We always used to soak Scarlet Runner pole beans in water overnight, and then we would get a jar and put some blotting paper rolled up inside the jar with sand in the middle and push the bean seeds down in the side of the jar. We would keep the jar in a dark place and watch the seeds germinate. You could see the little root come out and the top grow, and it was all great fun. Soaking seeds puts a real jump on how quickly they will get started. If you just put them in soil it will take them perhaps two to three days to absorb enough moisture for the seed to start to grow. Soaking them two or three hours will speed up that process. With seeds such as corn, peas and beans, I put them in a little tumbler, right on my kitchen counter or somewhere I can keep an eye on them. Then after they have plumped up a bit, take them out of the water, drain the water off and put them in an old pie plate or an old pie dish in between layers of wet paper towelling or wet newspaper. Lie them on your kitchen counter and keep the paper wet. Lift it up daily to see when they start to sprout.

Once they have started to sprout then you can put individual beans or corn into their own little pots, perhaps a 4 in. (10 cm) pot. You know they are going to grow and you can keep them on a sunny window sill. With corn, often I will put two corn seeds per pot and let them grow, maybe just to keep each other company, who knows? Eventually, when they grow one will be stronger, and when you plant them out in your garden, cut away the weaker one so that you are left with one strong plant.

One of the most important factors once you have sown seeds, whether it be indoors or outdoors, is to keep them really well watered. Without moisture they will not grow. Watering is easier to control in pots when you are sowing seeds indoors, but often it is forgotten outside and sometimes in the spring there is a continuation of those drying winds and sunny days which extends into a period of drought. It is very important at that time to make sure to keep the ground well watered. Do not water to the point that you wash the seeds out of their little seed drills, but make sure that you keep them nice and moist in order to achieve perfect germination.

Remember to lay down old twigs, what I call pea sticks, or branches over the rows or even chicken wire to keep off the neighbourhood cats at the initial stage. Otherwise they can do an awful lot of damage raking around in the garden when the seedlings are coming up.

Once the seedlings have germinated in the rows, when the seedlings come up and get to the stage where they will need to be thinned out to give them enough space to develop, you can use some of the thinnings as transplants. If you have sown just one row of lettuce, you can start another row next to them with the transplants. Or, you can use them as an intercrop in between some of the larger vegetables such as brussels sprouts which need to be planted at least 24 in. (60 cm) apart. So, when you are carefully thinning out your lettuce, make sure that you

get some roots on some of them and use them as transplants to put into other areas. I would never have believed it until I came to this area, but it is even possible to transplant beets, as long as you do not break their tap root.

When sowing seeds indoors use very similar techniques to those used when sowing annual flowers in a pot. Make sure that you have good-quality sterilized potting mix, good clean pots and, of course, handy labels. Make your potting mix nice and moist so that when you squeeze a handful of it, it just sticks together. Then fluff it all up nicely in a pile and mix a little bit of superphosphate through it, about a tablespoonful (15 ml) to a regular household bucket or pail full of soil. Mix this through and once that is done then fill your pots just by dropping the soil in lightly so that it piles up just above the surface of the pot. Rake it off level with a flat piece of wood or measuring stick, and then use the bottom of another pot to firm the soil down inside the pot, so that it ends up being about 1/2 in. (1 cm) below the rim of the pot edge and you have a nice flat surface to sow on.

As with flowers, tap the seeds out in the palm of your hand, hold this hand just above the pot and gently vibrate it by hitting it with the other hand. This way a few seeds will fall onto the surface. Some seeds show up very well, such as lettuce seeds which are often white so you can see how many have gone in, while others are black and almost impossible to see, but undersow rather than oversow. Lightly cover the seed with a little soil…if you can see a few of the seed poking through that is alright. Then put them in a warm place with black plastic over the top.

When sowing annual vegetable seeds indoors, sow one thing at a time and do it away from where your soil mix is kept. This way, different seeds will not get mixed up, and any seeds that do get spilled will not accidentally get into your potting mix so that all kinds of things come up in places where they are not wanted.

Once the seeds have germinated, which will take from a week to two weeks depending on what you are growing, they should be put in an area of good indirect light in the house, such as a north- or east-facing window sill, so that they do not get burned by the sunlight. They are large enough to transplant when the seed leaves are big enough to hold between your thumb and forefinger. Then, lightly lift them out of their pots and transplant them into individual little 4 in. (10 cm) pots, or recycle those little baskets from the garden centre that hold six plants.

Whatever you are transplanting make sure that you put them way down in the soil so that the little seed leaves are just resting on the surface of the soil. Lightly push them into place with a finger or pencil and then keep them, preferably, in a cold frame.

If you do not have time to sow your own vegetable plants, garden centres carry vegetables in the early part of the spring with their other bedding plants. A couple of little things to watch out for. When you select vegetable plants make sure that you choose the healthiest-looking ones. With some of the cabbages, certainly with broccoli and cauliflower, if they have been on the shelf in the garden centre for a number of weeks and look a little starved they become very root bound within their basket. If you take them home and plant them out they will immediately go to seed, forming miniature plants which are not usable, or they will just send up a spike and go to seed.

So try to buy good, healthy-looking plants as soon as they come into the garden centre, take them home and plant them as soon as possible.

Labeling is sometimes a problem in a garden centre, particularly with tomatoes. You will see a seed flat full of little pots of tomatoes. Usually only one of them has a label, so that when somebody buys the one with the label, then you are not able to identify the others. Make sure that you mark on the pot at the time of buying what it is that you think you are getting because it can cause you grief later on if you get the wrong variety for your garden. It comes down to common sense. You want to buy good and healthy plants, and any reputable nursery is going to sell good and healthy plants because they hope you will come back year after year to buy them.

■ VEGETABLE SELECTIONS

Listed below are some recommended vegetable varieties for gardens in this region. Some seed catalogues will give the name of the variety as well as how long you can expect them to take to grow from seed sowing to maturity. Some will say 45 days, others 100 days. It is important to know that those are just average figures for all of North America, and there is no guarantee that you will have a harvest within the time specified. This is where your log book will come in handy as a guide to how quickly they will mature in your own garden.

Asparagus. Asparagus is really a herbaceous perennial in that it will stay in your garden for a number of years. Choose a space that can be especially prepared for it and where it can be left for a long time. It is probably best to buy two- or three-year-old asparagus plants from a garden centre because they will give you earlier results, although you can grow them from seed. Good drainage is very important, and you should incorporate liberal amounts of manure when preparing the soil. In the wintertime, prepare a bed about 3 ft. (1 m) wide and at least 6.5 ft. (2 m) in length. Put some boards around so that it is about 12-16 in. (30-40 cm) deep, raised up so the soil stays nice and warm. In the spring work in some more well-rotted compost or manure and then buy your plants. Sow the plants in April in two rows about 18 in. (45 cm) apart each way. You do not have to plant them very deep. Do not plant the new plants or crowns any deeper than about 4 in. (10 cm).

In the first season be very careful about weeding the bed and avoid doing a lot of deep digging because these are very surface-rooted plants. Hand pull the weeds as they appear and shake off the soil, but do not disturb the surrounding soil. When asparagus grow they send up tall plumes of feathery foliage, so you will need to put some sort of staking around to stop them from flopping all over the place. When the foliage turns yellow in the fall, cut it right down and put it in a compost. At the same time top dress the bed, either with manure or with a 6 in. (15 cm) layer of seaweed over the top. Asparagus love a little bit of salt in the soil, so by putting the seaweed on the top, it will get rid of all

the slugs, and it will rot down and nourish some wonderful asparagus for cutting the following year.

Conventional wisdom says that you must not cut a crop until the third season, but none of us in this day and age can wait that long. We are always tempted to cut the odd one the first year and certainly expect to get a crop in the second season. As long as you are feeding them well there should be no problem with this. Never cut any later than mid-June. You should always let some of the shoots mature for leaves, otherwise you will not get very good asparagus. If you have the time to do it, it is worthwhile selecting the male plants, which are the plants that have no berries on them. The plants that have berries on them do not produce the best asparagus, so if you can bear to dig them up and get rid of them and just keep the male plants, they will be much better.

Broad Beans. Because many people in this part of the world came from the United Kingdom, this is a plant widely-enjoyed in this region. In North American catalogues they are usually listed under broad beans but sometimes under Fava. The variety recommended for this area is Broad Windsor Long Pot. If you live in coastal regions of the province where you have a very sheltered garden, you might try to sow these in November. It sounds strange, I know, but they are a good thing to sow where you have had potatoes, for example. Just work some well-rotted manure into the soil to about 6 in. (15 cm) deep, level it off, and then sow your broad bean seeds. They will start to germinate and stay as little seedlings throughout the winter. In a difficult winter you might lose them, but chances are they will over-winter because they like cold growing conditions. Otherwise, a good time to sow them is in February, as early as possible. Because they are large seeds, soak them for two to three hours before planting.

Bush Beans. Bush beans are wonderful. They are very useful for growing in containers, in barrels for example, or in raised beds. They are very fast maturing and best started off inside about the middle of May. Again, because they are large seeds, soak them for two to three hours. Sow them into little individual pots and then plant them out the last week of May or first week of June. Two good ones for this area are Contender and Improved Tender Green. While both of these are useful as an early vegetable, you can have very good success using them for late sowing in July when you have pulled up other vegetables in the garden and have some space. Try a late July sowing for some fall beans.

Pole Beans. These have always been magical to me because they grow so rapidly. It always reminds any of us, I am sure, of reading Jack and the Beanstalk. The traditional one to grow is the Scarlet Runner, or if you know some Italian friends they have probably introduced you to Romano beans. Scarlet Runners tend to get a little stringy when they are left on the vine, but Romano beans stay nice and tender and snap easily even when you can see the beans forming inside. Start off both varieties inside by soaking them, starting in mid-May, then plant them out in the first week of June.

Wax Beans. A good one is Honey Gold. Deal with them exactly the same way as you would the bush beans.

Beets. Beets are always wonderful to grow, not only for their tasty roots but also for their tops which can be used as greens. I happen to like those little early ones that you can cook and use in salads; the Early Red Ball is the best for this purpose because you are going to use them all early on in the season. But if you want one that is going to last a little later in the season, try Ruby Queen. Beets like cool growing temperatures, so the earlier you can get them in the ground the better. If we have a very early season, sow beets perhaps the last week of March, but definitely by early April they should be sown directly into your garden. Remember that you can transplant beets and they will grow mature roots as long as you do not break the tap root when transplanting them.

Broccoli. Everyone loves broccoli. It produces so early in the garden. One head of broccoli buds will form on each plant and then when you cut them off, more side shoots will grow, giving green vegetables to harvest as early as late June or early July. A good one is Italian Early Sprouting and another is Southern Comet. Both are good for this area. Broccoli should be started off inside a greenhouse or cold frame, or on a window sill. Sow them in the middle of March, and then when they are large enough transplant them into pots and put them into the cold frame, ready for planting out in April with the main part of your vegetable garden planting.

Brussels Sprouts. Because of our mild winters you can grow your own brussels sprouts to eat with Christmas dinner or whatever winter holiday you celebrate. The nice thing about brussels sprouts is that they can really stand the frost. Some varieties are extremely hardy. One that you might have a little difficulty finding is called Roodnerf Late Supreme, and another popular one is Jade Cross. I usually like to sow these in the garden either the last week of May or early June. For that purpose you will probably need to leave a little area of your garden as a seed bed so you can sow the seeds and then transplant them or thin them out so they make decent plants.

Cabbage. You can buy cabbage plants in garden centres or grow them yourself. A very good early variety is called Early Marvel. If you are going to sow it yourself,

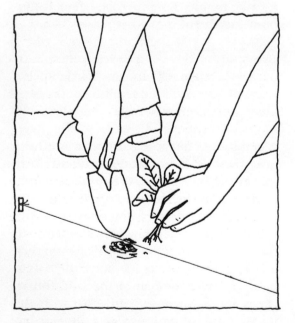

25. *Planting cabbages in rows.*

sow it in a pot inside in March, transplant it and have it ready for planting out in April. For summer or mid-season cabbages you could direct sow outside one called Danish Ball Head. It has very good firm heads of cabbage ideal for making coleslaw. Another nice aspect of cabbage is that in our mild winters they will stay in the garden and tolerate a tremendous amount of frost. One that I like is called Late January King. It is extremely tolerant of cold temperatures, and you would sow it in the same seed bed where you are going to sow your brussels sprouts, the last week of May or the first week of June.

Carrots. Probably the nicest early carrot is Early Bird Nantes. It likes cool germination temperatures, so if the weather is warm towards the end of March, you could sow some at that time. Then you could try another row or two in April. At that same time in April you could sow a good later carrot, ideal if you like to make your own carrot juice, called Royal Chantenay. The interesting thing about this variety is that it can be resown again in July. A late sowing of carrots is really super because that means you can have carrots that start to mature in the fall. If you have well-drained soil, you can put some leaves over the top of the carrots and leave them in the soil, digging them as you need them right into the winter. A real problem with carrots is the carrot root fly, and you would be wise to sow them under some Remay cloth.

Cauliflowers. Early Snow Crown is hard to beat for this area as an early cauliflower. Start it off inside in March in pots, transplant it, put it in the cold frame and then have the plants ready for putting out in April. There are actually overwintering cauliflowers that produce their florets very early in the spring. In Europe this is quite a common crop, in Holland and in Britain, and the seeds are available here for a variety called Armado. You would sow the seeds of this in an area of your garden that is free in July and August. Sow them thinly and transplant them into an area that can be left for a whole winter. They are very frost tolerant, known to withstand temperatures down to about -20° C (-4° F). They will produce marvellous heads of early cauliflowers in the spring. Do try them...they really are wonderful.

Celery. Celery is another terrific plant to grow here, but the slugs love the celery so you will want to refer to the section in this book on pest control to learn how to deal with these. For an early-maturing summer celery a good one to use is Golden Self-blanching. It could be started off inside in March in pots or in the cold frame so that you have little plants to put out in the spring. For your main crop, Utah Improved has to be the best for this area. Start it by sowing the seeds outside in April. With celery, both the self-blanching and the main crop, it is very important to grow it in a trench (see illustration for leek trench) so that you can throw earth up around it to blanch it and produce nice white stems. There are several ways of protecting it from the soil. You can save your milk cartons, cut the top and the bottom out and slide them over the plant when it is growing. You can also use lengths of plastic drain pipe, or you could wrap them in wax paper. Utah Improved

tastes best later on in the season after it has had the first frost on it. In fact, it is very tolerant of frost and can be left in the garden and used right up until the end of December for those early winter salads. That is the time of the year when you need some fresh greens.

Chard. Chard looks like giant spinach but has wide white centre stems. Fordhook Giant is a green form with very strong green leaves and white centre stems. There is also a red form called Rhubarb Chard. Both of these are delightful vegetables to grow. You can steam the green part separately from the stems if you want to. Direct sow early if possible. Chard is like beets and spinach...it needs a really cool start. So, as early as the weather warms up in late March or early April try to get them sown. Also, you might have success with a late sowing, particularly of the Fordhook Giant. When you do that July sowing of carrots try a row of chard. Chard is also quite winter hardy and in a mild winter it will send up little fresh shoots whenever there is a warm spell in January and February. So, it could be considered to be a winter vegetable too.

Corn. There are two varieties of corn that are good for this area. One is called Early Extra Super Sweet, which matures quite quickly. The other is Golden Jubilee. The Jubilee corn is widely grown up in the Chilliwack area of the Fraser Valley and it is so sweet and so good. The thing to know about corn is to start it off inside, soaking the seeds for two to three hours. Start it off inside about the second week of May so that you have some nice plants to be planted out in the first week of June.

Corn loves heat, and remember to plant it in blocks, not in a long single row across the garden. It needs to be in blocks, about one yard (1 m) square, so that the plants can get wind pollinated easily. If they are in a row they tend not to get pollinated and you will get no corn at all.

Cucumber. Cucumber is another hot-season crop but well worth growing in your garden. Start these seeds off mid-May indoors in little individual pots either on your window sill or in your greenhouse. They germinate very quickly, so do not leave them in the pots long. You need to time it so that they will be ready for planting out in the first week of June, so start them in mid-May. One that I love that is never bitter is called Sweet Slice. Another one I like is the Lemon cucumber. They look just like little lemons. These are excellent in a salad.

Kale. Kale is a must for a winter vegetable. Curly kale is the old name for it because it has very curled foliage that looks much like parsley and reaches the height of a brussels sprout plant, about 18 in. (45 cm). There is an excellent F_1 hybrid for this area called Winter-bor. It is extremely frost tolerant and should be sown at the same time you would sow brussels sprouts and January King cabbage, that is in May or June, in a seed bed in your garden. Then put it out somewhere where you had an earlier crop, where it can stay over the winter.

Leek. Leeks are a must for leek soup in the winter. Start the seeds inside and transplant them. Actually, you can get away with starting them in a pot at about the third week of March so that they can then be transplanted directly into the garden. A good one for this area is Giant Musselburgh, and another one very good for winter hardiness is Dorabel. Leeks need to be planted in the bottom of a trench. Dig out a trench about a spade's depth and two spades' width and work some good manure and organic material into the bottom. Plant your leeks in a double row in this trench, and then as they grow cover them up with earth. This produces those lovely long white stems on the leeks. Leeks are very good for winter use, so they are well worth growing.

Lettuce. Lettuce can be direct sown as soon as the weather warms up. It can also be sown on and off throughout the season. Great Lakes is a good head-type lettuce which has been very successful for years and works well, but I like a more crispy lettuce and go for the romaine types. A very nice one is called Volmaine Co. Some other vegetables, such as brussels sprouts, need to be spaced fairly far

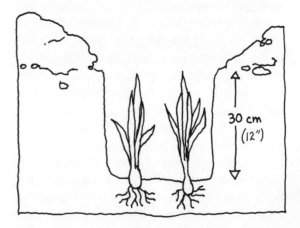

26. *Leek trench bordered by excess soil.*

apart because they are going to take up a lot of space, and they look silly when you first put them out. So, you could sow radishes in between them, plus a quick crop of lettuce. Lettuce are so easy to grow that you can do double-cropping all around the garden.

Onions. For a spring-bunching type the White Lisbon is the best to grow. Direct sow this in rows in the garden in April, and as they start to be a usable size you can thin them out. This is a nice bunching onion for those spring and summer salads. Start off main crop onions probably about the middle of March, with the leeks. Two goods ones are Canada Maple, which forms incredibly large delicious onions which you want to use before

wintertime comes around, and then, to be stored for later use, Autumn Keeper. If you sow them about the middle of March they will be ready for transplanting into your garden as little seedlings. Some people try onion sets which you can get from garden centres, but the birds are forever pulling them up when you put them in so I like to put in the little plants if possible.

Parsnip. Parsnip is another winter vegetable which is very tasty roasted around roast beef, if you like that sort of thing, and is great for using in soups. Parsnips should be sown early in the season, as soon as the weather warms up in late March or early April. It is a very sensitive seed that should be kept at a constantly cool temperature. Once the package has

As the leeks grow, gradually refill the trench with the soil. Covering the base of the plants like this produces long white stems.

133

been opened the seed starts to disintegrate right away and it can take sometimes two to three weeks to come up. To create a good setting for germination, take an iron bar, such as a crowbar, and push it down into the earth to make holes about 12-18 in. (30-45 cm) deep. Fill these in with some very fine sifted rich soil, sowing two or three parsnip seeds on the top of each one of these cores. That way, when they germinate you can select the strongest and let it grow and it will form a marvellous conical parsnip under the ground. Parsnips should be put in an area of the garden where they can stay for a long time for use in the winter, and they always taste better after the first frost.

Peas. Everybody loves peas. Sow them in March or April, the earlier the better. There are so many to choose from, but Sugar Snaps is one of the favourites. It needs plenty of room to grow because it gets quite tall, up to about 6.5 ft. (2 m) in height. Sugar Snaps tend not to get stringy, and you can cook the whole thing, pod and all. If, however, you like to have peas directly from the pod there is a strange-looking pea called Novella that has very few leaves and lots of tendrils and does not grow too tall, so very often you can get away without staking it. Remember, do not be too heavy handed with nitrogen around peas because they produce their own.

Peppers. Peppers are heat-loving, hot season crops, and they only do well in good hot summers. They should be started indoors about the same time as tomatoes, the middle week of April. Grow them in good light once they have germinated; a

greenhouse or a cold frame is ideal. If you like a semi-hot pepper, Hungarian Hot Wax is a great one. It has nice, conical-shaped fruit which goes quite an orange colour in the fall and becomes hotter with age. If you want just green peppers, Early Canada Bell is for you. By starting them in the middle of April, they will be ready for planting out the last week of May.

Potatoes. Potatoes should be started not from seed but from seed potatoes, and it is very important that you go to a garden centre and buy certified potato seed. Do not try to grow ones that are left over from the supermarket. You can run into all kinds of problems. There are two very good varieties for this area which should be planted as early as March or April. One is called Early Warba and is great for very early new potatoes. Netted Gem is another very good variety for this area. It is much more tolerant of potato scab, which might be a problem in your garden. You can take out a trench and plant these directly onto well-rotted compost or manure and they will produce very fine potatoes.

Pumpkin. Pumpkins are always fun to grow, particularly if you have children around, but they do take up an awful lot of room in the garden. Start them off mid-May because you want them to be just right for planting out the last week of May. There are many to choose from, and people do try to grow the Atlantic Giants here, but they need very hot temperatures and very rich soil. One that I like just because it has that lovely deep orange colour is called Jack O'lantern. It can be used for making pumpkin pie and is great to use for decorating around Thanksgiving and Halloween.

Radish. Radishes are one of those crops that you can start to sow fairly early in the season when the weather warms up and can continue sowing on and off throughout the season as intercrops between other crops. They take about a month to mature and are lovely for salads. They tend not to like the heat of the summer, so are best treated as a spring and late summer salad crop. You cannot beat Scarlet Champion or French Breakfast. Both are very good. They need lots of moisture in the soil, or they will get very hot and bitter.

Rutabaga. In the old country these are often referred to as Swedes. They are really like a winter turnip and are a great winter vegetable. Sow them in May and thin them out in the area that you want them. You cannot transplant them; they have to be sown directly. Sow them in little clumps about 6 in. (15 cm) apart or more. The best variety for this area is called Altasweet. They are just a marvellous vegetable if you like to make stew in the wintertime. Imagine being able to go out right the way through November to March and dig these from your garden for a fresh winter vegetable.

Spinach. Spinach is best sown as soon as the weather warms up in late March or early April. There are two good varieties for this area and both are just a one-shot deal which you harvest right away. I have never had much luck with what they call perpetual spinach in this part of the world because once we get into our hot sum-

mers they tend to bolt and go straight to seed. The best varieties are Melody and Olympia. With these, use some of the leaves to start off with and then eventually the whole plant.

Squash. If you want a vegetable to encourage you to become a gardener then zucchini squash are the best to start off with because they are always successful. They like fairly rich soil, with lots of well-rotted manure or compost worked in. Start them off indoors about the middle of May so that they are ready for planting out about the end of the month or the first week of June. A good bush zucchini is called Black Beauty zucchini. It forms many little zucchinis which are best harvested when they reach a length of about a little under 12 in. (30 cm). If you let them go any longer than that they can be used but are not really tasty. The other squash that a lot of people like in this area, especially to harvest and keep for winter use, is the Table Queen squash. This is an acorn squash which keeps well in a cool basement or storage room. I want to suggest one more and that is Vegetable Spaghetti squash. It is a marvellous thing because when you steam it the inside of it breaks apart like long strands of spaghetti and is very tasty. I have had lots of fun in growing it in this part of the world so I recommend it to you.

Tomatoes. Tomatoes are always a very "iffy" crop on the West Coast. It is a rare summer that you get lots of ripe tomatoes in your garden, unless you live farther inland where you get hotter days. In coastal regions I think that if you have the room you should definitely grow Sweet 100 tomatoes. They are cherry tomatoes that come on long, very beautiful trusses, anywhere from fifty almost up to a hundred on a truss. They taste the way old tomatoes used to taste and are great for picking and coming again because they produce tomatoes from the middle of summer right through until the frost. I did say if you have the room for them, because once staked and grown up as a single stem, they can reach a height of almost 6.5 ft. (2 m). If you like a regular-sized tomato then Early Cascade is an excellent choice for this area. Tomatoes should be started off indoors in April, plants planted in individual pots, and should be ready for planting out the third or fourth week of May.

Turnip. People often confuse turnips with Swedes, but turnip really is a summer vegetable in this part of the world. Purple Top White Globe is the best. Sow it directly into the garden and thin it out in April. You cannot transplant these thinnings, so sow them thinly to start. They are nice white turnips that you can use for grating...they are quite nice raw if they are not too old...or you can use them in summer stews.

No matter how small your garden I cannot think of anything nicer than picking and eating your own fresh tomatoes, beans or corn. There really is nothing to beat the taste of home-grown vegetables.

■ THINGS TO REMEMBER

1. Add well-rotted manure or compost annually.

2. Always rotate crops to prevent overuse of soil and to discourage disease.
3. Keep vegetable gardens weed-free by weekly hoeing.
4. Keep records of which vegetables did well and which did not.
5. Use top-quality seeds or plants for best results.

Greenhouses, Cold Frames and Cloches

Once you have caught the gardening bug and are really involved with it you are always looking for ways to overwinter things, to grow plants that are a little unusual, to try to grow some seeds for yourself, or just to make the season last a little longer. In this chapter, I am going to deal with three devices that help to make gardening a year-round activity.

■ GREENHOUSES

First and foremost you need to sit down and ask yourself why it is that you want a greenhouse. What do you expect it to do for you? There are various forms of greenhouses. You can have an unheated house, just a greenhouse built in your garden somewhere that has absolutely no heat in it at all. It will have its use, like a giant cold frame if you will. The only drawback is that as soon as it freezes outside it is going to freeze inside your greenhouse. It would only be useful in cooler areas for growing tomatoes and cucumbers in the summer.

Then you can go on to a cool greenhouse. A cool greenhouse means that it has some form of heating that keeps the minimum temperature around 5°-8° C (40°-46° F). This type of greenhouse will enable you to keep your fuchsias, your geraniums, your marguerites, all those sort of things inside for the winter. It will allow you perhaps to grow some late vegetables in pots, but most importantly it would allow you to start and grow all the bedding plants and vegetable plants that you need for the season. You will also be able to use it for raising cuttings of fuchsias and perhaps some houseplants, so it can be very useful.

A heated greenhouse becomes a rather more expensive commodity because what you are going to do is try to keep the minimum temperature around 10°-16° C (21°-61° F). With lights you certainly could grow some tropical crops. You could probably even grow tomatoes in the winter, and perhaps orchids. But then you would have to specialize in those warmer crops and would not be able to use the greenhouse for your bedding plants in the spring.

Probably for starting out the best one to have is a cool greenhouse, one that is slightly heated.

Having made that decision, how big do you want your greenhouse to be? This is always a difficult problem because no matter what you start off with it will never be large enough for you. When sowing seeds on the window sill, it will not take long to fill up the sill with two or three varieties of bedding plants, but the sky is the limit when you have a greenhouse, so where do you stop? You will have to set yourself some limits. A reasonable starting size for a greenhouse in a house garden situation would be 8 ft. wide by 11 ft. long by 8 ft. at the roof peak (2.4 x 3.3 x 2.4 m).

Having decided on the size you will next have to decide where to put the greenhouse. Various factors enter into your decision. First, you must have some form of heat, which means that it must be close to an electrical supply. If it is going to be a free-standing greenhouse, it can be sited just about anywhere in the garden. For example, if you have electricity in the garage which is at the bottom of the garden by all means put it near there. When making a decision about siting you also must think about how much light you get in your garden. Only you will know this best. You do not want to put a greenhouse under trees. It needs to be in an open situation where it gets as much light as possible because, while too much light or heat from the sun can be a problem, you can always overcome that by shading your greenhouse. Try to stand it somewhere where it gets all-day sunshine. It is better to align a greenhouse north to south so that it gets the broadest exposure to the sun in the morning and in the afternoon.

The next decision will be what type of material you will use to build your greenhouse. You could use either wood or metal. I prefer aluminum because it is easier to care for. The metal does not corrode and usually the glass fits better and you get fewer leaks. Certainly, a wooden greenhouse looks very nice, but it will leak and you have the problem of keeping it painted or preserved over the years to make it last. If it was my choice, I would definitely go with an aluminum greenhouse. The question often comes up at this point whether plastic or glass is best for greenhouse windows. Maybe it is just tradition, but I really do believe that glass is better. I have no scientific facts on which to base this opinion, but I just think that a glass greenhouse works best. I have seen orchids and other plants grown very successfully in plastic greenhouses, I must admit, but even though we are told that plastic lasts forever, it does break down eventually in the weather. So glass is the way for me.

If you buy your greenhouse from a builder then the design will already be in place. But if you are going to go ahead and try to build one of your own, likely you would not build it from metal but from wood. There are some things you need to think about. Good air circulation in a greenhouse is an absolute must. The reason for this is that if you have stag-

nant air the humidity from the plants and the stale air would be a haven for all kinds of fungus diseases. So, it is desirable that you have two vents in the roof of your greenhouse, one on either side. They can be hand-operated, or they can be automatic, but you definitely should have ventilation.

If money were no problem and I could afford it, then I would have a greenhouse that had a door at each end. I think that is very useful. It helps with air circulation in the summer. Greenhouse doors are manufactured now with a glass panel that slides up and a fly screen on the inside so that you can leave it open to facilitate good air circulation. If you cannot have a door at each end, then give some thought to having an automatic extractor fan at one end of the green-

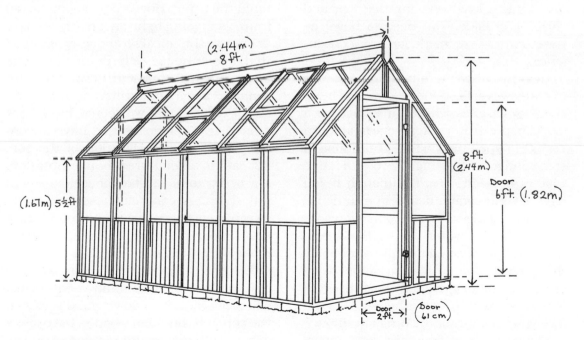

27. *Typical backyard greenhouse.*

house, at the opposite end from the door, so that you can pull air through it at those warm times of the year that start during April, and certainly in the summer if you are going to use it for growing tomatoes and cucumbers. You will need to have good cross-ventilation as well. A small greenhouse may not have side vents, but it is something to which you could give some consideration. If you can draw the air through from one end to the other that is usually sufficient.

Another consideration when choosing the site is that you should be able to have a water outlet, a pipe brought in with a faucet inside the greenhouse. This way you can fix up an automatic watering system quite inexpensively, if you are going to be growing some summer crops in there. Just for filling your watering can to water seedlings in the spring, you do not want to keep opening the door and running outside. You need to have the water right there inside for your convenience.

Heat can be brought to the greenhouse in many ways. Propane or kerosene heaters give off fumes. These can be used as a backup, preferably a kerosene heater, if a very cold spell puts your greenhouse in some danger of freezing. The best heating system is electric heat, although if you have a gas hot water heater in your house and are ambitious you could consider running a hot water line to the greenhouse if it is close enough. But probably the easiest way is to use some basal electric heating pipes along the full length of both sides of the greenhouse. This will give you a very good heating situation.

Electricity also becomes very important for light in the greenhouse. The first thing you think about a light is that you will need to put one up on the ceiling to allow you to work on the long dark evenings. But think about adding a light source to help your seedlings in dull weather, which we can have in the spring, or after you have put on your shading, or as supplementary light to extend the season. If you are going to do this, have some hooks put up where you can hang a light unit that can be raised and lowered. This enables you to have your light source close to your seedlings whether they be on the bench or down on the ground, at least as close as 12 in. (30 cm) above the seedlings so that they get full benefit from the artificial light. Definitely consider this when you are putting the electrical outlets into your greenhouse.

Once all of this is decided then you will need to think about how you are going to build the thing. How are you going to set it up? Is it going to be on a concrete base or open to the soil? I strongly recommend that a greenhouse be built on a concrete base. A soil floor could perpetuate, for example, a soil fungus disease or a bacterial problem that will come back year after year. Then you would have to contemplate liquid sterilization of the soil, not easy in a home greenhouse situation. Far better to have a solid base of cement put down. A concrete base is easy to sweep, easy to scrub down. If you do have a solid floor of concrete or other material, make sure that it is sloped for drainage, or better still have a drain installed.

If you buy an aluminum greenhouse it will probably be set down not directly on the concrete but on a wooden base of 4 x 4 in. (10 x 10 cm) pieces of wood sitting on the cement. This means that your greenhouse is more or less portable. If you sell your house and move away, it is possible to take apart your greenhouse and move it with you.

On one side of your greenhouse, preferably the east side, you should install a bench. The bench should be built to the most comfortable height for you to work at. You can use a bench to stand your seedlings on, your pots, your overwintering fuchsia and so forth. You can also hang or store things underneath the bench. Also consider adding some brackets along each side that would allow you to put up and take down some glass shelving, which is very useful when you are growing seedlings but which you may not need all year. You want to bring seedlings up as close to the light source as possible. A shelf is a handy place to have all your little seedling pots, and then when you transplant things they can go into flats down on the bench or under the bench for shade until they establish themselves.

If you want to grow a lot of seedlings then you could install a temporary bench on the west side too, which will give you as much space to work with as possible. However, I would let the west side be used mostly for some summer crops of greenhouse tomatoes. I mentioned in the vegetables section that tomatoes are sometimes a hit-and-miss crop in this area. If you have a greenhouse you can start them off nice and early in the season in those deep, black plastic nursery pots. You could also grow a crop of tomatoes and some cucumbers inside, down the west side of the greenhouse. The same nursery pots should be large enough to grow a decent plant as long as you give it adequate watering and feeding.

It is also a good idea, early on, to build yourself a bin on casters that can run underneath the bench on one side. This bin can be used for keeping your sterilized potting mix. When you mix it yourself it is nice to have it mixed ahead of time and kept in a bin under the bench so that it is the same temperature as the greenhouse. This is better than bringing in a bag of cold potting mix perhaps from a garden centre where it has been outside and trying to use it right away.

One essential instrument for the greenhouse is a maximum/minimum thermometer. This is a U-shaped glass tube filled with mercury with the temperatures marked on both sides, one for minimum temperature and the other for maximum temperature. Metal markers inside the tubes rise and fall, sticking at the day's high and low temperature. If you were concerned and wondered how cold your greenhouse got last night or how high the temperature inside reached on a sunny day, this thermometer will give you the only accurate indication. Even if you have an automatic system which cuts the heater on and off, if the sun comes out and the vent does not open properly it can get far too hot in the greenhouse. If the vent did not close properly at night on a very cold frosty night, then you could run into problems too and this is one sure way that you can keep a check on it.

If you buy a manufactured greenhouse, most likely it will have incorporated at least one automatic vent opening at the top. There are several on the market. There is one that has oil inside in a little cylinder that expands or contracts with the heat and automatically opens the top.

If you cannot afford to have an automatic vent opener then leave your greenhouse closed on very cold days. One nice aspect of the hand-operated ventilators is that you can open a vent on the side that faces away from the prevailing winds so that the cold wind does not blow in or you can open a vent just a crack. Automatic ventilators are the answer if you want to make things very easy on yourself, or if your leisure activities sometimes take you away for the weekend, or if you are just not going to be there on a daily basis to keep an eye on the heat in your greenhouse.

In the spring, as the sun starts to heat up, sometimes as early as March and certainly by April it can reach such intensity that it can burn your seedlings. Then you will need to shade your greenhouse. One solution is a whitewash-type material called Cool Ray™ specially designed to spray or paint on glass. It blocks out all the burning rays of the sun but allows the good ones through. In a climate such as ours where we get a lot of rain, certainly after our October or November rains, most of it will have washed off. Even if not, it is very easy to use a cleaning brush on the end of a hose to wash the excess Cool Ray™ from the glass later on in the season. If you can afford it, install automatic blinds that pull up and down as the light changes. Or use old bamboo or nylon window shades that roll up and down. These can be put up early in the season, either on the inside or the outside of your greenhouse. The advantage of shades is that on dull days when you need all the light that is around to get inside the greenhouse you could leave the shades up. Once you have applied Cool Ray™,

you have cut down on the light intensity on those days when there is no sunlight outside, when it is cloudy. That is when the added advantage of supplementary fluorescent light can be very helpful to your seedlings.

Cleanliness is very important to the everyday running of a greenhouse, and you must always get rid of garbage. There is a tendency to pick off dead leaves and various other things and drop them under the bench to be picked up later. Do not do this, because it will encourage bugs to come into the greenhouse and fungus diseases to get started. Have a little garbage pail and get rid of your garbage on a daily basis. Always use clean pots when starting out your seedlings or doing any potting up. Make sure they have been washed in some household disinfectant before you use them. If it is a clay pot this should have been done several weeks before use so that the disinfectant has had a chance to evaporate out of the pot. At least rinse out pots several times.

Always keep it clean under the benches. Do not pile things up and keep them there. Have a shed somewhere else, a potting shed for working in so that all pieces of soil and rubbish get taken away each time and are not left underneath the bench. The bench itself should not be a solid plank. It should be open to allow good air circulation up through the plants to cut down on fungus diseases. Sweep the floor regularly and scrub it down at least twice a year using a household bleach. Do this after you have moved your plants out of the greenhouse.

Some people think about having a lean-to or a sunroom extension put onto their house that they can use as a greenhouse.

But you know, it really becomes a whole different thing, an extension to a living space. First of all you will need to double glaze it to reduce heat loss. Certainly you will need some form of ventilation, but otherwise it will be a room that is run more or less at the same temperature and humidity as your home. Sunrooms are wonderful in the wintertime on a sunny day. You can put out a table and some chairs and eat meals out there, but you would not use this space as a growing greenhouse. You might have one or two pots of specialized plants in there, perhaps a bougainvillaea or hibiscus or flowering maple, but it certainly would not be used as a growing greenhouse. Then again, if you progress from that and want to specialize in a particular crop, you can build an extension which is more like a greenhouse. I have a friend who has a marvellous greenhouse for growing her orchids built as a glass room that runs off the kitchen. It is totally separate from the house so that if she needs to use any pesticides or anything that is going to be a problem within the house it can be closed off. It is not run as a room in the house but rather as a separate room with its own heating system, specialized misting units and circulation fans.

■ COLD FRAMES

A cold frame is most useful to a home gardener in the spring, when you buy your plants or grow your own seedlings and it is still too early to plant them in the garden. You need somewhere that is intermediary between the heat of a home and a greenhouse, which is around 20° C (68° F) and the 4°-5° C (39°-41° F) it still is outside at night. A cold frame enables you to "harden off" your plants, the term that gardeners use that means getting your plants used to outdoor conditions.

Cold frames can also be used in areas which never get very hot summers. Out at UBC the Food Garden is stuck out on a point of land and we get a lot of wind off the water, so it is always cool out there. Even if it is hot downtown, out on the point you wish you had brought a sweater with you. Using cold frames allows exposed gardens such as that to grow some of the more heat-loving crops. Aubergine,

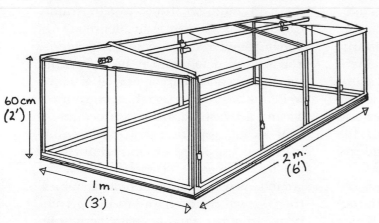

28. *Prefabricated aluminum cold frame.*

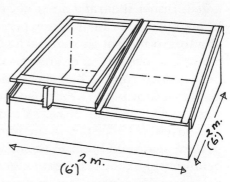

Home-made wooden cold frame.

143

or eggplant, do extremely well in a cold frame. You can use a cold frame to grow melons in that type of situation too, or a very late crop of carrots or lettuce. One year we had winter lettuce in a cold frame that we were able to cut and use over the Christmas holidays. A cold frame enables you to lengthen your garden season as well.

Traditional cold frames were called Dutch Lights in the old country. They were built 6.4 x 3 ft. (2 x 1 m) oblong, usually two, side by side. They had a clear sheet of plastic or glass on the top that was hinged so that you could lift it or close it. The back was 24 in. (60 cm) in height and the front 12 in. (30 cm) in height so that it sloped down to face the sun and also allowed the rain to run off the glass. Some people used old windows that were taken out of homes, or they simply built a homemade wooden frame with treated wood and a glass top that could be opened and closed. Now that gardening is becoming more and more popular, greenhouse builders and garden centres are bringing in other forms of cold frames from the United Kingdom and from other parts of the world. There is one on the market made from a type of aluminum which is like a mini-greenhouse; it goes under the trade name of Crittal™. It is put down in a more permanent situation out in the garden just for lengthening the season and for growing the heat-loving crops. It has glass sides and is higher down the centre so that the glass can be lifted on either side and you can have total access into the frame.

Here again, if I had the choice I would definitely use solid glass panes for the top as opposed to plastic. You run into innu-merable problems with light plastic in the wind; the top is forever blowing away. That is not to say that you should not use plastic, but if you do then you will need to put something like a bungie cord across the top to anchor it down. It is very disheartening to wake up one morning and find the lid of your cold frame in your neighbour's garden, so make sure that if you do use light-weight material it is anchored well. This goes for any frame in an exposed situation.

It is best to treat a cold frame as a permanent structure in a permanent site. If you are going to build your greenhouse on a cement base, why not extend the base and build yourself a little cold frame there? That will keep things really nice and clean and tidy. You could have a cement base for the frame, and you could extend the electric outlet in there and put a soil warming table in the bottom of the frame for the very coldest part of the year. Or you could use it as an extension for growing winter lettuce or for rooting some cuttings.

If you are going to use a glass-sided cold frame for heat-loving crops set out in a garden situation, they are best put down on some sort of open wooden frame. Choose your spot carefully, definitely full sun but sheltered from cold winter winds. You will need to change the soil within the frame each year or enrich it really well. It is best not to use the same crop in a frame all the time, so choose a couple of heat-loving crops and swap them frame to frame every other season so that you do not take the same nutrients out of the ground. As with your hardening off frames, try to set your garden frames in a permanent situation on a wooden or a solid block base so that they will not get moved around.

Like a greenhouse, a cold frame needs some way to regulate its temperature and humidity if it is going to work well for you. You need to be able to open the top on hot days, otherwise it will get so hot in there that your plants will suffer. Unfortunately you cannot put an automatic ventilating sytem in a cold frame. What you can do is cut notches in a wooden stake and attach it to the front of the structure, making sure the notches are deep enough for the lip of the lid to rest in securely. The notches on the stake will allow you to adjust the lid opening according to the weather. You cannot go away for long weekends and leave it closed up without having a neighbour come over to have a look inside. As with the greenhouse, around April the sun gets so strong that it can burn. You will need to put some sort of shading on the glass for the time that you are hardening off your plants. You could use Cool Ray™, or if you felt you could anchor it well, you could use an old piece of material like an old sheet or some burlap which cuts out the intense light but will give enough so that the plants will not get all drawn and leggy.

Hardening off seedlings should be done during the latter part of April and early May. The process takes about three to four weeks, so you will want to put plants out in the middle week in April. In the first four or five nights, leave the top closed. Close it about a half hour before the sun goes down so that you trap some heat inside. After that period, leave the top open a crack at night for the next four or five days. For each successive four or five

day period, leave the top open a little more, so that by the last four days the plants are in the cold frame with the top left off completely. This will gradually introduce them to the outdoor environment, the cooler nighttime temperatures that they are going to have to deal with out in your garden.

If you have a free-standing glass cold frame sitting out in your garden you could start to use it for crops very early in the season. On this coast, even in February if a little frame is kept closed the sun starts to have enough heat to warm up the soil. As early as the last week of February or the first week of March you could put in some early carrots or some lettuce seed. You could certainly put in radishes and would be harvesting these at least one month to six weeks before any of the other crops are ready outside in the garden. And at the same time, you could be starting off eggplants or melons in your greenhouse, so that when the early crops have finished in a frame you could add a little bit more fertilizer to the soil and plant your heat-loving crops in there for the summer. By the same token, when the eggplants have finished, perhaps during September, you could transplant some lettuce seedlings started off elsewhere in a pot or in a container into your cold frame. There is a very good romaine-type lettuce called Winter Density that does extremely well and can be planted in October to grow on through to November for harvest sometime in December. So, you can certainly utilize a cold frame for a much longer season than you would an ordinary open piece of ground.

You can use the cold frames that you have set up near your greenhouse—the same ones you have used for hardening off in the spring, for rooting shrub cuttings which you take in July or August. These cuttings will root much better if they are in some sort of a cold frame situation, and you can keep an eye on them, especially in the lean-to or Dutch Light type of cold frame.

In the cold frame near your greenhouse, if you want to chance it, it is possible to overwinter some fuchsias and geraniums or similar plants in pots. Leave the plants you want to overwinter out in the garden as long as possible and then trim them all back as if you were going to be burying them for the winter. Put them in pots and place these inside the cold frame. When you are raking up your leaves, particularly when they are dry, fill in all around the pots with dry leaves from the garden and put some on the top. Leave the plants in the frame with a barely opened crack so that they get some air circulation. In an average winter that does not get too terribly cold, you would have fairly good success overwintering some of your plants in a cold frame this way.

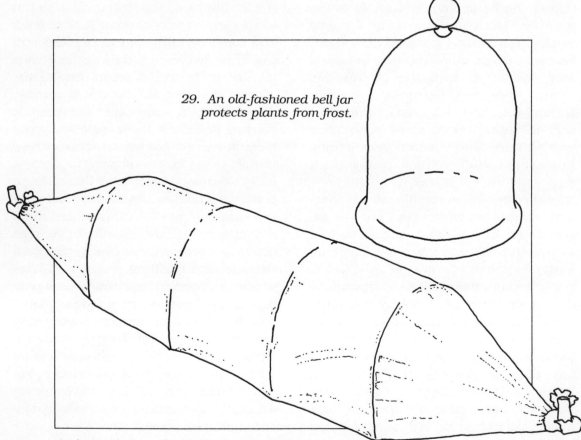

29. *An old-fashioned bell jar protects plants from frost.*

A plastic cloche extends the planting season.

■ CLOCHES

The name "cloche" is European and the idea certainly came from French and Belgium gardeners years ago. When I was a little boy you could buy vast cloches that were real difficult things to deal with. They had a strange little wire clip with a handle on the top and you would clip them all together and carry them very gently and put them over the rows that you had just sown. Inevitably, until you got the hang of putting them together you broke little panes of glass like crazy.

There were also some wonderful bell-shaped cloches left over from Victorian or Edwardian times that were made of blown glass with a little handle on the top which allowed you to lift them and put them over a plant. I have even seen in some gardens recycled big old clear-glass commercial pickle jars put upside down over the top of tomatoes when they are first planted out in the garden, and while they do not look nearly as elegant they work for a little while. Today, the widespread use of plastic and polyethelene makes it very easy to make frames just by stretching everyday plastic over wire hoops.

This has been done widely in New Zealand, where you see acres of fields with rows and rows of these plastic cloches. A company named Kerilea now manufactures a little whole cloche kit that you can put up in your garden. It has four grooved aluminum hoops of about 4 in. (10 cm) wide wires that fit into the grooves that clip at the base of each of these hoops. The four hoops make an area of about 6.5 ft. (2 m) in length, then you anchor the clear plastic at each end with some stakes that are pushed down into your garden,

and tie it up so that it looks like a big long Christmas cracker.

This type of cloche can be put up on prepared soil as early as February, meaning that in March you could sow your crops in the cloche which you would normally be sowing outside in April. Once the cloches have been up for a month the soil has warmed up that much more, so you can really get a jump start on the season. Sow your seeds, whatever crops they might be, and then leave the cloches completely closed until you start to see germination taking place.

Then, on sunny days, simply unclasp the wire on one side of the hoops all the way along and push the plastic up on the side that is away from the prevailing wind so that some air can circulate inside and the sun will shine in making a little sheltered environment. Then close it down at least half an hour before the sun goes down to trap the heat. This is a marvellous way of getting a jump on the season.

One year at the Botanical Garden we built a step planter. It was 3 ft. (1 m) wide and 6.5 ft. (2 m) in length and had three steps on each side. The tallest step was about 24 in. (60 cm) in height, the next one was 12 in. (30 cm), and the last was almost at ground level. The planter was built on an open area that had once been lawn, and we filled it up with some pretty decent soil that we mixed ourselves, putting in some humus. Then we got some very heavy gauge wire and made strong hoops that went right up over the stepped planter and tied the plastic over this frame. In February we filled up the steps with carrots and beets, and in the top we put parsnips because they needed greater depth for the roots. We could have been much more imaginative with our choice of crops. We could have had lettuce or spinach or chard. That thing produced so much food in a small space, certainly enough for a family of two, perhaps with a child. I would strongly recommend that you try something like this to extend your season if you have only a small garden. While we used long-term crops like the parsnips in the middle, once the carrots were finished on the lower steps you could put in a late crop of lettuce or some other late greens. Or you could put in some radishes very early on and then replace them with one of the more warmth-loving crops, perhaps some little cucumbers on the bottom step. A step planter is a marvellous way of having a very productive area in a small space.

You could also build wire hoops over your raised beds and start off some early crops much more quickly than in a regular ground-level gardening situation.

It is also possible to use plastic to extend your season at the latter end. I am a great believer in temperate climates such as this in putting in late crops, such as a July sowing of carrots or bush beans or chard. If you live a little further away from the coast and are going to be bothered by cold weather later in the season, plastic tunnels could be most helpful to lengthen the time that you can grow vegetables in your home garden. Definitely consider putting in plastic cloches.

Recently, experiments have been done with a type of plastic that is perforated. This allows the air to circulate and come through. I have a friend up in the Chilliwack area who has used this to great success in his garden. With perforated plastic you do not have to worry about putting in wire hoops. You simply prepare the soil early, then cover it over to warm it up with a flat sheet of regular plastic, it could be black plastic if you want. When it comes time to sow your crops remove this sheet and sow your plants in rows. Then, spread the clear perforated plastic over the rows and bury it along the sides and at each end of the sown area. It is important to anchor the plastic firmly because wind could be a problem. Once the plastic is well secured just leave it there. As the crop grows it pushes the plastic up and the plants hold up the plastic cloche themselves. The perforations allow air to circulate and the plastic cover amplifies the sun's heat and allows you to extend your season. It does not look attractive but it does work, so it might be something to experiment with in your home garden.

The obvious advantage of using either a cold frame or greenhouse is that you can extend the seasons so nicely at both ends. Once you have invested in a greenhouse you will never look back when it comes to producing your own bedding and vegetable plants in the spring. If you cannot yet afford a greenhouse, with cloches you can be starting and harvesting vegetables a month before everyone else.

CHAPTER 12

Weeds

Weeds are an integral part of any garden, and whether we admit it or not, we all have weeds in our garden. There, does that make you feel better? They really are only a major problem when they get out of hand, and the ones that do are usually the perennial kind such as Bishop's weed, buttercups or couch grass.

If anything about gardening is therapeutic, weeding is. It is so satisfying and you can see your results right away. If you are a little bit mad at the world, you go out and weed your garden and look back and see what you have done, and you feel so much better. The more cultivated areas in your garden, the more open ground there will be for weeds to grow in. So, perhaps it is time to think about reducing the areas that you cultivate. Perhaps it is getting too much for you to do the whole garden, or maybe you like doing other leisure activities and do not have all day, every day to spend in your garden. So why not put more of it in lawn? You could certainly grow vegetables in raised beds and that can cut down tremendously on the maintenance.

Around your patio and sitting-out area, you could have an arrangement of patio pots and tubs filled with colourful annuals in the summer and bulbs in the spring. Then all around the edge of your garden and lawn, along fence lines to hide your neighbour's yard or the street, you could dot in a mix of ornamental and fruit trees together with one or two areas of colourful shrubs that give you seasonal colour. Underneath that you can have ground cover. If you plant your garden for a more diverse planting and reduce the area in cultivated beds, you can reduce the effort needed to control weeds.

■ WEEDING BY HAND

In the opening chapter I wrote about winter digging in a vegetable garden. This can be done in a newly formed flower bed as well. At the end of the season, totally bury all the weeds upside down at least 12 in. (30 cm) deep and most will not come back up again. Some perennial weeds will find their way to the top, but all the annoying annual weeds such as groundsel, chickweed and that wretched stuff called pop or snap weed will go away as long as they are buried roots up. Admittedly, when you turn the soil over you will not totally cover every weed seed, and when the spring comes around and the weather starts to warm up, weeds will start to grow. When they just begin to germinate on the first warm sunny days get out there with your hoe and just hoe them up so that they lay in the sun and shrivel up and die. They will not have a chance to grow and form seed. If you practise winter digging and pounce on the few survivors in early spring, you

should be able to keep down the annual weeds in any cultivated area.

Having mentioned hoes, there are three kinds widely available. There is a draw hoe with a blade like a crooked neck, and as you work forward along the rows pulling the blade towards you in tiny strokes, it chops the weeds as you go. The only problem with it is that you walk on the ground you have hoed. Another is the Dutch hoe, or push hoe, with the cutting blade on the front. There is another type of hoe called a Swoe,™ which has a blade joined in the stem in the centre of the blade so that all the edges are cutting

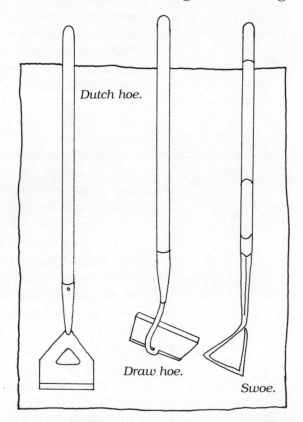

Dutch hoe.

Draw hoe.

Swoe.

30. *Invaluable tools for a weed-free garden.*

edges. As you push and pull it you are actually severing the weeds at ground level. You should always keep your hoe clean and fairly sharp. If you are hoeing in among crops, it takes a little while to develop the proper technique. If the hoe blade is sharp, it is very easy to chop off flowers and newly planted vegetables. When I first started in horticulture as an apprentice gardener I had to hoe in a very formal planting of marigolds. Not yet being able to control my hoe I cut off several marigolds and stuck them back in the ground, hoping no one would notice. Of course they wilted right away and the head gardener soon had to give me a second lesson on how to use the hoe carefully.

Quite honestly a hoe is invaluable. If you find it difficult to bend down and pull weeds and have a large area to deal with, definitely invest in a hoe. You will always have to pull out a few weeds that occur in a row of vegetables or right next to the base of the flowers, but for the open areas, if you hoe once a week, the weeds will never have a chance to grow. My old head gardener believed that and it really is true.

Where do weeds come from, especially if you keep your own garden nice and clean? In your neighbour's yard or an empty lot down the road dandelions, thistles and various other types of weeds grow and the wind will send their seeds into your garden. Or, manure which is straw based or which contains a lot of the weed seeds that have passed through the animal's system without breaking down will introduce the seeds as you spread it around your garden. This is often why something totally different that you have

never seen before will come up the season after a fresh load of manure has been put down.

Hand weeding goes along with this weekly activity. Try to go out in your garden on a daily basis, perhaps first thing in the morning, as I do. Whenever you see a weed pull it out. Particularly in the summertime, if you do this on a daily basis, weeds will have no chance to build up in your garden.

Perennial weeds are tough to get rid of. Bishop's weed got its name because it was the only weed that made the bishop swear. Its botanical name is *Aegopodium podagraria*. There is a cultivated variegated form of it that people plant in gardens. Putting it in a bottomless container such as a barrel and sinking the barrel down in the ground will prevent it from spreading all around the garden. I would never introduce it into an area, particularly a shrub bed or perennial bed, because it would be very difficult to keep in control.

There was an old gardener named Fred Streeter on the radio when I was young in England. He was a great believer in mulching, and he maintained that if you kept mulching an area where a problem weed like *Aegopodium* was growing, and you kept pulling up the weed every time you saw it, it would eventually all come up into this lovely soft mulchy area over a period of years. The weeds would spring up readily and their roots would be easy to pull out from the top layer of soft material. Over the long term, all of the problem weed could be contained and eliminated.

Another perennial weed that is a dreadful problem visually, especially if it gets into shrubs or into a hedge, is the white Morning Glory or *convolvulus,* which is fairly common throughout this area. It has long white runners that seem to go down forever, at least a yard (1 m) down into the soil. In the little house where I live in Kitsilano, there is a bit of bind weed that has been in the garden for the two years that I have lived there. When I first moved in it was all the way up through a rhododendron, and I managed to pull it out by hand as best I could down at the bottom of the rhododendron, but there is a piece of the root that lives underneath the patio and it still surfaces two or three times a year with a lovely new tendril, which I pull off. We have an ongoing relationship.

■ HERBICIDES

Hand weeding is fine for an isolated, individual weed such as this, but if you are driven to distraction by a whole backyard full of something like bind weed, you will have to resort to using a herbicide. The most common herbicides are a hormone weed killer that works down through the leaves to the stem and eventually into the root system and kills the weed plant.

There are several herbicides on the market, some of which still have a 2,4-D base. This is a very dangerous herbicide. Read about it well before you use it so that you are quite clear on what it can do and how much you are supposed to mix up. Then when you mix it be very careful to stay well away from any favourite plant because one or two little drops splashed on its leaves would kill the plant. With rubber gloves on take a little paint brush

and paint the leaves of the weed. Some people put the weed in a bucket of mixed herbicide while it is still attached to the ground and let it soak. But you must remember that whatever leaf it gets on it will kill. So it is only as a last resort that I would suggest that you use any herbicide to get rid of a weed like bind weed, particularly in an area where you are going to be growing vegetables. If you can, just keep pulling out, and pulling out, and pulling out the weeds—eventually you are going to win.

Couch grass or crab grass, or any of the perennial grasses that propagate by underground rhizomes, are best dealt with in a prepared bed by lifting them with a hand fork as they appear. If they get in amongst plants or bushes like currants or gooseberries, little pieces of the root can hide right in underneath the crown of the bush where it is absolutely impossible to dig them out without digging up the bush. In this case, in the fall, sometime during October or November depending on where you live, lift that bush, prune it right back, wash all the soil off the roots and just hand pick out the couch grass that is in amongst the roots. This is a labour-intensive solution but is the only way to stop it from growing up through the bush. Then replant the bush with some fresh soil around it, maybe some well-rotted compost or well-rotted manure. It will take a year to get over being moved, but the weed will be gone.

In areas on the coast and in isolated areas throughout the interior, a marvellous weed that has survived since prehistoric times, Mare's Tail or Horse Tail (*Equisetum*), is the bane of a gardener's life. It is extremely difficult to eradicate. In our roof garden at the CBC Mare's Tail got in underneath the patio blocks and ran along an automatic watering system, popping up in every available bed. All we could do was keep pulling it out until the garden was totally redone, and all the old soil was taken away. Old Fred Streeter's method of deep mulching works for *equisetum,* but it is a long-term job. Applying an herbicide would be the simplest solution. For a garden with a lot of perennial weeds, consider hiring a professional to apply a herbicide. Even this might not be successful after the first application, and you would not be able to grow anything for a season.

In recent years it has been a common practice when planting a shrub border to put down black plastic on the ground around the shrubs and bark mulch on top of that, to hide the plastic and make it look more aesthetically pleasing. This certainly does help to keep the weeds down in a large bed, although it is not always very attractive. Remember to keep enough space open around the bottom of each shrub for water to penetrate and to permit feeding. When it comes to mulching, I prefer to put well-rotted compost or old mushroom manure about 2 in. (5 cm) deep on an annual basis over the area. It looks nice, helps to feed your plants, and helps to improve the quality of the soil in and around your shrubs. But go ahead and use the plastic if that is an easy way for you to deal with this problem.

■ LAWN WEEDS

For some people it is very important to have the perfect lawn. The chief enemies of the perfect lawn are the broad leaf grasses, such as crab grass, that run by rhizomes underneath the ground. These are probably among the most difficult weeds to eliminate. There are selective weed killers to use on the lawn, manufactured to kill only broad-leaf weeds. But anything that is not going to kill your lawn is not going to kill a weed grass.

If you notice broadleaf grasses coming into your lawn early enough in the spring, make a special effort to dig out those areas. Take out a square of turf around the weed and pull the whole thing apart, getting rid of the broad-leaf grass. Fill up the resulting hole in your lawn with some decent soil, level and firm it well and sow a little bit of fresh grass seed mixture on the top or put down a fresh, newly grown sod from a garden centre to replace it.

One of the reasons that I am against using herbicides on a lawn is that lawn grass is a marvellous ingredient to make compost. If you treat a lawn with any weed killers, and then use lawn cuttings in a compost pile, there is a tendency for some of those chemicals to concentrate. A few years ago, a friend of mine asked me if I would come and take a look at a camellia bush in her garden. When it came out in the spring it was totally distorted on one side. On that side of the camellia bush was where the compost pile had been for a number of years. She had been using an all-purpose feeding and weeding fertilizer herbicide combination, and putting grass cuttings on the compost. Over the years the chemical residue had concentrated enough to cause deformity in the camellia bush. Now that was an ornamental plant. If you are going to be putting compost into your vegetable garden, some plants such as tomatoes and cucumbers are very sensitive to herbicides. Herbicide damage can show up in tomatoes several years in a row if compost has been affected. If it upsets the tomato's growth, goodness knows what it does to our insides. So try to keep herbicides off of a lawn if it all possible.

Dandelions also have a great time getting established in a lawn. You can spot treat them with a herbicide, but that means that you cannot put the grass on the compost. Better to dig them out using a long narrow trowel. Try to get as much of the root as possible, or they may come back up. If your lawn is more perennial weeds than grass then really the best thing to do is to rototill and dig the whole area in the fall and start from scratch.

Clovers and trefoils, pretty little things that come into the lawn, are not as easy to control, and if you get a lot of clover in the lawn then it is difficult to treat. Selective lawn herbicides that include MCPA, usually the trade name is Mecaprop™, used in the spring preferably just after a rain when all the weeds are growing on a warm day, will work down through the roots. But again, be warned about the compost pile.

While I am not a great lover of putting copious amounts of high nitrogen on a lawn, a high-nitrogen fertilizer, in theory, should deter trefoils and clovers from coming up because they are legumes. Legumes produce their own nitrogen nodules from their roots and if you add more nitrogen to them, too much will kill them. The grass will get stronger and will crowd them out. An application of a high-nitrogen fertilizer early in the season, followed in the summertime with a more balanced fertilizer that will build up

the roots and make for healthier grass, is a more satisfactory form of control. Weeds will return after a herbicide application, but a stronger, healthier lawn will be more resistant to weeds.

In coastal areas in British Columbia one of the major weed problems in the lawn is moss. Moss in itself is a very beautiful thing and I have always felt that we do not use it as well as we could. Japanese gardens really take advantage of moss and use it as a ground cover. If moss takes over a lawn and you use the lawn for picnics and barbecues, moss will not be durable enough to withstand heavy traffic, but as a ground cover under trees it can be quite attractive. However, if you want to have a nice lawn then moss will drive you to distraction.

In coastal regions, not in the interior, if we do what everyone else does across Canada and apply lots of high-nitrogen fertilizer to our lawns it adds to the acidity in the soil. A typical lawn fertilizer analysis is 10-6-4, the first number representing a high concentration of nitrogen that makes the grass nice and green. But on the coast with our high rainfall the soil is very acidic in the first place, and so if more and more nitrogen is added to the soil the salts will eventually build up and the soil will become very sour. This can lead to all kinds of problems, ranging from moss to slime mould fungus. This is the end result of sour soil in a lawn.

With a new lawn there is a better chance to control this. On the coast people will put down lime in the spring. This helps to sweeten the soil and in theory helps to keep down the moss. Also, instead of using a fertilizer on your lawn, use a more balanced all-purpose fertilizer such as

6-8-6. This will build up the roots which will make for stronger, healthier grass that will choke out moss.

If you move into a new house, and the lawn has a lot of moss in it either because it has too much nitrogen or has been neglected over the years, then in the spring rent a rotary rake from any garden centre, and rake over the lawn. In Victoria and the Gulf Islands you would do it in April, perhaps in Vancouver in early May, up in the interior in late May or early June. Get rid of as much moss as you can. The moss you remove can be composted or used for lining hanging baskets. Remember if you use moss for hanging baskets to pull out all the weed roots first—otherwise they will grow in your hanging basket. After rotary raking, treat the lawn with some lime. Do not put lime and fertilizer down at the same time because the lime has a very adverse effect. It will lock up all the phosphate in the fertilizer. Always apply lime earlier, and at least three weeks should go by before you put down any fertilizer. This can help get rid of moss.

The ferrous ammonium commercial compound mixture sold in garden centres in the spring as a moss killer will give only temporary control. Raking, spiking and aerating the lawn, brushing in some fresh soil and fertilizer to improve the quality of the grass, will help to control the growth of moss.

When a new lawn is sown from seed, no matter how careful the cultivation and preparation of the soil, weeds, mostly annual weeds, will come up. Do not be tempted to put a selective weed killer on a newly sown lawn. Most annual weeds cannot tolerate much cutting back, so the first two or three mowings should get rid of them. Just turn a blind eye to them, forget they are there, because the grass will start to grow and it will choke them out.

There are other areas of the garden where weeds can occur and be a problem. When sowing seeds, always use some form of sterilized potting mix. With new seedlings it is very difficult to distinguish which are flowers and which are weeds. So it is very important to use sterilized potting mix for any seed sowing, or any greenhouse or houseplant potting. This will also help to avoid fungus problems.

The bottom line with weed control is a little bit of hard work. Wherever possible, try to eradicate weeds by hand or by using a fork or spade. If you feel that you must use some herbicides then consult books or Ministry of Agriculture publications on safe herbicide handling. A little bit of hard work and perseverance will give you much more satisfaction and make your garden a much safer place to be.

Pests and Diseases

In recent years there has been much publicity about the overuse of chemical pesticides both in home gardens and commercially. Thank goodness, gone are the days when we felt, as gardeners, that we could go to a garden centre and ask for some sort of spray to put on the garden to keep the plants, whether they be flowers or vegetables, pest free for the whole season. Of course, there is no spray that will do that, and that is totally the wrong way to deal with pests, You only need to go after a pest as it becomes troublesome in your garden.

I stress the importance of non-chemical control wherever possible. There will be times to use pesticides, but only as a last resort. In a commercial garden, cutting back on using sprays can be devastating because if a particular pest comes in it can wipe out a season's crop, meaning lost profits. But in a home garden, pests are more easily controlled. Admittedly, in a large garden it is hard to stay on top of all the problems, but if you keep an eye on things in your garden everyday, you will be able to take care of pests and diseases before they get out of hand.

Certain times of the year bring certain problems. For example, in the summer if cabbage white butterflies are fluttering around, then check the big-leafed vegetables in your garden. If you turn up a cabbage leaf and see a little cluster of orange eggs on the underside, then just squeeze them with your finger and thumb, wipe them off and you have eliminated the whole problem of having to deal with caterpillars at a later stage. There are all kinds of home remedies that you can use for spraying on pests, and I will deal with these later in the chapter. Also, remember to practise crop rotation, for example with vegetables. Sometimes there are overwintering eggs or overwintering spores down under the ground. If the same crop is planted in the same place year after year, it can harbour that pest or disease. Moving it around will cut down on the problem. Correct planting distances are also important to allow good air circulation between plants. This helps cut down on fungus diseases, but it can also help keep pests down because the plants are easier to observe. And, keeping weeds down gives bugs fewer places to hide. Observing these simple gardening practices leads to better control over the whole garden.

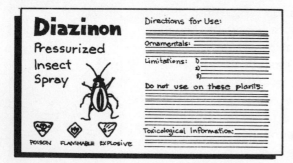

31. *A typical pesticide label. Read the instructions carefully.*

Certain pests seem to come and go in cycles, perhaps over five to ten years. Some years ago in British Columbia we had a plague of crane fly, sometimes called daddy long legs. Large gangling bugs flew around in the summer, banging into lights. But in recent years they do not seem to be as evident. Recently there have been awful problems with scale. Scale sometimes occurs on fruit trees and then moves into the garden onto all kinds of other plants. It can become very debilitating to a tree. What I want to say is that even if you did nothing to control these pests, chances are that the plant will survive in the long term, and the invasion of each pest will subside. The other side of that coin is that when we have gone out and sprayed these particular pests over the years, we end up killing them but also killing all the good little predator bugs which nature provides to keep everything in control. In this way we unbalance nature's own way of controlling its problems. Those little grey larvae with orange-coloured dots that you see when you are out there working in the garden are lady bugs and they actually live off aphids. So for goodness sake, do not go spraying with something that is going to kill them because they are keeping the aphids down for you. More and more, garden centres will be selling predator larvae and bugs for us to introduce into our gardens. In a greenhouse situation it is easy to introduce these predators because it is a controlled environment, and in actual fact many large commercial greenhouses do a lot of their crop protection this way. So think about that when you go out and spray. You are not only killing the bad guys, you are actually killing the good guys too.

I know that in some cases you will be driven to distraction and will feel that you must use a pesticide. In my own home garden just last year, I had a terrible infestation of sow bugs. They were everywhere. Sow bugs are those cute little armour-plated things that hide under old pieces of wood and leaf mould and do not look as if they are going to do a lot of damage, but when my ornamental plants started to grow, like Astrantia which I really love and other little plants, sow bugs would eat off the entire flower bud. I hate to admit it but I used granular Diazinon™ in that situation to try to control the damage that was happening to my perennials.

If you do resort to using chemical sprays in your garden, always wear rubber gloves, and always wear a mask when you are mixing them. Do not do it anywhere near where you are going to have food. Read the instructions on the label extremely carefully, not at the time that you are going to do it but perhaps a day before so that you are very clear about the exact proportions to use. Then, only use it as directed and do not spray on a windy day so that poisonous chemicals drift all over the place.

As we discuss the various pests and diseases that occur in your garden, I will pass on some homemade remedies that work well. You may know of some others. The only warning I would give concerning these is that if someone gives you a homemade remedy, always test it on part of a plant or part of a crop first to make sure that there are no adverse effects. There are some very fine recipes, and some rather odd things to control bugs

and diseases, and I will mention them as I go.

■ PESTS

In a book this size there is no room to discuss every pest that could attack your garden. Refer to the recommended reading section for other works that can help you in this field.

Ants. Ants are not really a major pest in a garden. True, if they decide to build their home, a little ant hill, underneath your favourite plant they can disturb the soil, and they will be very visible. They love to go after sweet things. They actually like to get the sweetness that exudes from aphids, so that is why you will often see them scurrying up trees. They will sometimes go after the stickiness and sweetness of fruit, and that can be a bit of a problem. I would not spray ants with any pesticide whatsoever. They are just not a major problem in the garden. They do not eat plants. They just go after the sweetness that exudes from plants. If they become bothersome, perhaps coming into a greenhouse or sometimes even into a home, mix borax and icing sugar. They will take this back into their nest and it will kill them.

Aphids. Aphids can do a fair amount of damage to a plant and they look awful...everyone gets upset when they see them. There are many, many different forms of aphids. There are green aphids which attack roses and vegetable crops. There are grey aphids which go after cabbages. Then there are black aphids which go for nasturtiums, and they will

159

also attack soft-leaf plants such as beans.

Here is a non-chemical treatment for black aphids that works extremely well. Pick leaves that are covered with black aphids, put them in a blender with some water and whisk it around so that it looks like an awful grey-green daiquiri. Strain this liquid, add it to some water and put a little soap in with it. Soap always helps to make it stick onto the plant. Then spray this back onto the plants and, believe me, within hours they are gone. It is the most effective spray I have ever seen. If you start using your kitchen blender for putting bugs in, it is probably going to split up a happy home, but because it is such an effective method, I would suggest that you get an old blender from a garage sale and keep it specifically for this purpose. I have only tried it for aphids, but this method could work well for other pests, too.

Aphids are also controlled by soap...an old-fashioned soap, not detergent...because they breath through holes in the side of their body and when the soap sticks to them they suffocate. Some people swear by putting in mashed garlic with the soapy liquid and say that it really helps to control aphids.

Then there is the famous rhubarb recipe. Boil 2 lbs. (1 kg) of rhubarb leaves in 2 qts. (2.2 L) of water. The rhubarb leaves have oxalic acid in them and this can burn and be quite dangerous, so it is important to be absolutely accurate about the measurements. Once the leaves are soft and have gone a dark colour, then cool the liquid and strain it. Then add a further quart (1.1 L) of water to the liquid and add some soap flakes. Use this as a spray on plants that have been affected by aphids. Putting more leaves than recommended into the mixture can burn the entire plant. When I was a child a local publican used this liquid to spray the roses in front of his pub, wonderful climbing roses, and although it killed all the aphids, all the leaves fell off the plant too. This is a hazard, and the liquid would be poisonous if you drank it, but it works really well for controlling aphids.

Cabbage Root Maggot. Cabbage root maggots can be quite devastating. What happens is a little fly comes along and lays its eggs and they hatch out as root maggots which go down and feed on the roots of the cabbage or cauliflower or related crop and cause the plant to die. These flies are usually around from April to June in British Columbia. Try to put something around the base of the plant that will deter the fly from laying its eggs. Some people make little collars out of very fine cloth, such as Remay™ cloth. Also, any flies that are attracted to a particular crop are often drawn by the scent of that plant. For any flies that come along and lay their eggs in the soil, something that I found works extremely well is to save coffee grounds at least once a week and that very day go out and sprinkle them around the plants. The smell of the coffee will deter the fly and keep it away. Lastly, if none of these remedies work then use granular Diazinon™.

Carrot Fly. The carrot fly behaves much like the cabbage root maggot, and it can be equally devastating to crops in this part of the world. The fly lays its eggs, not only around carrots but also around parsnips and celery, anytime from around mid-June to mid-August. It can be heart-breaking because your carrots are looking beautiful and coming along really nicely and you think you will leave them in the ground just a little bit longer before harvesting them. Then when you come to harvest you will find that this little larva has eaten down around the surface causing the root vegetable to go a rusty-brown and start to rot. The great revelation in recent years is this wonderful Remay™ cloth to put over carrot crops. It is like a big sheet of muslin except that it is much more finely woven so the little fly cannot get through. Put the sheet of Remay™ over the top of your carrot crop, burying the edges but leaving enough room to expand as the crop grows. It keeps the carrot fly away, and it will keep the fly away from your parsnips too. Coffee grounds sprinkled along carrot rows certainly will keep the fly away. Also, when sowing carrots, sow them very thinly, extremely thinly, because if they need to be thinned out the smell of the pulled carrots will attract the carrot fly.

Cabbage Caterpillars. When the cabbage white butterflies are around, that means they are laying the eggs that will become cabbage caterpillars. The problem with using a chemical spray to eliminate any kind of caterpillar is that it will only be effective if it contacts the caterpillar directly. This is so difficult to do because caterpillars hide on the underside of leaves and can be terribly difficult to get rid of. So, if caterpillar damage or droppings are evident the most direct way of dealing with caterpillars is to go looking for them and pick them off. They are a lovely green colour and blend in with the cabbage. When I was small my father used to give me a penny for every caterpillar I found in the cabbages or brussels sprouts.

Cut Worms. Cut worms go through cycles and are particularly bad some years and not so bad others. They are very much like leather jackets in appearance...about 1-1.5 in. (2.5-3.8 cm) long and a grey-brown colour. If they are present in the soil they eat the stem of the plant at ground level. The plant then falls over and that is the end of it. Cut worms are usually around in the early part of the season, April to June. Some people make collars by recycling cans. Take the tops and bottoms out of cans, or milk cartons, that you use in the kitchen. When planting push these collars down into the ground around the plants so that they are at least an inch (2.5 cm) down into the ground. These will stop cut worms from having a chance to get to the bottom of your plant. If you are driven to distraction then use granular Diazinon™,

Earwigs. Earwigs are those little brownish insects that run around with pincers on the front of them, and they really can pinch you if you pick them up. They are not a major problem to most vegetable crops but can be a problem with dahlias. Also, they can be a nuisance to trees and shrubs. My father used to put a stake in the ground to support a dahlia. He would then put a flower pot filled with straw upside down on the stake at the level of the flowers, and the earwigs, which love straw, would run inside. Then he would go out and burn the straw to kill the earwigs. That would be an alright sort of thing to do in a home garden. If not, use something like Sevin™.

Flea Beetle. Flea beetles are a visible pest that does damage which really looks awful, but the plants, if left, usually grow out of it. Flea beetles attack potatoes and tomatoes specifically. They are a tiny jumping black beetle that comes out when you disturb the soil around these crops, usually from around May to July. They eat little holes in the foliage. People say "Oh, my tomatoes look awful this year because they are full of holes," but quite honestly, even without treatment, as the tomatoes grow, the problem goes away and the fruit will not be affected. It is the same with potatoes: the leaves will be affected but the potatoes will not be. Sevin dust can be applied, but better just to leave it. Crop rotation will take care of them in a year or two.

Close-up of an earwig trap showing straw.

32. Dahlias with an earwig trap on a stake.

Leather Jackets. Leather jackets have become less of a pest in recent years. The major problem that they cause is that they eat the roots of grass plants which can cause great brown patches in the lawn. A good indication that they are present is that when the starlings are around they spend their time pulling them out of the lawn. This is a great biological control. If you feel that leather jackets are a major problem in your lawn, lift a piece of turf about 12 in. (30 cm) square. If you see more than about twenty in this small space then you will need to do some spraying. Spray the lawn once between the first week of October and the end of May with Diazinon™.

Leaf Miner. Leaf miner is a devastating pest. There are three different forms that cause a lot of grief in our province. In recent years the one that attacks beets, chard and spinach has been especially troublesome. A fly lays its eggs on the surface of the leaf, and when the worms hatch out they go inside and start to eat the cells away, leaving the skin of the leaf intact but covered in big brown blotches. Because the problem is inside the vegetable leaf, it is very difficult to control, and it is best to go out and pick off the leaves as soon as little yellowish blisters appear. Pick off those leaves and get rid of them. If you are allowed to, burn the leaves. Do not put them in the compost pile. Consider giving the affected crops a rest for a season. The recommended chemical spray is Malathion™. Another host plant for this problem is what we call lamb's quarters weed. If you keep this weed down it will break the life cycle of the pest.

Leaf miner on marguerite daisies is a different story altogether. They will go inside the leaves and make little squiggly tunnels, usually a pale colour, and they can almost defoliate a plant. Again, pick off and destroy the affected leaves as they occur, to break the life cycle. Also, since this is not a food plant it is not as dangerous to use Malathion™. Not so much on the coast but in the interior, birch trees in the garden are beset by a birch leaf miner. The recommended control for these is a systemic pesticide called Dimethoate 2E™. This is painted on the trunk when the leaves start to open in the spring and gets taken up on the inside of the tree, making the tree toxic to this particular bug. It will also control aphids but should be used only on ornamental plants, never on vegetables. Lilac leaf miner is similar to the birch leaf miner and can be treated in the same way.

Narcissus Bulbfly. Narcissus bulbfly is something that I have never actually seen in all the time I have lived in British Columbia, although I have met people that have had the problem. What happens is a large fly lays its eggs and the worm hatches out and tunnels down to live on the inside of the bulb. It does not actually kill the bulb but stops it from flowering, resulting in clumps of daffodils or snowdrops that are all leaves and no flowers. The only way to find out if it is present is to dig up the bulbs and see if there is actually anything inside. If there is, then you should destroy those bulbs. Get rid of them in the garbage or burn them if possible. This will help to break the cycle. If you are driven to distraction by this particular problem then put granular Diazinon™ around the foliage and into the soil starting in May and repeating every ten days until July.

Sawfly. Sawfly is a problem that occurs specifically on currants and gooseberries. Early in the spring when the bushes start to leaf out, something begins to chew on them. If you look closely the affected branch will be covered with little green worms that are eating and eating like crazy. If left, they can defoliate a bush. They will not kill the bush but they will defoliate it and severely reduce the crop within a matter of days. What happens is that large flies lay their eggs and then the worms appear, usually during the last half of May. Cut off the affected branch and get rid of it. Step on the caterpillars and just get rid of it. However, if it seems to have gotten a hold in the bush the only recommended pesticide is Methoxychlor™. Use it as the caterpillars appear. I have never tried the blender method with this pest, but it is something that you might like to try.

Scale. There are many different forms of scale. The ones that occur on fruit trees can be very devastating because they suck the sap out of the tree and reduce its vigour. The best control of scale is a winter dormant spray on deciduous trees and shrubs. Toward the end of the season, after applying lime sulphur, do a dormant oil spray just before the buds start to open. This usually controls the problem nicely. There is nothing you can do about scale in the middle of the summer when it is present. You could spray until you were blue in the face with all kinds of pesticides and you just could not control it. The scales that are visible are usually the old ones. They have gone brown and are no longer active, but there are little new ones being formed on the branches further up, and if you see them you can scrap them off with your thumbnail. But that is not a very great way to control this particular problem. The other scale that becomes a problem with

evergreens, particularly on the coast, is commonly called a sooty mould, which is a secondary stage. The evergreen leaves of plants such as camellia or holly become totally covered with a black sooty mould substance. This happens because the shrub has scale on the underside of the leaves. If you pick up the leaves and look, you will see little bright-green scales active on the underside of the leaves, and as they suck the sap they exude a stickiness. You may have parked your car under a tree that has been infected by bugs and the windshield gets covered with this sticky substance. To treat sooty mould, spray the underside of the leaves with Malathion . Spraying with soapy water on a regular basis will help to clean up the leaves. If scale is controlled, particularly on the new foliage, eventually the sooty mould problem will right itself.

Slugs. When you first move to the coast you discover the large banana slugs, but they really do little damage. It is the little black slugs that can devastate crops in the early stages because they come out at night and feed on new seedlings. Freshly gathered seaweed for the first couple of weeks has enough salt in it to deter slugs, and a band of it around a vegetable plot will keep the slugs away. But after the rain has washed out all the salt it becomes a haven for slugs. There are many slug baits available on the market, but one of the problems with using them is that they are bran based. If they are sprinkled openly around the garden, cats, dogs and birds can come and eat the poison bait. The solution is to make what I call a little slug jail. Recycle plastic containers that have had yoghurt, margarine or ice cream in them. Wash them out and make holes on the side of the containers just near the bottom so that they are at soil level and large enough for the slugs to slide in. I usually put four holes to a container. Then put a table-spoon (15 ml) of slug bait in the middle, put on the lid and hide them underneath large plants. The slugs are attracted to the bait, which lasts a little longer be-cause it is kept dry. When the container is full of dead slugs dispose of them, then wash and re-use the container. This is a safe and effective way to deal with slugs. People still do go out at night with a salt shaker and sprinkle it on slugs. This is one way of killing them...not very nice, but it does work. Another recipe is to put down a saucer of beer. The slugs are attracted to the beer, fall in and then drown.

Spider Mite. Spider mite is a problem that occurs primarily in the interior parts of the province of British Columbia. Spi-der mites get their name because they form webs in a major infestation. In ac-tual fact they are not spiders at all, but mites. The thing to know about spider mites is that they hate water. Evergreens or any other shrubs that are susceptible to being attacked by mites should have a heavy jet of water sprayed through them daily. This will help control the problem. Otherwise you can use Malathion™ or Safer's Insecticidal Soap™. Spider mites do not usually occur in the vegetable garden, so keeping the foliage moist in the early part of the day in drier areas should take care of it.

Tent Caterpillars. Tent caterpillars are terribly visible and can be a problem on an annual basis. One day you look up in an ornamental tree in your garden and there you see an enormous tent full of caterpillars that have hatched out. Get a pair of long-armed pruners, prune out the branch, light a little pile of newspa-pers and burn the problem if you are allowed to burn in your garden. If not, put them out with the garbage, first making sure that they are killed. Late in the wintertime, just before the foliage starts to come out, spray with a dormant oil spray. This can help to control tent cater-pillars. If you are up a tree when you are

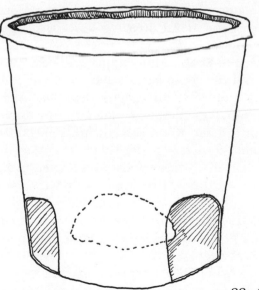

33. Slug trap made from a recycled yoghurt container.

doing your pruning in the wintertime and notice on the small, pencil-thick branches a little cluster of eggs, sort of like brown styrofoam running around the outside of a branch in a cluster, cut off the affected branch and burn it or get rid of it. If only one branch is infested with tent caterpillars, there is no need to spray the whole tree with pesticide.

Web Worm. Another similar problem which is closely related to the tent caterpillar is the web worm which occurs on Cotoneaster. In years when it is bad, cut the affected branch out, burn it or get rid of it in the garbage to cut down on its life cycle.

Weevils. If you live on the coast and grow rhododendrons or other evergreen shrubs you will find that at certain times of the year, usually after the new growth has appeared, while it is still nice and soft, you will go out into the garden and find that a beetle has eaten all around the outside of the leaves. They make a nice pattern, taking little bites all around the rim of the leaves. If you were to go out at night with a flashlight you would find slow, snout-nosed weevils actually eating the leaves. If you have rhododendrons and shrubs that are on a single trunk, and none of the outer branches come down to touch the soil, then the trunk is the only way for the weevils to go up at night. Paint the trunk with a sticky substance known as Tree Tanglefoot™ that is used on fruit trees to control coddling moth and similar pests. It prevents the weevils from getting up into the shrub and they cannot do any damage. I have also seen people use steel wool wrapped around the trunk. The weevils cannot crawl up over this. There is a pesticide on the market called Weevil Bait™, or a sprinkling of Diazinon™ crystals around the base of shrubs when the weevils are active can help control them. Or, you could simply go out at night and by hand pick off the weevils and step on them. The overwintering form of this insect is a grub that will eat the roots of strawberry plants. Unless this is a major problem I would not worry about it, but granular Diazinon™ will help keep them away.

■ DISEASES

Most diseases that occur on the coast are fungus diseases that result from high humidity. In drier regions fungus diseases are usually brought on by overwatering, which creates the conditions for fungus diseases to spread. Mildew, for example, can be a real problem in the Okanagan. Following are a few of the major diseases which affect the home gardens in our area.

Apple Scab. Many apple and pear trees and the stone fruits such as plums have a problem with fungus diseases. Apple scab, for example, can deform the apples and make them look awful. The known long-term control for this is to make sure that all of these trees are sprayed in the wintertime with lime sulphur. Lime sulphur is a natural fungicide and when sprayed on the trees in their dormant stage it burns all the overwintering spores that occur on the fruit trees. Even after spraying, a wet spring, particularly in coastal areas, will make the fungus diseases run rampant. You can do everything that is recommended in any book and, if it is a bad season, you will still get scab on the apples. So you live with it, cut out the scab part, eat the apples, make the pie…there is nothing wrong with it. If you want to do some control 90 percent sulphur sprays are available from garden centres. These sprays should not be used when the temperature rises above 26° C (79° F). This will cause burn damage on the trees.

Black Spot. Black spot looks just like it sounds. Big black patches appear on rose leaves. It is usually worse in wet seasons. Always pick off the leaves and burn them as they appear. Never let them drop off and fall back into the soil. If it seems to be a major problem, a regular spraying program with a product like Benomyl™ will work fairly well, although you will have to do it every ten days to control the problem. Again, you can spray roses in the wintertime with lime sulphur, and you can spray the soil around them which will help to cut down on the problem.

Dogwood Leaf Blotch. There is no known control for dogwood leaf blotch. Some trees are more susceptible than others. The most important thing to know is that if the leaves drop off any fungus-infected plant and fall to the ground, then the spores can overwinter in the soil. So any leaves that drop off should be raked up and burned or put out with the garbage, and not put back into the compost pile because this can regenerate them. In the centre of the compost pile, when it heats up they will get killed, but the ones around the edges will survive. The only thing that I can recommend is a dormant spray with

lime sulphur when spraying fruit trees. Plants are a bit like humans, you know, survival of the fittest. I think if you have a tree that is a little sad and weak, it will be much more susceptible to fungus diseases than others, and therefore it is very important to fertilize your trees. I am a great believer in fertilizing to make a stronger plant.

Peach Leaf Curl. Peach leaf curl is a miserable problem on peaches, and one of the reasons that it spreads so readily is moisture. In coastal regions it is advisable to plant peaches against a south- or southwest-facing wall under the overhang of your house to stop the rain from splashing down on the tree. This will reduce peach leaf curl. If the leaves start to curl, they become all bumpy on the surface and are sort of a red-orange colour, pick them off and burn them as soon as they appear. Sometimes if a tree is badly infected that means picking off most of the leaves. On the other hand, a good winter wash with lime sulphur is a great way to control it, making sure to thoroughly cover the stem and all the nooks and crannies in the bark to kill these overwintering spores. In the summer as it appears, if it becomes a major problem, the Ministry of Agriculture recommends copper sprays which must be used very carefully but do help to control it. Try to plant the tree where it is not going to get a lot of overhead water on it, and that will help control the problem.

Powdery Mildew. Some seasons powdery mildew is really bad, while in others it is not. On the coast, large-leafed maples are particularly susceptible to powdery mildew. In a bad season, the air becomes full of the spores flying around. They will start to grow on any soft-leafed plant they land on. Use sulphur spray or one of the recommended fungicides every ten days. Good air circulation is the key to keeping down this problem, and also not watering at night so that the plants stay wet overnight because this gives the spores a chance to develop. A good overhead watering in the morning will wash off some of the spores that may have landed on the leaves. The leaves dry throughout the day and this can help reduce the problem. But if it is a bad season for powdery mildew it will get on your peas, it will get on tomatoes, it will get on roses, it will get on all kinds of crops and there is very little that can be done to control it. Make sure that you have good air circulation. The same applies to begonias. If you grow the tubers for begonias in a patio of stagnant air without much air circulation, mildew can be a problem, but if you follow some of the controls recommended then you can cut down on it.

Rusts. Rusts, such as raspberry rust, come particularly in wet seasons. It is a very pretty fungus because it is a rusty orange colour and occurs on the surface of leaves. Pick off infected leaves and spray with a recommended fungicide every ten days in seasons when it really is bad. Also spray raspberry canes and the soil around the area with lime sulphur after pruning out the old canes in the wintertime and tying up the new ones. Many other rusts occur in our gardens. Hollyhocks are almost impossible to grow on the coast because of rust, whereas in the interior they thrive because of the drier

conditions. Some of the older varieties of snapdragons will succumb to rust in coastal gardens or gardens where heavy watering takes place. Grow rust-resistant varieties, particularly if you are growing your own from seed.

Often with diseases, if you catch them when they first appear, picking off and destroying the leaves or cutting off the infected branch when you are doing your winter pruning, you can limit their spread. They will always be around, but really, what is wrong with a little scab on an apple or a little blemish on the surface of fruit? If it tastes good then there should be no problem at all. I hope that this chapter has made you more aware of the pests and diseases to be found in your garden. Read about pesticides and herbicides and all these other things before you start using them liberally in your home garden.

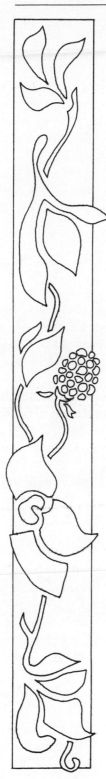

■ JANUARY

Vegetables and Flowers. Planning is all part of gardening fun. January is a great time to collect and read seed catalogues to plan and order seeds for the season ahead.

Fruit Trees. In milder coastal regions there is still time to carry out pruning until the end of the month, and to apply dormant sprays on calm, frost-free dry days which are rare on the coast.

Greenhouse. If you have a cool greenhouse with a little heat, sow pelargonium seed, and as you lift your forced bulbs for bringing into the house let them have a few days in the greenhouse to allow their leaves and flower stalks to develop before bringing them inside.

General Maintenance. Either fix or build new wooden patio planters and hanging baskets, and treat with wood preservative in the dryness and heat of a basement or garage. Clean and oil tools; get the mower sharpened. In coastal areas keep a weather watch by protecting patio pots which might have been left out during frosty weather, and by knocking heavy wet snow from trees and shrubs.

■ FEBRUARY

Vegetables and Flowers. Continue planning as in January. Try to send out mail orders for seed by the middle of the month.

Fruit Trees. In coastal areas if the winter is still frosty you could do a little late pruning. But if it is mild and the buds are beginning to swell do not prune. Apply dormant oil spray for scale.

Greenhouse. If you have a cool greenhouse with a little heat, sow lobelia, fibrous begonias and other slow-growing annuals. Take cuttings of houseplants.

Prepare potting mixes for next month's sowing and let them warm up in the greenhouse.

General Maintenance. Repot houseplants in the earlier part of the month. In milder regions if the weather is reasonable move trees and shrubs or plant new ones if required and available.

In milder coast regions, rake and aerate lawns and apply top dressing and lime during the last week of the month.

■ MARCH

Vegetables and Flowers. Sow broad or fava beans if soil is workable in coastal areas. Also spring-dig on dry days. Trim back old stems on perennials and divide if necessary.

Fruit Trees. In the interior and northern regions prune fruit trees and apply dormant sprays in the first half of the month. In all regions apply a mulch of well-rotted manure or something similar to bush and cane fruits.

Greenhouse. Start up begonia tubers. Sow most annuals and vegetables requiring some early heat during the latter part of the month. Remember not to oversow.

General Maintenance. Depending on where you live, as the weather warms tidy up debris left from last year. Start a new compost pile. Be careful of bulbs coming through; stake with pieces of brushwood.

Start lawn maintenance in interior and northern regions. Do not add more lime to already alkaline soils.

This is a great time for moving and planting trees and shrubs.

Prune roses.

■ APRIL

Vegetables and Flowers. Sow peas and early vegetables such as spinach, chard, beets and onions. With flowers, if soil is prepared and warm sow annuals like Bachelor's Buttons or Shirley and California poppies.

Fruit Bushes, Canes and Plants. Plant new berry bushes and strawberries. Place something like an old bucket upside down over rhubarb to force early sweet stems. Feed established fruit trees and bushes with a general fertilizer at a handful per square yard (1 m²).

Greenhouse. Transplant seedlings and resow failures. Sow tomatoes. Also apply shade to the exterior of the greenhouse by using Cool Ray™ or a similar product.

Cold Frames and Cloches. Prepare and clean up cold frames for hardening off seedlings. Sow early crops under cloches in the garden.

General Maintenance. All spring digging should be completed by the beginning of the month. Start to feed lawns and mow in milder regions. Feed established clumps of bulbs to help build them up for next year. Plant potatoes.

■ MAY

Vegetables and Flowers. All general planting takes place this month of both flowers and vegetables with the exception of the hot crops (see greenhouse). Plant new perennials also.

Fruit Bushes, Canes and Plants. Place straw as a mulch along strawberry rows. Watch for pests and deal with them organically before they get out of control.

Greenhouse. Sow hot crops such as pole beans, zucchinis, cucumbers and corn in pots for easy transplanting the first of next month.

171

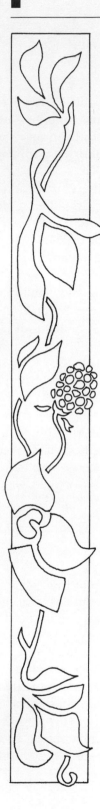

Cold Frames and Cloches. Depending on the weather and where you live continue using as last month.

General Maintenance. Use an all-purpose fertilizer at a handful per square yard (1 m²) before carrying out any planting. Dead-head rhododendrons. Place slug traps around as needed. Hill up potatoes. Do not let early sowings and newly planted plants dry out.

■ JUNE

Vegetables and Flowers. Plant out the heat lovers. With vegetables this means tomatoes, corn and zucchini and all its relatives. With flowers it is zinnias, impatiens and gerbera.

Fruit Bushes, Canes and Plants. On fruit trees, thin heavy crops of fruit on apples, pears and plums. Keep up the pest watch and deal with them organically.

Greenhouse. In cooler coastal regions greenhouses can be used for growing tomatoes and long English cucumbers throughout the summer.

Cold Frames. In cooler coastal regions cold frames are great for growing hot crops like melons or okra all summer.

General Maintenance. Feed flower and vegetable gardens once a month now through September with an all-purpose fertilizer at a handful per square yard (1 m²). Harvest early radishes. Resow salad crops as needed. Keep down the weeds. Keep containers and hanging baskets well fed and watered.

■ JULY

Vegetables and Flowers. Sow late vegetable crops. Remove old and decaying leaves. Stake and support as required. With annual flowers keep the dead heads

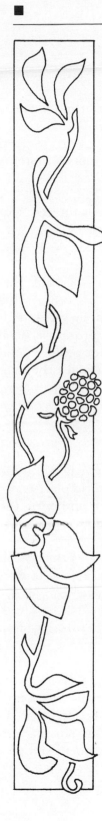

picked off so they will keep blooming.

General Maintenance. As last month. Always watch out for pests and diseases. Keep up the watering and feeding, and of course the mowing.

■ AUGUST

Vegetables and Flowers. Harvest and enjoy crops. Let some of the older varieties go to seed if you like to save your own. Some of the early annuals like nemesia and schizanthus will be finished now, so remove and replace with something from your local garden centre.

Shrubs. This is the month to propagate shrubs from semi-hardwood cuttings.

Hedges and Evergreens. Trim all evergreen hedges this month including cherry, laurel and cedar. Also top evergreens.

General Maintenance. As last month.

■ SEPTEMBER

Vegetables and Flowers. Harvesting continues. Save seed of both flowers and vegetables.

Bulbs. Order spring bulbs such as hyacinths, daffodils, etc.

Greenhouse. Clean out the greenhouse ready for winter storage of plants such as fuchsia, etc. Do not bring them in yet; it is too early.

General Maintenance. Summer is not over yet. Keep feeding and watering container plants and keep the dead heads picked off to keep the show going. Tag shrubs that need to be moved either next month or in the spring, depending on where you live.

■ OCTOBER

Vegetables and Flowers. Harvesting continues. Those vegetables to be stored should be lifted.

Bulbs. Plant bulbs in the garden and in pots for forcing for indoor enjoyment.

Greenhouse. Bring in plants to be overwintered. Cut them back and repot into smaller containers first. If you have lights in your greenhouse sow some late lettuce.

General Maintenance. Start digging the vegetable garden as soon as the summer vegetables are out. At this time you may add fresh manure if available. When tidying up the garden use leaves as a winter protector. Keep them in place with chicken wire. Do not remove dead stems completely to the ground on perennials; they can protect during winter and be removed next spring.

■ NOVEMBER

Vegetables and Flowers. Plan for next year. Evaluate which ones you liked or did well for you and plan where you might plant them next season, remembering the importance of crop rotation in the vegetable garden.

Shrubs. May be transplanted at this time of the year in milder areas. For other areas it would be best to wait until March or April.

Greenhouse. Check thermostat and heating system regularly.

General Maintenance. Continue digging. Start pruning ornamental trees and shrubs. Prune raspberry canes, cutting out the old and tying in the new. In areas of high snowfall tie up your evergreens and shrubs with binder twine to stop snow damage (remember to remove the twine in the spring).

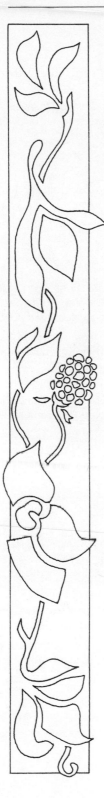

■ DECEMBER

Vegetables and Flowers. Bring in some of the earliest forced bulbs to bloom for the holidays.

General Maintenance. Always keep a weather watch and protect planters, etc., accordingly. Expensive ceramic planters should be emptied and brought in during the winter months. Prune fruit trees in milder areas. Wash and clean pots and seed flats which are to be reused this coming season.

In the gardening world there is always something new to read about. If you would like to expand your knowledge on some of the topics dealt with in this book, here are some suggestions.

Annuals

Crockett, James. *Annuals*. Alexandria, VA: Time-Life Encyclopedia of Gardening series, 1971.

Fell, Derek. *Annuals: How to Select, Grow and Enjoy*. Tucson, AZ: HP Books, 1983.

Jones, Carolyn. *Bedding Plants: The Complete Guide for Amateurs and Experts*. North Vancouver: Whitecap Books, 1989.

Sinnes, A. Cort. *All About Annuals*. San Francisco: Ortho Books, 1981.

Taylor's Guide to Annuals. Boston: Houghton Mifflin, 1986.

Bulbs

Crockett, James. *Bulbs*. Alexandria, VA: Time-Life Encyclopedia of Gardening series, 1978.

Horton, Alvin. *All About Bulbs*. San Francisco: Ortho Books, 1986.

Owen, Rosemary. *The Pacific Bulb Gardener*. Sidney, B.C.: Gray's, 1971.

Taylor's Guide to Bulbs. Boston: Houghton Mifflin, 1986.

Perennials

All About Perennials. San Francisco: Ortho Books, 1985.

Crockett, James, and Oliver Allen. *Book of Perennials*. Alexandria, VA: Time-Life Encyclopedia of Gardening series, 1978.

Harper, Pamela, and Fred McGourty. *Perennials: How to Select, Grow and Enjoy*. Los Angeles: HP Books, 1985.

Taylor's Guide to Perennials. Boston: Houghton Mifflin, 1986.

Trees and Shrubs

All About Trees. San Francisco: Ortho Books, 1983.

Crockett, James. *Flowering Shrubs*. Alexandria, VA: Time-Life Encyclopedia of Gardening series, 1972.

Fell, Derek. *Trees and Shrubs*. Los Angeles: HP Books, 1986.

Taylor's Guide to Shrubs. Boston: Houghton Mifflin, 1987.

Taylor's Guide to Trees. Boston: Houghton Mifflin, 1988.

Pests and Diseases

A Gardener's Guide to Pest Prevention and Control in the Home Garden. Victoria: British Columbia Ministry of Agriculture, 1986.

Ware, George C. *Complete Guide to Pest Control*. Fresno, CA: Thomson Publications, 1980.

Seeding

Bubel, Nancy. *The New Seed-Starter's Handbook*. Emmaus, PA: Rodale Press, 1988.

Vegetables

All About Vegetables. San Francisco: Ortho Books, 1985.

Chan, Peter. *Better Vegetables the Chinese Way*. Pownal, VT: Garden Way Publishing, 1985.

Crockett, James. *Crockett's Victory Garden*. Boston: Little, Brown, 1977.

General Reading

Tarrant, David. *A Year in Your Garden*. North Vancouver: Whitecap Books, 1989.

Willis, A.R. *The Pacific Gardener*. 11th ed. North Vancouver: Whitecap Books, 1987.

Page numbers in italic refer to illustrations.